Married Under The Influence

Married
UNDER THE INFLUENCE
A true story

Harmony Rose

ARCHWAY
PUBLISHING

Archway Publishing books may be ordered through booksellers or by contacting:

Archway Publishing
1663 Liberty Drive
Bloomington, IN 47403
www.archwaypublishing.com
1-(888)-242-5904

Because of the dynamic nature of the Internet, any web addresses or
links contained in this book may have changed since publication and
may no longer be valid. The views expressed in this work are solely those
of the author and do not necessarily reflect the views of the publisher,
and the publisher hereby disclaims any responsibility for them.

Any people depicted in stock imagery provided by Thinkstock are models,
and such images are being used for illustrative purposes only.
Certain stock imagery © Thinkstock.

ISBN: 978-1-4808-1050-1 (sc)
ISBN: 978-1-4808-1052-5 (hc)
ISBN: 978-1-4808-1051-8 (e)

Library of Congress Control Number: 2014915165

Printed in the United States of America.

Archway Publishing rev. date: 09/05/2014

Acknowledgments

I would like to give a very special thank you to my dearest childhood friend for over thirty-four years of friendship. She has always encouraged me and would never let me give up on myself. Words cannot express my gratitude to this beautiful soul! She is always the first hand to reach for me when I am down. Without her through the years, I don't know what I would have done.

I would also like to give a special thank you to another friend for taking the time to share his honest opinions as I was writing this book.

I want to thank both of them for the countless conversations that helped me through the darkest time in my life!

Special thanks also to my family: my daughter, my father, my mother and her husband, my brother, and my older sister-in-law. I love all of you and cherish you with all my heart. Thank you for always standing by not only myself but my husband! You have encouraged me when I needed it, believed in me when I didn't, and loved me when I couldn't love myself. Thank you all for being the support I needed.

I would also like to thank those who took the time and allowed me to interview them for opening up and sharing very personal details about your life or addictions. You are so courageous!

Most of all, I am grateful to my beloved husband for his dedication to his sobriety, his friendship, love, and encouragement in my journey writing this book. Thank you for believing that together we can make a difference in the world of alcoholism. I am so proud of the man my husband is today, and the passionate love we are blessed to share with one another is more than we could have ever hoped for. With all that I am, I love you! Thank you for believing in us!

Love always …

Dedication

I would like to dedicate this book to my beautiful daughter. You have been with me every step of the way. You have no idea that you are my strength to keep going when I am weak. Always believe in your dreams, and know that you can do anything you choose to do. I have made mistakes in my life and you have witnessed many of them, but I hope that I have been a good example and have shown you how to love unconditionally, how to find hope when you feel hopeless, how to always stand by what and whom you believe in, and how to forgive even the most unforgivable things. My wish for you is to be your best self that you can be; to always be loving, openhearted, and quick to forgive; to never be judgmental; to often say, "I am sorry"; never be afraid to be wrong; and to know that sometimes the worst situations have the best endings.

I wish love in abundance for you. You will always be the greatest miracle that ever happened in my life! I love you with every breath I take. You will always be my baby girl, and yet I am so proud of the young woman I see before me today, and I can't wait to see where your journey in life takes you because I know wherever that is, it will be nothing short of extraordinary!

Love always,
Mom … XOXOX

Contents

Introduction

Please allow me to introduce myself. I am the wife of an alcoholic, but I am also so much more than that. I am a mother, stepmother, daughter, sister, cousin, friend, and animal rescuer. My husband and I have been together for over fourteen years, married eleven of those years. I have come to realize that my story is not in any way unique. I am just one of thousands of people in the world that have been affected in one way or another by alcoholism. However, alcoholism does not define my marriage nor who we are as a family. My story is about how alcoholism has affected us *as* a family.

I am not a doctor or psychologist; I don't have a degree. I have no professional background where alcoholism is concerned. What I do have is the everyday real-life experience of living with an alcoholic. I am just an ordinary woman who feels her story needed to be told for the world to hear so that other women, men, children, mothers, fathers, and so on who are going through a similar situation will know that they do not have to feel ashamed, alone, or defeated anymore because they are in the company of so many others who are going through the same thing that they may be experiencing at this very moment.

A few months back, our daughter said something to me that I found to be very powerful that I would like to share. She said, "Growing up with an alcoholic dad and a mother who lied to us kids for him has made me more closed off and skeptical of people." This is a great example of the collateral damage caused by one person's addiction.

I would like to welcome you to share this journey with me. *Married under the Influence* is a true story of being the wife of an alcoholic. Inside this book, you will find that nothing is ever as hopeless as it seems, forgiveness can free you from your own emotional prison, and believing in something greater than yourself may be just what has been missing in your life. You may find that some chapters seem to be repetitive; however, alcoholism is just that—repetitive. I encourage you to read from beginning to end to experience the years and events that occurred in their entirety. You won't be disappointed (I hope)! You will read interviews with wives of alcoholics, an adult son of an alcoholic, a recovering female alcoholic/addict, as well as an interview with my own husband. You will learn the difference between true sobriety and what it means to be "dry and sober." All of the journal inserts are from my own journaling through the years; some names may have been excluded or changed for privacy, but all the events are true to the best of my recollection. (My husband can attest to this!)

This book will make you smile, laugh, and cry; it may even make you angry; but most of all, it will bring you hope and give you insight on what life can be like living with an alcoholic and how you don't have to be a prisoner to this disease. There is help all around you. You can find strength in your darkest moments, and you never have to do it alone.

If you yourself are an alcoholic or know someone who is suffering, you may be able to identify with some of the behaviors or situations in this book, which I pray will lead you to seek the help you may need. I hear this quote all the time in meetings: "Today is the day you don't have to drink or drug no matter what." My wish for all of you is that you take that first step.

Our hopes in sharing our most personal intimate details of everyday life with the world is that we will help one couple or even one person who is still suffering. I wish you all a safe journey. I hope it leads you to some form of recovery. I hope I will somehow make a positive difference and touch someone's life, because for me the loneliness was the worst part of all. I now know that I am no longer alone and I don't have to feel ashamed—nobody does! Now I even have strangers reaching out to me, which truly shows me I am not alone in this world after all. There are so many others who really do understand, because there will always be a piece of everyone's story that we all share. Remember, you are the author of your own life; tomorrow starts with a blank page, and you decide how it is written.

Chapter 1

I had just celebrated my Thirtieth birthday four months before my husband and I started dating. My husband and I are exactly six and a half years apart to the day. Here is how we met. I was friends with his older sister. I went to her house one day, and my future husband happened to be showing off a new motorcycle he had just purchased. When we were introduced and our eyes met, it was as though time stood still in that moment. We just stood there gazing at one another like we were the only people around! I often wondered if anybody noticed or if it was just us reacting to our chemistry?

For the next ten months, we would run into each other at his sister's for barbeques and things like that, and our daughters would play together. He would always come up to me and offer me a beer. My reply was always the same: "No, thank you, I don't drink." Then he would take my hand and compliment me on my fingernails because they were always done with designs. I thought to myself, *is this man flirting with me? He always wants to touch my hands and offer me a drink even though I tell him every time I don't drink. It's cute!* I went with his sister out to his house a few times (she would make me go with her; I know she was hoping we would get together). One time in particular, he was putting up a fence around the back porch. He asked me to hold a box of screws for him, so the inside joke for years to follow was that I was his "screw girl." As a matter of fact, years later at our wedding, that exact comment was in a wedding toast given by his sister!

From the second we met, it seemed our destiny was to be together. One night his sister and I went out to meet some family for dinner, and the only ones who showed up were me, his sister, and him. We hung out, they had a few drinks, and from there we went to a bar to play pool. By the end of the night, he was way too drunk to drive home, so his sister asked me if I would mind driving him home. We sat and talked for hours until the early morning. I had to get myself home, so I borrowed his truck. Later that day I dropped it off at his sister's so he could pick it up after work, and I made sure to leave a cute little note for him to find. It said: "Hi there. Hope I didn't keep you up too late last night. It was nice to sit down and talk with you. Anytime you want to talk, just give me a call. Thanks for trusting me with your truck last night. I appreciate that, and I promise I didn't go four-wheeling or anything. Ha-ha. Thanks!" That note is in a collage of pictures framed on our wall in his office. For some reason he kept that note. He told me it's special to him because it reminds him of our conversation. (Little did he know that would be the first note of thousands yet to come!)

Shortly after that, we went out on our first date. From that day forward, we were inseparable. We didn't spend one day apart. Each time I spent the night at his place, I would put my belongings in the corner of his room. One day not long after that, he said, "I need to make room in the closet for you!" Three short months after our first date, we moved in together. We knew from the first moment we met that there was an undeniable amazing connection that just couldn't be ignored.

I knew it would be an amazing journey, so I began writing a journal. Day one of my journal reads like this:

May 30, 2000

I have had the best two weeks of my entire life! The man I started dating and I have been together every day for the past two weeks. How incredible is that! He doesn't seem selfish, and he has passion for me. We sit and gaze into each other's eyes for hours. I am falling in love. He is the most wonderful man! How is this possible?

I wish I could put into words how I feel. It's very hard because I have such a deep feeling of closeness with someone I just met. Is this crazy? It seems crazy. Is it safe to say I have found my soul mate? He tells me he feels exactly how I do. It is phenomenal! I am just so thrilled to have met someone who seems to feel the same way about me as I do him and wants the same type of love in his life! I am so excited my heart flutters. I have butterflies. This is insane, but in a good way! I know the beginning is always the honeymoon phase, but I wish relationships could always stay this way. I know I am jumping in very fast, but that's okay. Why not? Maybe this time it will work out. Sometimes you just know, and this time it has to be different!

We went out of town for a few days to get away. We went to visit his dad, and we also went to an amusement park. I will never forget this day because, when you don't know someone, you want to get to know all there is to know about him or her. I *do not* go on roller coasters or any high-adrenaline rush rides *ever*! I like the water rides, the animals, the gift shops, and the food, but I am terrified of heights; they make me feel woozy and unbalanced. I used to love them as a young kid, but I just don't like them anymore. I will never ever get on an airplane and fly either, it's just my thing. We got into a disagreement about it. He got so angry at me because I wouldn't go on any of those rides with him. Right then I thought, *we have only known each other a short time and you're pissed at me, I mean legitimately pissed, because I won't go on a roller coaster?* I told myself at that moment that if he was going to get that mad about something as simple as that and not understand, then what was going to happen when we had serious issues? He apologized, so I forgot about my concern.

I didn't realize it until many, many years later, but during that visit he and his dad were pounding down the alcohol. I didn't think anything of it at the time, but it was a mirror image of himself and what he would become not to many years later.

July 13, 2000

My daughter and I moved in with him. I must be nuts! We haven't known each other that long, but we connect in such an incredible way, I just feel it's the right thing to do. I am putting my faith in this man! I know this is it: he is the one for me! I have known his sister the past few years, and I already feel like family with her. Others, like his mom and oldest daughter, were pushing for us to get together, so hopefully they will all come to love me and my daughter.

I have wanted this kind of love all my life. It's what you dream of. I can't believe how much I love him. I just look at him, and I find myself falling deeper in love every day. He tells me that he is going to love me forever, and I believe him! Finally a man who promises to love me and can say, "I will love you forever." All my life I wanted this love, and now we have it with each other! No more being alone, ever! My heart melts. Could this be my one? Yes, he is my one and only! Am I jumping too fast before really knowing? I have to take a chance just like every time before, and hope this is it for me. I have finally found the love of my life, and I am going to enjoy every minute of it!

Our relationship moved very fast as you can see. We all had to adjust. He had his teenage daughter and granddaughter who lived with him full-time. His other two kids came every weekend from

Friday night to Sunday night. My daughter went from being the only child, having her own room, and having a mom all to herself, to sharing a house with four other kids. That was a lot for her to take in. She was only six years old, and now there was a man in her life in the daddy position! Meanwhile, he liked to go to bars to play darts and pool, so we would go often. We also played shuffleboard. We had a lot of fun, so we did this all the time. I didn't really worry about the drinking much because I didn't think it was a problem and he never went without me; we always went together.

I thought I knew what an alcoholic was. To me it was someone who drank every day, was falling down drunk, had no job, looked like a bum, and lived under a bridge—the total cliché of what we were always led to believe. An alcoholic certainly didn't look like a man who kept the same job for twenty-five years, wore a suit, paid his bills, took care of his family, and only binge drank every few months—it certainly couldn't be that guy! I had no clue it could exactly be that guy. You do not have to drink every day to be an alcoholic—what? Clearly I had no idea what an alcoholic really was. I had a lot to learn!

One time before we moved in together, we were drunk; that was unusual for me because I don't usually drink. Not too many years before, in my late twenties, I started to suffer from terrible debilitating panic attacks so badly that I became afraid to leave my house. I also found out that I had a heart arrhythmia, so drinking was not a good idea for me.

Anyway, that night I had three beers, which was way more than I could handle. We decided it would be a good idea to drink, get on our kids' skateboards, and try to skate down the ramp they built in the backyard. We crashed so badly! I have never had a bigger bruise in my life than I did from that night because I landed on my shoulder and he landed on top of me. We lay on the ground laughing hysterically. It was 3:00 a.m. At the time it was hilarious; we were so drunk!

I will never forget what happened to me, though. After falling asleep for like two hours, I woke up. I stood in the bathroom, and my heart went so out of rhythm, it was crazy. It scared me I thought I was having a heart attack or something. I had no idea what to do, and then shortly after, it was back to normal.

Honestly I thought my future husband had picked up drinking as a very bad habit because of things that had happened in his life, so I thought if I was patient enough, loved him enough, and gave him what he hadn't had in his life, he wouldn't need to drink so much anymore. There wouldn't be a reason for him to self-medicate, right? I obviously had no idea what would happen. I was just giving myself credit for "saving him" before it even happened. I didn't know he was, in fact, an alcoholic. I thought he just drank a lot!

After my parents got divorced, I became a martyr. I was the one who took care of my brother, me, and later my father—that was my job. I was a sister, mother, friend, daughter, and caretaker, all in one, at the very young age of sixteen! I even quit my last year of high school to work full-time so I could buy groceries.

Just after my parents split up, the boyfriend I had at the time started to physically abuse me. I was confused at first because he never "hit me" per se, but he sure loved to grab me by my upper arms, shake me, and throw me up against the corners of walls and leave bruises in places you couldn't see, like the middle or upper back and the upper arms. See, physical abuse to me meant you had to punch or hit; it didn't mean throwing me around or slamming me against walls or calling me nasty names, it wasn't until I got older and realized it was all abuse.

One night I woke up with him holding a pillow over my face. I couldn't breathe. I kicked and fought him off and said, "What the hell are you doing?" Was he trying to suffocate me and kill me? He played dumb, pretending he did it in his sleep, like he was "dreaming." Please, how stupid do I look? I knew what his intention was. I was too afraid to tell anyone. My best friend knew because when I was changing clothes one day, she saw the bruises on my back, but I made her promise not to say anything.

On Thanksgiving Day in 1986, I was almost Seventeen years old. My boyfriend had been living with us for about a year and a half at this point. My father came to pick up me and my brother to take us out for dinner. (Dad no longer lived with us due to him and our mother divorcing) and my boyfriend was waiting for his sister to come pick him up. I sat on the bed and I mustered up all the courage I possibly could because I couldn't live that way anymore; I feared if I didn't get out now, I might end up dead one day. I said, "I need you to pack your things and move out." He poked his finger into my forehead so hard it knocked me back onto the bed. I got up in his face and said, "Get the fuck out of my house now!" He grabbed me with one hand by the throat and threw me up against the wall with my dad waiting in the living room. He closed his other hand into a fist, and he said, "If you say one word, you know what will happen." He finally let go, packed his clothes, and left. I swear to God I thought he was going to choke me to death; I thought I was going to die that day. I had to put a scarf around my neck to hide the red around my throat from where his hand held me so tight. I swore to myself I would never ever again put up with anyone touching me like that! This was the same guy who wrestled me to the ground, sat on top of me, and spit in my face a year after we broke up because he wanted me to give him back a birthday gift he gave me when we were together. I was almost Eighteen years old. Talk about feeling like a total piece of shit!

My parents never knew any of this until I was in my twenties. Once I took a look at the men in my life that I had relationships with, it seemed most of them had a problem with some type of addiction. I don't know if that is because the very first boyfriend I had was the first guy I drank with, smoked pot with, and so on, or if I just feel I can rescue people. I started dating when I was thirteen years old. I was young and did things I never should have for such a young girl, but the one good thing is I was able to be honest with my daughter and stepchildren to share things with them from my experiences so maybe they wouldn't repeat that same type of bad behavior at any age. How many of you can relate to these feelings and thoughts? I took my shame and turned it into lessons I have learned, and instead of hiding them, I am open about them. It took me a very long time to grasp that the actions someone else takes are not my fault, and I still at times struggle with that to this very day. We all have the ability to make someone feel happy, sad, mad, joyful, disappointed, loved, and so on, but each of us as individuals must be accountable ourselves for what we choose to do with that.

December 26, 2000

The holidays, especially Christmas, have always been huge at my house. It's all about family, friends, and good times! Christmas here this year was crazy big. I am talking huge! The presents covered half of the living room; you couldn't walk around them. His kids said they had never seen anything like that before, and I thought that it was so cool I could bring my touch on the holidays here and the kids would be so happy. Not that it is about the gifts, but it is so exciting to watch their faces as they open their presents, especially when they are little and so grateful for what they get; they are still innocent. Christmas takes me back to being a kid; I am so jolly and happy I love to give. Hands down, Christmas is the best time of year. To sit and watch our families join together and become one big family is precious to me. It seems to me that this is the beginning of our forever for us. I couldn't be happier. It especially warms my heart to watch my daughter be part of a whole family. This is what life is all about. We are home, baby girl. I found where we belong!

This is my interview with a young adult son of an alcoholic. The son is just shy of his twenty-first birthday.

Question: *Did your dad drink your whole life?*

Adult Son: *Yes, he did drink a lot! He has been drinking for as long as I have known him. From what my mother tells me, he is now sober and wants a new start in life.*

Question: *How do you feel having an alcoholic parent affected you growing up?*

Adult Son: *I don't feel having an alcoholic parent affected me in my stages of growing up. I mean it affected me, but not daddy issues; it was more of self-worth issues. I was angry a lot when I was younger. I knew for a fact that there were other kids in the same situation as me, so I felt like I didn't need anyone's pity. What did affect me was the death of a dear friend back in my sophomore year in high school. I saw him as a mentor, a great kid, but he loved to party. He invited me to a party one night, but I couldn't go because I had an exam the next morning. So what ended up happening was he gave his keys to a friend of his because he was too drunk to drive. He was in the passenger seat, and his buddy went to pass the car in front of them. He swerved off the edge of a cliff, and my friend was the only one who died on impact. His death hit a lot of us hard, especially other students in the area and those who went to school with him.*

Question: If you have a relationship with your dad now, how is it different?

Adult Son: I haven't spoken to my dad since the end of my junior year in high school. I am not ready to talk to the guy. I don't know if I ever will be! From what my mom has told me, he doesn't remember most of what he did in the past, but since I do it is very hard to deal with that. My mom divorced him when I was fifteen years old. He was never a father to me, and what I did learn from him was what kind of man not to be. The worst memory I have of my father is him telling me he didn't love me, he didn't want me, and he wanted nothing to do with me.

Question: What happened when your father did leave?

Adult Son: After my mom divorced him, we got into an argument after a football game. He was talking crap about how I played that game, and I told him to "F**k off!" He grabbed me by the throat and lifted me off the seat of my mom's car. I haven't talked to him since.

Question: Do you have a problem with addiction now, or do you see an issue with it in the future for yourself?

Adult Son: I have no addictions other than believing my best is never good enough so I push my body and mind past their limits. I feel if my dad isn't proud of who I am, what I am, who I've become, then no one will be. It's a father-son thing. I have a mentor who I call dad now who has definitely had a positive impact in my life.

I know this kid pretty well, and I thank him for sharing his personal emotions with me and allowing the world to read it, hoping it helps someone else who may be in a similar situation.

In this case, just as many others, living with alcoholism really plays with your self-worth. You question yourself and wonder if you're "good enough," not only for someone else but at anything that you do. I believe this has affected him more deeply than he realizes, and as he gets older, he will start to get in touch with those emotions. Many times you are always feeling like you fall short of what you should be.

This can be so traumatic for people. It doesn't matter if you are a child, wife, husband, mother, father, sister, brother, or friend, living with alcoholism really impacts people in different ways. Be assured that everyone in an alcoholic's life is affected by this in one way or another. It is my hope that through reading this book, you can relate to myself or to one of the people I had the pleasure of interviewing, all of whom were gracious enough to share their stories of strength, hope, forgiveness, love, and recovery. You'll know you are not alone and there are people who understand and can help.

We all deserve to feel loved and accepted. We all have to remember that we have to love ourselves no matter how bad we feel or what our situations may be. There are people out there who, from the outside looking in, appear to have it all, but they may have the same low self-worth that you or I may have or have had at some point in our lives. Material things and money don't give you self-worth.

You will notice who the true people in your life are; even on your darkest days, they love you and stand by you. Even when you feel as though you don't love yourself, they will hold out a hand to help you up. Be careful, though. There are only so many bridges you can burn before it all comes crashing down around you. Now I don't mean that these people will just coddle you. As a matter of fact, the ones who stand up and call you out on your wrongdoings, the ones who challenge your lies and are willing to be brazenly honest with you even when you don't want to hear it, those are the ones that you need to listen to the most because one day you will come to understand they were not being mean or trying to harm you in any way. Actually it is completely the opposite: they are trying to help you because they care, and sometimes honesty really hurts but it is the only way to heal and see things for what they truly are.

Chapter 2

In May 2001, I went to bed with some stomach discomfort only to wake with high abdominal pain. I got out of bed and started getting ready to go to work. Eating crackers and drinking water didn't help. I called my boyfriend (who is now my husband) and told him that the pain was still there and how it was high up under my breast bone and it was concerning me. He said if I couldn't get in to see my doctor to go to the ER.

At the emergency room, they gave me what they called an intestinal cocktail, which helps to calm things like ulcers and other stomach issues; if after forty-five minutes the pain went away, they would know it worked and what they were dealing with. No such luck for me! It didn't work, so the next step was an ultrasound. After my ultrasound they took me back to the room I was in and said the doctor would talk to me after he got the results. As we all know, that usually takes *forever* ... Not this time! Within five minutes the doctor was in my room. I instantly knew something was terribly wrong; I got a really bad feeling in the pit of my stomach when he walked in. The doctor sat down and said, "You have a large tumor on your left adrenal gland."

I said, "How big is this tumor? Is it cancer?"

He said, "Almost 11cm big, about the size of a small grapefruit."

I about freaked out—a tumor the size of a what!

He said they didn't know yet if it was cancer, and that was all I heard. I went into complete shock. Kind of like when you see people in the movies; they just go someplace else in their minds; they freeze and hear nothing else—that was me.

I called my boyfriend. He came right down, and from there it was a whirlwind of events, doctors, and tests. I was there for eight hours that day! I also saw an endocrinologist, and he explained to me that he was hoping that the tumor was what is called a *pheochromocytoma*. Wow, say that three times fast! All I know is he said they are benign, so I wanted that one!

I finally left the hospital in a complete daze. My boyfriend left to go back to work, and honestly I don't even remember how I drove home that day. It was a complete blur.

I thought about my daughter. What would happen to my daughter if I died or if I was sick? Who was going to take care of my baby? This was not a good thing at all.

I sat on the front porch. There was a light breeze that day. I just sat there with the sun on my face, tears rolling down my cheeks, watching the leaves blow, and thinking I could die. Oh my goodness! How would I tell my dad? He always worries about me. We told my family, and I made arrangements for my daughter to go and stay with my mom in Florida for about six weeks while I recovered from major surgery. I would need to have my left adrenal gland and the tumor removed. I found a surgeon who had some experience with performing adrenalectomies and she made me feel comfortable. I trusted her.

I went for several opinions before I found her. The first surgeon suggested she cut me open from my breastbone down to my belly button and then remove half my spleen. I thought, *Oh hell no. This doesn't sound right. Can it be this bad?* We couldn't run out of there fast enough. That was a scary appointment! Thank goodness I found my surgeon, who was a lot more reassuring that she would do her best to do it laproscopically, but if that were not possible, with the most minimal invasiveness she could. She said that they had to biopsy the tumor and I had to wait for the results to find out if it was cancer; then we could go from there. She said once she was inside, she would have a better idea once she saw what the tumor looked like and could check my other organs.

Having to say good-bye to my daughter was the most heartbreaking thing I have ever done in my life, and I never want to experience that feeling again. Picture this: I went to the airport with my daughter and my mom. My daughter was only seven years old, so she didn't really understand. I hugged her so tight, kissed her, and cried. I didn't want to let her go, fearing it would be the last time I saw her. I asked my mom to promise me that if anything happened, she would take care of my daughter for me, that she would raise her and never let her forget who her mom was and how much I love her. Hugging my mom and saying good-bye was so hard, not knowing if I would ever see them again; but I knew that if anything happened, she would protect my daughter with her life and never let my memory fade. I had my hands pressed up against the glass watching the plane leave (that was when we were still allowed to walk people to the gate), bawling my eyes out standing there feeling so alone.

I had a positive attitude, but I was scared. It happened so quickly and unexpectedly, doctor after doctor, test after test for three weeks until it was time for the surgery and the premedication for the two weeks prior to lower my blood pressure. It made me feel worse than I have ever felt in my life. It was awful to feel so weak I was like a zombie!

The surgery was June 1, 2001. It lasted six hours. My surgeon said I did great, but it was very painful to move afterward. I could see this would take some time to heal. She said that the tumor was encapsulated, which was great news because she said she was sure it wasn't cancer. The tumor was all smooth, with no rough edges. Awesome! *Awesome!* No other organs were affected by it.

I wouldn't be leaving this earth today. It was a good day! Thank you, God!

June 9, 2001

Eight days after my surgery. I can't believe it. He didn't come home last night! How do you not come home at all, especially to the one you love who just had surgery and needs you, needs to be taken care of? Why would he do this to me? What is happening? I don't understand. Is he having an affair? He wouldn't do that to me. It couldn't possibly be that, but then what? Why is he not home? I am so confused. This isn't who he is. He doesn't treat me this way. He loves me!
He called me at 3:38 a.m. saying he was drunk and gambled his whole paycheck. Not his whole paycheck! That is a lot of money. I can hardly move! Now I am obviously not able to work, and we only have his paycheck to live off of. What the heck are we going to do now? And why am I thinking about this major stuff when I am on pain medication and trying to heal and relax days after a big surgery? And why would he put me through something so stressful? How selfish of him and thoughtless!
He got mad at me and said that he is sick of my poor-me attitude, to get off my pity pot, that I will be just fine, I just need to recover and get over it! Are you kidding me? I had surgery one week ago. I am scared. Do you think he could give me a break and stop thinking of just himself? I just had surgery. It is going to take me a few months to recover. I had to send my daughter away, and he's treating me like this? We have been together for over a year. What is wrong with him? I need him to take care of me and love me. I would do anything in this world for him; I would support him 100 percent! Sometimes life gets unbearable, but we have to hold each other's hand and take one step at a time together. This has never happened before.
God, please let him be okay. Bring him home soon. I need to tell him I love him and that everything will be okay, it will all work out.

He finally came home at 8:15 a.m. He was still drunk and said he took about eight Xanax because he was so upset. Who does that? We have a family, young kids. Where is his head? Mixing Xanax with alcohol in the quantity he did, he is lucky he isn't dead or in a coma. Is he trying to kill himself? What the hell is wrong with him?

Even in my times of need, I worry about him and whether he was okay. I wanted him to know how much *he* is loved. What about me and what I was going through? He didn't seem too worried about that. He got so stressed out with work and life he needed to drink to make it feel like it was more tolerable. It just created more of a problem, but during this time I was trying to focus on me getting better. You have no idea how bad it hurt when I would cry, the physical pain was almost unbearable.

Being able to hear my daughter's voice every day on the phone was the highlight of my days. I missed her so very much! My daughter said to me, "Mommy, I got upset about Father's Day." I asked her why. She said, "Because this is the first Father's Day that I have a daddy who really loves me, and I can't be there to spend it with him." How precious is that?

June 11, 2001

We got to spend the weekend alone. It was way overdue for us as a couple! It was so wonderful. We needed that; I could tell he really needed it! We have so much to be thankful for. I need to feel his love because I have been feeling a little lonely; he is working so much, and with the surgery, I am just needy, I suppose. I feel kind of helpless because I can't do much. It will be a tough couple of months, but we will get through it together. My aunt was here for two weeks taking care of me. I was so grateful she was here to do that. She stayed with us during the week while he worked, and then stayed with my dad on the weekends to go out and have fun since my boyfriend would be here to take care of me.

June 12, 2001

Today is his birthday! My aunt is going to take me to the store so I can get a few gifts and his favorite pie. I love to do things like this, but we have no money and I just had surgery eleven days ago. I am feeling better every day, but I have to stay in bed and rest a lot. I way overdid it at the store, and now I am in pain! I must get back in bed and just relax, take it easy before I hurt myself.

June 14, 2001

My surgeon's office called and said they need to send me to an oncologist … a what! *I started freaking out. I said, "Wait! That means cancer. I have* cancer? I have cancer? *What happened to* benign? *I need my doctor to call me as soon as she can!"*
She is such a great doctor. She called me at noon, knowing I was panicking. She said, "I know you're freaking out, but I know when I did the surgery, I got it all; no other organs were affected." She said if you have even one atypical cell, they have to call it a cancer."
This is not making me feel at ease at all! She said, "I think they are wrong, but this means you need to be carefully monitored for a period of time."
I will keep a positive attitude. I will be fine. I know that this is part of my lesson in life. I will live a very long healthy life for my daughter and my true love. We just found one another. We have many years to be together, but for right now, I am going to allow myself to freak the hell out and know it is okay to be scared. It is okay to be concerned, but I will stay positive; I will stay focused and take care of myself.

June 16, 2001

I keep hearing the pathology report in my mind saying it is adrenal carcinoma, which is cancer. I have had many doctors and nurses tell me that an angel was with me the day I went to the hospital when I had the pain, because they estimate that it had been growing for at least ten years, probably much longer. They said if the tumor had burst, I would have died. Thank you, my guardian angel, for saving my life! Thank you, thank you, thank you!

My surgeon told me that she wanted me to go back to my life before the tumor. She said she is so confident that it is just a precaution and that she got it all. I miss my baby girl so much; a month is way too long for her to be away from her Mom. I need to hold her and hug her, to see her adorable smile. She is so full of life!

My boyfriend is upset with me again, and I truly don't know what I did. I am dealing with a lot right now. Why can't he have compassion for me? How about empathy for what I have endured, for how I feel? I really thought he had shown me so much love and passion in the beginning that he would be so grateful that I would be okay, and that he would always be by my side and take care of me. Sadly, that wasn't really the case. We talked before the surgery, and the emotions he was showing me showed he was scared that he would lose me. Before my surgery I had asked him to make sure he put Chap Stick on my lips because I read surgery can make them dry and crack; and also to please be by my side when I wake up. When I opened my eyes I was all alone and I reached up and touched my lips and they were dry. Sounds silly I know but a tear rolled down my cheek I just felt like in that moment I really didn't matter.

One time in the first few days of being home, he got in the shower with me and washed my hair because I couldn't even lift my arms up to do it myself. As I stood there crying, he comforted me. He loves me so much. He will take care of me. He was so gentle and kind, but then that was shattered when he didn't come home. It has been hours since he has talked to me. The sad thing is he has been gone for three days for work and obviously he has forgotten how much he missed me. I guess it was only me that missed him. I put my all into our relationship, thinking it would be received and given back in the same ways, but it never seems to work that way for me. Why? What am I doing wrong?

June 21, 2001

Twenty days after my surgery. I miss my little girl so much I can't wait. She comes home Tuesday! I want my baby girl home with me where she belongs. This has been so hard not having her here, but I did it for her!

June 26, 2001

My baby girl is finally home! I was standing on the front porch waiting for her to arrive and when she pulled up in the driveway with my mom I started to cry I was so happy. She jumped out of the car and ran up yelling "mommy, mommy" and hugged me so tight. She was happy to be home, a month and a half for a seven year old is a long time. I know for me it was hard not having her here.

July 6, 2001

I have an appointment in another state to see a specialist who deals with adrenal cancers. I am so upset with all of this. I just want it to be okay. I don't want to be sick. With all my heart and soul, please hear my prayers. I want to live to a very old age to watch my daughter grow up. I want to see my grandchildren and great grandchildren. I want to grow old hand in hand with the man I love. At times this has been pretty scary, not knowing if I'm going to live or die!

July 9, 2001

I talked to my brother today. He and his girlfriend reserved a room for us on the Russian River; it looks very relaxing and romantic. What a nice thoughtful thing for them to do!

My baby was sick last night. She threw up four times. Poor honey; maybe she got too much sun today. I don't like it when she is sick. In fact, I hate it!

When I feel sad or scared, I mostly read a book or write in my journal mainly to clear my mind.

My boyfriend and I went up to Boca Lake today and sat by the water. In the sand he wrote, "Every day I love you more." I started crying it was so sweet. Really! That would be like a scene in a romance movie. I want every day to feel like that! These moments are the ones I cherish and wish would never end. To feel that connection with him and the way he loves me, it's just so incredibly strong. We are amazing together. We truly are. We sure got lucky to have the special love that we do! I am so scared, though. I try to push it down and hide it, but I am. I just want to know that I can trust him and count on him to always be here for me, no matter what situation comes up, that he will be by my side.

July 12, 2001

I don't know what his problem is the past few days, but he is lashing out at me for everything. Like the girls took showers, and I dried my daughter's hair first because she came to me and asked me too and to curl her bangs. Then he comes up to me and says, "The next time you have the girls take showers, you dry my daughter's hair too!" I will take care of my daughter and your daughter like I have since the day I moved in here! Like I would be mean and not take care of his kids; this house and everything else every day. He needs to back the hell off of me and get a grip on this bad attitude he has with me! I am waiting to go see a specialist about cancer. Could you give me a damn break here? Oh, and by the way, I am trying to help you raise your kids! You'd think he would be more grateful.

July 31, 2001

The specialist explained to me what he wanted me to do when I get home, like having a PET scan, and if there are no signs of cancer he wants me to have scans done every three months to monitor me. There is a lymph node that is enlarged in the middle of my lower back, and they don't know why so this is what they have a concern about, that the cancer spread. My golden year will be five years. A PET scan is where you have to lie still for hours, and they inject you with nuclear medicine, which highlights any cancer in the body.
When we first got there, I went into the bathroom dropped to my knees, put my hands together, cried, and prayed to please not let anything bad happen to me. It has been pretty terrifying at times!
While we were out of town seeing the specialist we decided since my brother reserved a room for us spending some alone time together for a few days would be so nice. So I had my boyfriend try to highlight my hair.... Yikes, *that went very wrong! I ended up with an orangey reddish look. Oh my goodness, it looked terrible. What a blast! I had tinfoil all over my head. We were laughing and acting like we knew how to highlight hair. It was fun to spend time together being happy even if we did ruin my hair. Being alone was good for us; we got to relax and reconnect. We have a beautiful relationship. I don't believe he would ever lie to me or cheat on me. I think he is a good man, and for that I am lucky and so grateful. I put bubble bath in this huge Jacuzzi tub and turned on the jets when I left the bathroom. When we came back in, there was a tower of bubbles taller than he is. It was crazy funny! In the midst of bad times, there are really good times. I*

wish they could all be good loving fun times! God, I love that man!
He has my heart.
A really neat thing they do at this place we stayed is they have a
journal in the rooms for anyone who wants to write in it. We read
from others who were there before us. I found it to be so touching
to read personal thoughts of people you will never meet. It was so
beautiful right on the river. When you stepped out onto the back
deck, you could see the seals in the river lounging on the rocks and
the walruses making loud noises. It was so tranquil!

August 3, 2001

He got home around eleven o'clock at night. He was so drunk he
was falling into the walls and computer desk. He was very mean
with his words. The few days away, even with me having cancer
didn't change the way he was drinking or behaving. I was trying to
help him up, and he kept pushing me away, saying, "Don't touch
me!" Then he said, "I want to go home." I said, "Honey, you are
home." He said, "I love you. Don't ever leave me." I said, "Of course
not. I will never leave you. I am always here for you!" How do you
not see that you get so drunk you fall into walls and you're cruel to
people? How many times do you have to make yourself sick just to
feel better, only to go back at it again the next day or next week? I
know I am not perfect. I have my flaws, but this fight was not my
fault. There are no winners when we argue because we miss out on
precious time. Sometimes life kicks our ass. We need to get back up
and keep fighting!

September 11, 2001

Today is a day that will go down in history as one of the worst attacks
ever on the United States! As I was lying in bed still healing from

my surgery, my boyfriend called me and said, "Are you watching the news?" I said, "No." He said, "Turn on the TV. A plane just crashed into the Twin Towers!"

I couldn't believe what my eyes were seeing. It was a catastrophic disaster, and massive numbers of lives would be lost today! I watched as they played the news footage of the exact time that the first plane crashed into the tower. I really couldn't believe what I saw! As the day unfolded, I kept my daughter home from school, and watched hours and hours of the destruction that terrorists have caused. Planes were hijacked, the Pentagon was hit, and the Twin Towers crumbled before America's eyes. Our hearts were breaking coast to coast!

As the tears poured down my face, I grieved for the people who lost their lives today and for the families that would never be able to hold their loved ones again. I held my daughter so tight and asked my boyfriend to come home early from work. As the day went by, we saw footage of people actually jumping out of the towers to escape the fire from a hundred floors above, the giant cloud of ash covering city blocks, the countless rescuers and people helping the injured, and all along hearing the death toll climb higher and higher!

Things like this are beyond what the word devastation means. It really brings what is important in life into perspective when innocent lives are lost and families are destroyed by an act of terrorism. This is a tragic day for the entire world! It makes me feel very grateful for what I do have and to be able to be lying here in my bed healing and holding my daughter, but in the same breath, I feel so helpless and my heart aches for those going through this terrible tragedy. I wish I could do something to help those in need. All I can do across the miles is to send healing prayers and thoughts for the lives that have been lost. Like millions of others, we will watch and grieve for days, weeks, even years to come and do all we can to help. There just aren't any words to describe what has happened today, but I know as an entire nation, this will affect every one of us.

September 28, 2001

When I tell the kids to do something and my boyfriend goes against me, he shows them how to disrespect me. We should be a team. He knows damn well I take good care of them. I am trying to do what's best and what I feel is right. Where is the support? If we argue, he just blames me. It is always my fault. Then he threatens me that he will leave. How ridiculous is it that we have been together one and a half years, and he threatens to leave me for a silly argument? I know he has his defenses, but all that does is create a lot of insecurities on my part. Really, how controlling of him! Do you know how hurtful it is for someone you love to constantly threaten to leave you—and for no reason at all? It's like his weapon, but he is hurting my heart. Why not have healthy discussions like two adults and compromise? Sounds fair to me! I know he doesn't want to leave, but I suppose he thinks he can scare me into not arguing maybe? It has been a long day. I just need to relax!

After my surgery, I spent years going for test after test, doctor after doctor. Choking down this unbelievable nasty concoction you have to drink before you have certain scans, it made me want to throw up, and I certainly dry heaved! If it wasn't a drink, then they were injecting the fun stuff that warms you from head to toe from the inside out and makes you feel like you peed yourself, and the aftertaste is metallic like you just sucked on a penny! See, there was one enlarged lymph node in the middle of my lower back, and they weren't sure if it was from the surgery or something of concern, so besides keeping an eye on that, they had to make sure no cancer cells popped up anywhere in my body.

The first year I went every three months. I went for cat scans, MRI'S, X-rays, PET scans, ultrasounds, and blood work; specialists followed me for five years! There was never a test I went for that didn't cause me great anxiety. Waiting for those results, you hit your knees and pray! Things like that sure teach you the lesson of what is most important and what has true value in life—and it isn't anything with a price tag. That is something I will never ever forget!

Chapter 3

November 4, 2001

He asked me to marry him! I am getting married! *We are getting married! I am marrying my true love. Oh, life is so good for us. Even through the bad times, we sure love the hell out of each other! Holy crap! I am getting married. Yeah!*

I can't wait to be his wife and spend my life with the one I love. That is so awesome! He told me when we first got together that he would never get married again because he was married twice before. I would say, "Well, I want to get married one day. You will ask me someday. You'll see!" Here is how it happened…. He said he wanted to go up to the lake, and I really didn't want to go. He had been acting really weird, but I reluctantly agreed to go. We were looking out at the lake talking about how peaceful it was, and then he said, "Your dad wishes he was a bird today." As I turned and said, "What are you talking about?" he was down on his knee and said, "So he could see the expression on your face when I ask you to marry me." He was trembling and had tears in his eyes. I yelled and said, "Are you serious? Are you serious?" I started crying. I jumped at him and said, "Yes, yes, of course I will!" It was the most beautiful moment that I will never forget!

He asked my dad for his permission. That was so important to me. I know that meant a lot to my dad!

Finally a man who truly loves me wants to marry me, and he wants to adopt my daughter. We finally have our forever, baby girl! He said he never met an angel until me and that he could search his whole life and he would never be able to find a woman like me who loves him so much and treats him so well, that I am so committed to us! I know we have had our share of problems, but we have managed to work through things and stay together, so I am hopeful that we will have a good life together. If he could slow down his drinking, that would be even better! I just want him to be healthy so we can spend as many years as possible together.

When I get lost in life, he will be there for me; he will wait patiently as I will for him. I know no matter how hard I push, he will never leave me; I feel so secure knowing that. Thank you, God, for saving us last for each other! I will never be alone in my life again. When the kids are grown and starting their own lives, we will have one another. When our parents age and pass on (God forbid), we can hold each other up. I can't wait to be eighty years old sitting with him laughing! We will tell our great grandchildren all about how we persevered through the difficulties and that at the end of the day, love is all that matters! That's what love is about: being there when times get tough. In your darkest hours, you're one another's best friend. You share your secrets, dreams, and hopes and help each other make them a reality! Here is to the future! Our future …

The story behind my daughter is that she had emergency open heart surgery at seven weeks old. She was flown to a specialty hospital on the West Coast. The day after her surgery, she had a serious complication. She almost died. They had to use an experimental drug to save her life. Thank goodness it worked, and ten days later, I got to bring her home.

Eight weeks after that, my ex threw us out of the house. I had no job, no car, no money, and a sick infant. My daughter ended up with severe stomach issues after the surgery. She had a bit of a rough time at first. At three months old, she was the exact same weight as when she was born; she had not gained one ounce! Do you know how crazy that sounds that she lived three months and hadn't gained an ounce? Thank goodness my baby girl clearly had a team of angels watching over her!

This was scary for me as a young mom, and her biological dad wanted nothing to do with us. My best friend drove into town to pick me up with my daughter, my dog, and our personal belongings and I left. Before I did, he threw $300.00 cash at me and said, "Here. This is all you will ever get from me!" I will never understand why he wouldn't want to help take care of his child. Needless to say, this was a very stressful time for me. I had a sick baby I was taking care of all by myself, I had no money and no place to call home. Essentially I had nothing, but at the same time, I had everything. I had my baby girl, and that is what mattered most. The rest would fall into place with time. I had to believe that!

My ex liked to threaten me a lot that he would kidnap my daughter or he would turn her against me or if the state came after him for child support, he would make sure he would work under the table so I couldn't collect support from him. Take care of your responsibilities! He liked to verbally attack me to make me feel very insecure about myself. He would tell me my hair looked like crap or I was fat. He would say to me, "Look at yourself. No one would ever want you." Then he would laugh at me. It was cruel, and I was devastated. I had no self-esteem! I believed what he had said to me for so long.

He ended up signing away his parental rights when she was about ten months old. I never knew someone could sign a paper and say, "Hey, I don't want to be a parent," so they are by law no longer that child's parent and no longer financially or legally obligated. How does that happen? It is called terminating your parental rights. Well, okay, then that is how it will be! Sad as it was at the time and the emotional damage I knew it would inevitably cause my daughter, it was the best thing that could have happened; otherwise life would not have been the same for us. One day when she is an adult, if she wishes to find him and talk to him, then that is her choice, and I would support her and would even be there with her.

Even after he gave up his rights, I tried so hard to allow him to be a daddy, but it never worked out. The broken promises, lies, and inconsistencies just weren't part of a life we needed for us to be healthy. My daughter deserved so much better than that. Over the years when we would move, I would only allow him to have our phone number. I had to stop letting him know where we lived. We always met him out somewhere. I guess in some way I thought this would help protect us, and I think it really did a little because he couldn't harass us in person. I have had to get several restraining orders against him, and even had one served when he lived in another state. How crazy is that?

I had to have him arrested one time when she was three and a half years old because he came to my house freaked out and started banging on the roof of his truck. He was yelling, "Why don't you love me? Nobody loves me." He threatened to kill himself and told me it would be my fault, so the police showed up and put him down in the driveway. They cuffed him, took him to jail, and put him on suicide watch. It turned out that he had become a serious drug addict, and I had no clue this was happening. He called me the next day after he got out, and I told him that if we were going to be friends and he was going to be part of my daughter's life, then he needed to go to a rehab facility and be evaluated for his drug use and get help in some type of program. He never got into a program; he never got help for himself.

This went on until she was five years old. His grandmother called me then to tell me he was in jail again for drugs; according to her, I think this time it was meth. At that point when he called me, I accepted one last collect phone call from him. I told him this was it; he would no longer be allowed to have a relationship with my daughter. He was doing nothing beneficial for her. I had given him every opportunity to be her dad, but I was not going to let her go through life allowing him to constantly disappoint her. I made the decision to cut a very toxic person out of our lives. He was never a dad to her, and whenever it was convenient, he would want to see her or come by, but that was only a few times a year and it didn't come without serious consequences. So I refer to him as "the sperm donor." She doesn't remember him, and she hasn't seen him since she was five years old. This is why I was very careful about the man I chose as a partner. My daughter and I are a package deal, and I just wanted a good loving environment for her to grow up in with a family that loved her as much as I do—and my family does!

December 12, 2001

Today is my birthday, and I am miserable, me and my big honest mouth!

I started an argument last night, not meaning to, but it turned into that about the kids again. What the hell is wrong with me? I have been so worried about everything lately, and especially worried about the cancer, so instead of being close I feel like I am pushing him away. I need to change the way I do some things, but I know it isn't all me because he says a lot of cruel things. We all have our defenses. I feel like I am hurting our relationship and he is the last person I'd ever want to hurt. I have a man I want to spend my life with and who wants to spend his life with me. I want to be the best wife that I can! I have had a miserable day, and I only have myself to blame. Happy birthday to me!

Sometimes before we would go out, he would drink a lot at home, and then while we were out, he would always drink so much more. Let me put it this way: almost every time we were out, he got drunk. He would either stumble or be really loud and rude to people. It wasn't funny; it was humiliating. I frequently mouthed a silent "I'm sorry" to people, who would just shake their heads looking at him. I never said anything in the beginning to him, because well, I am not sure why, but a combination of not realizing it was a problem and feeling like it wasn't my place to say something, I suppose. Because after all, he just drank heavy on the weekends, so that was normal, right? On the weekends, though, when we did recycling, the kids would count all the beer cans or bottles, and the one that sticks out in my mind the most was when I heard the girls counting seventeen, eighteen, nineteen. Holy crap, are you kidding me? You have two young girls here counting Daddy's alcohol. Yep, it was all his. He drank alone, and that was just for one night!

My husband doesn't believe AA works; he says it isn't for him. I believe that is because he really didn't give it a fair chance to work. I have asked him so many times over the years to get help and go into treatment, but he always tells me that he could stop if he wanted to and that he isn't an alcoholic. I used to believe him, but over the years, the many failed attempts to quit drinking kind of speak for themselves. I know some people have the ability to stop cold turkey and never drink another drop again. My aunt's husband was an alcoholic, and one day she couldn't take it anymore. He was given an ultimatum: alcohol or her. He chose her and got help and was sober for over twenty-plus years; he swears by AA. Sadly, he passed away recently, but like anything, if you don't want to stop and you're not willing to, then you won't! I know you have to do it for yourself first and foremost. He was just ready to change his life!

January 3, 2002

I have this feeling that my fiancé is at the bar again. We will see. He was really mean to everyone last night. He snapped at his oldest daughter, and then he snapped at my daughter. He is so pissy. I don't know why; it's just one of his moods again! Well, now it has been fourteen hours since he has been gone, which is always my indicator that I know he is drinking. Yep, he is drinking—great!

Finally a phone call at 12:30 a.m.—from the bar, surprise. I had to go follow him home. Yes, he drove home drunk. Otherwise he would have done it without me, so to make sure I could watch him, I did it. This totally sucks! I don't believe or agree with drinking and driving for any reason ever! He has driven home intoxicated more times than I care to admit, and when I refuse to rescue him, he drives home drunk, so at times I feel responsible for the safety of him and others, and I go and get him and follow him or take him home, and we get his car the next day. Either way, it is wrong!

I feel like he puts me in these positions where it's like a rock and a hard place: if I don't go get him, then he drives drunk; and if I go and ask him to ride with me and he doesn't want to, then he gets in his car to leave, so I guess I figure the lesser of two evils is to follow him closely and pray he doesn't hurt himself or anyone else. What an awful place to be emotionally! I am so disappointed that he doesn't consider my feelings at all, but that is part of the alcoholism—pure selfishness! I'm sad and hurt. I feel neglected. I don't feel important, and some days I wonder if I should reconsider this life with him.

January 7, 2002

What a weekend! My daughter started having stomach pain when we were coming out of the pizza place where we were having lunch; she collapsed in the parking lot! My fiancé caught her, and we took her to the

ER. She had to have her appendix removed. We got there around two thirty in the afternoon, and she didn't have surgery until about ten o'clock that evening. What a long wait for a nine-year-old in pain with a high fever! She was so brave in the pre-op; they were explaining everything to her, and she just listened and trusted them to make her feel better.

I stayed the night with her at the hospital. I held her hand. The next day he and the kids came to get us, and they bought her a fish. She was so excited! She named him Fin. So cute ... When things like that happen, he is so good. I just wish it was all the time.

January 10, 2002

Suddenly he wants me to show him receipts for everything I buy, like I am a child and can't be trusted. So sorry you feel that way. How about you show me all your drinking and gambling receipts first, then I will show you mine! Please, I do everything around here, including work. The only thing I don't do is his job! I will be damned if I allow him to treat me like that. He has no right! He doesn't seem too focused on us anymore; he has lost sight of what's important. Us, our family, getting married! I feel pushed aside. Hell, he pushes everyone aside, even the kids! I want us to keep the passion we share fresh and make each other a priority. Don't get me wrong. We love each other, but sometimes when life gets tough and finances get difficult, you stress and lose sight of each other, and that isn't good. Always be willing to be the one to hold out your hand and not give up.

January 11, 2002

He apologized for putting work first and losing sight of our relationship. He said he has been so stressed with work, he is just overwhelmed. He said, "I want to be more normal, like we used to be." He said he loves me and wants us to be happy.

I love when he takes my face in his hands and we get lost gazing into each other's eyes. I know he loves me so much. We can't lose sight of what is important—each other! I breathe in and out every day like everyone else. I put one foot in front of the other and just take it day by day. At times I don't understand his bitterness toward me. It is almost like he is punishing me for something that I didn't even do. I don't like this, and I can't be treated this way for the rest of my life! The rest of the day was great. We were close and loving. We went and walked around the mall together, talking and laughing. It was nice to be together!

Life can be so unpredictable living with someone who has an addiction problem; one minute they love you, and the next they hate you. It feels very unstable; there is no security, only broken promises and lies. You feel like at any time it can all come crashing down, and no matter how much you try to prepare for it, you can never really prepare for something so devastating. I read a quote on the Internet that said "to be in a constant state of intoxication with total disregard for the negative consequences." Sounds like an alcoholic to me.

The Internet also shows there are four characteristics of alcoholism:

1) craving,
2) loss of control,
3) physical dependency, and
4) tolerance

It seems to depend what site you go on and what book you read as to what they say about what the definition of an alcoholic is or the definition of alcoholism. Some believe it is a disease, and others say it is not a disease, it is a choice. I got the following information online from various websites that discuss alcoholism.

Alcoholism is when you have signs of physical addiction to alcohol and continue to drink, despite problems with physical health, mental health, and social, family, or job responsibilities. Alcohol may control your life and relationships. Alcohol abuse is when you're drinking leads to problems, but not physical addiction. Support groups are available to help people who are dealing with alcoholism. The following are three such support groups:

Alcoholics Anonymous (AA)
This is a self-help group of recovering alcoholics that offers emotional support and specific steps for people recovering from alcohol dependence. The program is commonly called a twelve-step approach. There are local chapters throughout the United States. AA offers help twenty-four hours a day and teaches that it is possible to participate in social functions without drinking.

Al-Anon
Family members of a person with an alcohol abuse problem often need counseling. Al-Anon is a support group for partners and others who are affected by someone else's alcoholism.

Alateen
Provides support for teenage children of people with alcoholism.

I did an interview with a woman in her early forties. She has been sober for almost one year. She is an alcoholic/addict, and this is her story.

Question: When did you first realize you had an addiction problem?

Recovering Female Addict: *I knew I had a drinking problem for a while. It started out socially, but as my job got more stressful, the self-medicating really kicked in! I was given Xanax for severe anxiety, and* *it went downhill from there. I was drinking about two bottles of wine a night and taking tons of pills. I would then start waking up shaking and have to drink more. Then I suffered a nervous breakdown and tried to kill myself a little over a year ago.*

That still was not my rock bottom; the addiction became much worse. I was in and out of the hospital for a couple of months, but continued to use every time I got out. In May 2012 I decided to try and kill myself again and took an overdose of pills and drank for three days straight. I got behind the wheel and was attempting to drive off of a cliff and took down a light pole and some other cars.

I believe that is when God intervened. I was, of course, arrested. I spent the night in jail and checked into rehab the next day. That was the best thing I ever did. In rehab I was introduced to AA/NA. It has changed my life! I have not used since, nor do I have the desire to.

Question: Have you been married or in a serious relationship while you had your addiction problems?

Recovering Female Addict: *I have never been married. I was in a relationship when this happened, but I am no longer with that person. It was a very unhealthy relationship. I had to get rid of a lot of friendships. You really find out who your real friends are when you go through something like that. A lot of people liked me better when I was sick, so they could feel better about themselves—clearly toxic people!*

Question: How long have you been sober, and what changes have you seen in yourself from before and the way you are now?

Recovering Female Addict: *I have been sober for over ten months; I am coming up on my one-year anniversary! I am a completely different person. I have changed everything! I no longer work at the* *stressful job. I was making a lot of money, but walked away from it. No job is worth losing yourself or your life over. I have made new and wonderful friendships and relationships. I am a much kinder and more honest person. I can go to bed at night knowing I have not hurt anybody and I have done my best for today.*

Question: Did something traumatic happen that caused you to start using?

Recovering Female Addict: Yes, a lot of things happened that caused me to start drinking. I had a very hurtful relationship with my mother. She was very controlling and consumed with me! She wanted me to be perfect and beautiful. She made me take laxatives and fast when I was in high school. Our relationship is much better now. I have had hundreds of hours of therapy learning how to deal with her. She is very supportive of my sobriety. I was raised to be perfect, and nothing but perfect would do. There is a lot more to this story, but I can honestly say I have never been happier in my life.
I have found my higher power and he is guiding me through. Life is amazing! My dad is my biggest supporter; he is so proud of me. He helps keep me sober because I never want to hurt him in the ways I did ever again. I am happy I went through all I did because I am a much better and happier person because of it.

As you can see, there are many people of all different walks of life who turn to self-medicating due to traumatic things that may have happened in their lives. Nothing traumatic at all has to happen to self-medicate either!
Instead of continuing to self-medicate, the woman I interviewed above found something to believe in that was greater than her. She turned her life around and found happiness without the use of substances in her life. The hope and strength she found to take

this journey began with the first step of self-realization: that she in fact had to admit she did have a problem and she was not able to manage her life. Recovery is a lifelong journey, but one that will bring renewed hope and faith back into your life with the very first step!

Chapter 4

We weren't even married yet, and look at all these problems we were having. I know we all come with emotional baggage and I understand about what he went through in his past, but I also had a past and baggage. We had to be on the same team here, be here for one another. However, if this was a preview of our future, we would inevitably have serious problems. I just wanted us to be able to communicate on an adult level and be able to resolve our issues together. Some relationships are stepping-stones to finding your true love; others find it right away. We have a passionate love that is a blessing and comes around only once in a lifetime!

May 10, 2002

He is moody again! Why? I can't answer the reason this time. I don't understand. He got upset with me because I was busy doing laundry. He came in and said, "I thought we were having tacos tonight." I said, "We are." He said, "Really? When?" Hey, here's an idea: if you want them now, go in the kitchen and make them yourself.
I said, "Have you taken a Xanax yet?" He said, "No. I haven't picked up my prescription." I said, "Maybe it will help you with your mood because you're being rude." He said, "How about this? Fuck you!" I said, "That's really nice!" Obviously I was right about him needing the medication. Then he started putting on his shoes like he was going to leave. I said, "You better take all of these kids with you if your leaving!" He gave me

*a nasty look and just took his son—*shocker! *Way to abandon the girls and me again. Look how you're teaching your son to treat women! I am so tired of his moodiness and taking it out on me for no reason. Hey, bad day at work or not, I am not his punching bag to take his frustrations out on every day. It is not okay to be so disrespectful and hurtful!*

May 17, 2002

Late again coming home from work. He is at the bar again drinking, and as usual, I have all the kids. I have been calling him and paging him, but he won't answer.
I just don't understand. He should want to be home spending time with his family, not out getting drunk all the time! You know, like sitting in the pool in the backyard playing with the kids. Just him and I going out to a movie, playing darts, having dinner, anything that doesn't include him drinking. Sadly, all these things do in fact include alcohol, and only on a very rare occasion, he may only have like three drinks instead of thirty.

May 19, 2002

Surprise! He is at the bar again. He just called; he is drunk. I am not happy at all!
I had been trying to do something with him all day, and he either wants to nap or drink. I just want to spend some time together. Is that too much to ask? I try talking with him about wedding plans, but he doesn't seem interested. I feel sad as I sit here alone in our bedroom writing in my journal wishing he would pay more attention to me. I want to plan our wedding and make it an amazing day for us! It is so sad that the man I am planning on marrying doesn't seem to have much interest in our own wedding, that's a shame. I am so excited to become his wife

and for him to be my husband. This is our forever, our special day. I wish he were more excited and more involved in it. It really hurts my feelings because I don't care where we do it and it doesn't have to be expensive. I just want to share that commitment with him for the rest of our lives. I hope he gets more excited as it gets closer.

You know if he was just a social drinker and not an alcoholic, I wouldn't have such an issue with him drinking, but when it becomes more important than your family and there is substantial money loss and so on and so forth, it becomes a real problem. I love this man with all my heart and soul. We really are so good together, our personalities compliment one another but the drinking is an issue. We have so much love. He is my best friend, and no matter what happens on our worst day, it is better than not being with him at all because I believe that we can get through any storm together.

June 1, 2002

This weekend was his son's birthday. So all day up until now, 10:37 p.m., he has had about fourteen beers (yes, I count them often). He is drunk, yet he left and took his son and his friends to go have pizza. How foolish can you be? It is bad enough to do that to yourself, but to involve your kids and someone else's kids is just unbelievable—that is how people die.

Oh, and then he brought the boys to the skate park earlier, and about an hour and a half later, the kids came home but he didn't. Yep, he went to the bar! Really, it is your kid's birthday and you can't stay out of the bar? You can't control yourself to not drink for one day? Tell me again how you don't have a drinking problem!

I could smell the smoke from the bar, which had seeped into his clothes and body, and the stench of the booze was just gross!

He started with his rude selfish attitude for no reason. He said to me, "You self-righteous bitch." I said, "Don't you dare call me names.

You not only have one child at home that is sick, but three kids at a park, two of which aren't even yours, and you're out drinking. What if something happened? I had no idea where anybody was. What the hell is wrong with you? You leave all this in my hands all the time and have no appreciation for what I do or the situations you leave me in." I just want him to care. Screw this! I am so pissed off I am going to bed. I can't write anymore; I'm too angry! Why can't he just be a good husband, a good father? Why can't he do what is right for his family, for himself? Why is it so hard for him to make the right choices? I am so disappointed!

June 22, 2002

Surprise, we are arguing again! Part of me feels like this happens often so he can use it as an excuse to run to the bar and drink, because that is how he deals with things: he self-medicates. He creates an argument so he can leave and blame me for his behaviors. My husband is having an affair. It is with the bottle; alcohol always comes first! This is years and years of this behavior. It certainly isn't anything that I have caused, although he really likes to try and blame me and everyone else.

June 23, 2002

He walked to the bar late last night. I fell asleep only to wake up later and find him passed out on our bathroom floor. I have no idea when he came home. Can you believe he is drinking again today? He has already had a six-pack. Christ, it's like he just woke up! We haven't spoken much. I am so hurt by his actions. I can't believe he can live like this and not feel bad about how he treats me or the kids.
It is a roller-coaster life being with an alcoholic, and it isn't a fun ride. Give him the strength to stop drinking and hurting me and us in the process. I want him to stay healthy and show me I am important, that

I matter, that our life matters, that the kids matter. He finally meets me a woman who gives him love in the way he has said he has wanted all his life, so why is he not able to cherish it? I forgot to mention he left around six o'clock to bring the kids home but hasn't returned yet. Yep you guessed it, the bar!

I must be insane to consider marrying him when I see what life is like now. Maybe I am hoping that it will be different somehow. I don't know what I am thinking. I am just a believer that all things can be better. We do spend a lot of time together. It isn't all bad. We have great fun times. I just wish the bad times weren't so bad! We do family things with the kids. We spend some time alone. I mean, I go with him to the bars to play darts and shuffleboard, because if I don't, we would never be together. I really enjoy it. We have played in a few tournaments. He often goes to the bars alone too.

I just wish he was sober more often. Sometimes I try and bite my tongue and not complain about his drinking, and at times I talk myself into being okay with it because, after all, he does work hard and he deserves to have a few drinks on the weekends, right? Does that mean he always has to get so drunk, though? There are times when I am embarrassed because he is falling into things or falling down, being loud and rude. It makes me feel sad inside. I know he is worth more than his last binge. I just wish he knew!

July 3, 2002

He stayed out till 1:30 a.m. last weekend drinking, and then the next day didn't come home till the afternoon. He said to me, "Would it help if I said I was sorry and if I stop drinking?" He said he can feel that his drinking is killing him and he doesn't want to do this anymore; he knows he has been hurting me and the kids. He said we are all he has in this life and he doesn't want to lose us! He got emotional and started to tear up and said, "I love you so much I never

want to lose you. You're the best thing that has ever happened to me.
You take such good care of me. I promise to do better!" Dare I say
that I have some hope that he realizes what he is doing and is going
to change? That somehow someway he will find the strength to stop
drinking and control it this time? Maybe go to some meetings or seek
counseling to help him with his binge drinking? I hope so. I will help
him through it and be here for him.

July 18, 2002

Finally everything seems to be straightened out with my fiancé and
me. It is about time. He has been a bit moody because he hasn't had
a drink in about two weeks. I know it can make him irritable, but
he is lashing out a bit at me and the kids. I am so grateful that he
has not had a drink. I know his moods will even out. I just need
to be supportive and be there for him! I am so proud of him for
not drinking. I think we are going to be okay. This is it—no more
alcohol—now we can work on our closeness again and be happy! I
love him so much. I want to spend our lives being in love, laughing
going through all life has to offer together, the ups and downs, all of
it, as long as we have each other and we are best friends!

For me it seems like there isn't anything worse than a wife waiting
to see if her husband is going to come home drunk again, if he
gambled away his whole paycheck, what excuse she will have
to make up to cover for him, what lie she can tell everyone this
time. It is a horrible emotional cycle, and I for one have never
felt more alone in my life than dealing with this and trying to
educate myself on what alcoholism and alcoholics are. I was trying
everything in my power to help him, only to realize that I had
helped to enable him. I had become an enabler, and I didn't even
know it—go figure! I thought an alcoholic had to drink every day

and be drunk. Turns out I was wrong. They say that when people can't control how much they drink after the first drink and always have to get intoxicated, that is an alcoholic.

My fiancé is a binge drinker first and foremost, even if he went months without a drink. When he did have one again, it wasn't just one. It was an enormous amount, and I think he consumed until he just felt like he couldn't consume anymore. I can't tell you how many times he has gotten sick, and I can't understand why he would want to go back and do it time and time again. I mean, how many hangovers, how many blackouts, how much lost money, and how many times do you poison yourself and throw up or have to make yourself throw up to realize, "Hey, I have a problem." He always defended his actions and insisted he was in fact *not an alcoholic*! Denial is a huge part of alcoholism! The absolute worst part is the selfishness, the self-entitlement, it's all about me mentality is just sickening!

October 23, 2002

It has been awhile since I have written in my journal, and the day started out great! I went and tried on a dress for our wedding. I got some material to make a train, and so far I have had so much fun with it. I am trying to save money by making my own train— probably not a good idea since I failed sewing classes in high school! I called my fiancé around eleven o'clock. He said, "I was just going to call you." I asked why, and he said, "Because I miss you!" Awwww, how sweet, he misses me—now that makes me feel great! Things are good! We met for lunch and decided we would go out tonight; all is right with the world again! At least in our world, it is.

But I spoke too soon. He saw a phone bill in the truck and got stressed out, so he started fighting with me, and I was explaining that it would be okay, we would catch up. He turned it into a huge ugly problem and got mean. He said, "*Before you I was maintaining.*" I said, "*Then maintain.*" He said, "*I can't because of you!*" I replied, "*This has nothing to do with me. You can't maintain financially because you have a drinking problem, and you also have a gambling problem!*" He said, "*I can't even pay the IRS bill.*"

But of course when we got home, he got in his car and left. I am sure he went drinking. He leaves me and drowns his sorrows and wastes money on his addiction, yet he creates an argument with me about money. It really has nothing to do with the money. It is his escape to run and drink! Hey, he can't pay the damn bill, so let's piss it away on booze—now there's a concept!

Before he left, he came into the house and in front of his oldest daughter he called me an asshole; he said I am an idiot and I am stupid. Then he threw the dog leash at me and left! I am so angry at him for treating me that way in front of the kids. He was completely out of line; this is bullshit! What is wrong with him? That was so disrespectful to do to me!

November 22, 2002

Last night we had a big argument. He said so many mean things to me, like "*Pack your stuff and move out of my house!*" Then today he called and asked me to bring him lunch. Crap! Talk about confused! So we talked a little about what happened. One minute it is "*Get out of my house*"; the next it's "*Come have lunch with me.*" That plays with my emotions and can be so exhausting! Then after work he goes to the bar instead of coming home! What the hell? I don't get it. I just don't understand how he thinks at all. I always know when he goes to the bar because of the amount of time he is gone and his phone is off. I am so disappointed in him, and he wonders why I feel like he doesn't care about me.

I can only imagine what this is doing to the kids; I know what it is doing even if they don't! I just can't understand how he doesn't see it!

He has me, a woman who loves him and would do anything for him, and this is how you treat her? I mean, I take care of his kids way more than he does. Why? Because it isn't fair to them that he leaves them. But then people talk about me like I am a mean awful bitch! Please! People have no idea what is really happening, so it is easy for them to place judgment and listen to gossip. These certainly aren't the actions of a man who is concerned about his family, and frankly, it makes me feel like I am worthless!

December 7, 2002

His brother called him, and it seems like as soon as he hung up, he was trying to fight with me. That way he would have an excuse to leave because he was going to stay home and spend time with me, but with the enticing draw of the alcohol, he just couldn't say no! So we went in the bedroom to talk. He was being a total jerk, calling me a bitch for no reason. I said, "Excuse me." He said, "I said 'bitch.' How many more times do you want me to say it?" Then he proceeds to call me a fu**ing asshole, and says that I am f**ked up in the head. Why the need to be so verbally abusive? All this so he can go drink—seriously? How can he feel good talking to me like that? But more importantly, how can he hurt me like that and not seem to care what it does to me? Does he enjoy hurting me? Does it give him some sense of control? We were talking earlier about our past relationships, and his final comment to me was, "This is why I don't want to know about your past, because you're used and used up." Talk about a very mean thing to say to your soon-to-be wife! Probably a good thing he left, because for a moment I wanted to slap him in the face for talking to me like I am a piece of used crap! Tonight I don't want to see him at all, which I am sure I won't anyway. He will probably "pass out" at his brother's, or at least tonight I hope he does. Even thinking that makes me feel like a terrible person because I love him so much, but he seems to have *no regard for how he hurts me. His actions quite frankly when he drinks are very selfish, and it isn't right!*

If you know your life is a journey, you must learn how to travel lightly. If you keep what doesn't make you happy, then there is no room for the good things to come in. Change can make those bad things turn happy if you put in the effort! I know I am guilty of this, but if we go through hell, we all take mental notes and remind ourselves frequently of things that happened, don't we? We should shift our focus onto the great things in our life that are happening or have happened, instead of dwelling on the bad. However, you do have to do some emotional work here. You have to make things right with yourself and others, or that hell you live in in your own mind will never be a place of contentment, but one of mental torture. Nobody wants or deserves that.

Do what it takes to be the best version of yourself that you can be just for today, even if that one small step is to have two drinks instead of four, to refrain from calling your spouse nasty names, to go to bed early, to have dinner with your family, or to try going to just one recovery meeting. Whatever your small step is for you, try it. If you like the results, do a bigger step tomorrow, or just keep repeating the small steps until they become routine and you do them automatically without thinking about it. I know without a doubt that it will start to create a confidence and a happiness in you that will make you want to strive to do more. Maybe one day you won't even want to pick up that drink because you found something worth so much more—your life!

Chapter 5

February 13, 2003

I am the only parent around here who is a parent and not a buddy. I have to enforce everything. I don't understand it at all! Why can't he be on my side and see that I am trying to raise the kids the best I can so they can grow up to be healthy adults? Children should have boundaries and consequences. We as parents are supposed to teach them these things while they are little so they don't grow up thinking they don't have to follow rules and can treat people anyway they want. They need to know the world doesn't owe them anything and that they have to earn things, right?

Maybe it is me with the wrong beliefs about raising kids, but I don't think so. It is very hurtful that he makes me always look like the bad guy intentionally and allows the kids to mistreat me instead of teaching them how to have respect. I am going to be their stepmom. That is hard enough on me, but to have my fiancé make it even harder is just wrong. It isn't their fault. They are just kids. It is his fault. He is the adult and should know better. He is a grown man, and it is time he stopped acting like a spoiled child that does whatever he wants without any concern for how it affects others. It makes me very sad feeling like I am doing something wrong, but I know I am not. I am trying to fit in to an already made family. I just want to be treated with respect and to be cared about. I want my daughter and I to feel like we belong and we are loved after all this is our home too!

I found something on the Internet about house rules, and I thought that it would be helpful for our family; after all, there are four children in the house—five if you count my fiancé, which sometimes I do because of the way he acts. I started to read them to him. When I got about halfway through, he grabbed the remote and turned up the TV. I said, "What are you doing? I am trying to read something important to you. Maybe if we had more rules around here, we would have a better structure for our family!" After a few meaningless words, I started getting, "F**k you, f**k off, stick it up your ass, you don't know when to shut the f**k up", and all this because I want to find a better way to raise our children together. We are getting married in four months, and I can't even talk to him. I can't have my own feelings or opinions about something he doesn't agree with. Really, who the hell does this man think he is, talking to me in such a disrespectful way? He isn't even home half the time! No wonder that the kids do the same; they live what they learn! How do we parent together if he isn't even in the right frame of mind to raise kids? I have never been married before (well, not for love anyway—long story), but I am pretty sure your spouse should be your best friend and the one person you can talk to and count on, right? Trying to dodge his insults and protect the kids is what my job is here, but no one protects me. I take the brunt of everything thrown my way. Does anyone stop and think of how this hurts my heart? Of course they don't, not for one second! Maybe that is my purpose with him: to take care of his kids in a way he is not capable of at this point. Maybe one day he will look back on these years when he is sober and feel grateful for all I did all those years for our family, things that he couldn't really see until he was clean and sober, and he will find a way to make amends and to say thank you and I love you in a way that he never has before. Now that would be something truly amazing!

I was working full-time, paying the bills, keeping the house clean, doing laundry, cooking, shopping, planning all the wedding stuff, and taking care of all the kids (I already considered them my kids too, but what I am pointing out is how unfair he is). I was unappreciated and taken for granted, that is for sure! I kept telling myself that part of this was the stress of the wedding and his work and just life in general, but who was I kidding? Anytime he could drink, he would; he didn't need an excuse, but if he had any excuse, he wouldn't have to take accountability or responsibility for his actions. He could blame someone else, mainly me!

In April of 2003, we drove to another state to be on a famous talk show. Yes, you read right. I was on a talk show with my brother and his fiancée called *Family Grudges*. My fiancé got to sit right up in the front row in the audience he didn't have to sit on stage like me, but during the show the doctor did ask him some questions and brought him into it just a little. Oh my goodness, what a wild experience that was! Family grudges— go figure! My brother had written a letter to this particular show just looking for some advice on how to communicate and handle our brother/sister issues. He thought at best maybe he would get an e-mail from someone with suggestions on what to try, but what he got was a phone call from the producer asking about our story then I got a phone call asking my side. Next thing we knew, Hollywood here we come! In a million years, I would have never thought I would be on a talk show sharing my personal issues with the world. Now I am putting it all in a book! It was crazy! My brother and I had not talked for a year; it's a very long story. Needless to say, the show opened a door for communication. Sometimes all you need is an opportunity for a new beginning. That was a total trip to meet someone famous and sit in front of an audience full of strangers talking about our family problems and emotional baggage. I was so damn nervous! After I was asked to come onstage, maybe fifteen seconds into the show, I was crying like a baby.

April 18, 2003

What can I say except for the fact that I feel like leaving because he is sitting at the bar again? Really, is that all this man thinks life is about, getting drunk and sitting at a bar? Life is passing him by every single day. There is so much going on in the world, and he doesn't see how precious time really is. We are never guaranteed tomorrow! Seriously, what is the excitement about a stinky smoke-filled bar? I mean is this what my life will be like for the next twenty, thirty, or forty years? All I get to look forward to is him sitting in the bars and getting drunk? Two days ago we got into the worst fight ever! He slammed a door in my daughter's face and made her cry, then threw the comforter across the room and knocked a lamp and other things onto the floor. What kind of man makes a little girl cry and just leaves her to feel bad? What kind of father does that to his daughter? He called me some names too. He was a nasty jerk and told me to give him back his ring because our relationship was over; he told me to pack my stuff and leave.

We talked a long time the next day. I cried a lot and told him how much he is hurting me and the way he treated my daughter was wrong. He promised he would work every day on our relationship. More empty promises?

I hope not; I can't take more broken promises. I mean, we love each other, we have so much passion, and our good times together are amazing! I believe he will be better. I really think he wants to be! We are getting married in two months. I know he is a good man; he is a great man. He just has to change his behavior; he just has to see that what he is doing is damaging.

April 19, 2003

Another short-lived promise. He is at the bar again. I mean, not even two days later. What the hell is this? I paged him, and he called me from the bar down the street. I asked when he was coming home, and he said he didn't know. Why do I bother asking? He always does whatever he wants with no regard to others anyway. I don't understand how he can tell me how much he loves me, he never wants to live without me, and then he treats me this way! I wish someone could explain it to me.

I will always feel second to his alcohol. It's not fair he is treating me horribly; his actions are not showing me he loves me. I feel unloved, neglected, abandoned, and useless! What a sad way to feel from the man who is supposed to be my husband in ten weeks! We have so much fun when we are together and things are good. It doesn't matter if we are out playing darts, having lunch, watching a movie or whatever—we are very close, and then other times, it is as though we couldn't be further apart. I really don't understand it.

Three months before we were to get married, his ex-wife called me and told me that my ex worked with her and he wanted to see "his" daughter. First of all, he gave up his parental rights legally when *my* daughter was less than a year old, so he doesn't have a daughter; he is simply a sperm donor. And secondly, it is none of her damn business! This dang town is just too small! He wrote a little note and asked her to give it to my daughter; it had his phone number on it.

I talked to my daughter about it; I wasn't going to let her see him. She was only nine; she wasn't ready for something that confusing. She was not interested in talking to him anyway, but asked if she could write him a letter.

I called him and arranged to meet with him. I brought the letter she wrote, and my fiancé insisted on coming with me. I met my ex outside his work. It went really bad. He was nasty, and honestly I wanted to knock him out for the heartache he had caused my daughter. He started calling me names, and then he got in my face. My fiancé grabbed me by the waist and pulled me away because I was getting ready to hit my ex, and I know he wanted to do the same to me. Hey, if some jackass is going to physically threaten me, I am going to defend myself. I made it very clear to him that he would not speak with my daughter, and once she was eighteen, she could decide for herself, but he gave up his parental rights a long time ago. It was his choice to walk away, and my soon-to-be husband was going to adopt her. He is her father!

On June 22, 2003, we were married—even though the night before, we had a terrible argument. It turned out to be a beautiful day! Most of our family and friends were there. When we danced, we became lost in one another, feeling the strength of our love. As I was walking down the aisle and our eyes met, we knew we wanted to be together. We just needed to find a way for it to be better! I have never doubted my love for him, and I have never doubted his for me. It sounds strange, I know, but we are the love of each other's life. This I know with all my heart and soul to be true! I guess in that moment you feel so much love, acceptance, and hope for the future, you feel as though all the bad will disappear. I suppose part of me truly believed that his drinking would get better, he could control it, and if we didn't have arguments he wouldn't need to drink so much. But he would celebrate his good days with alcohol and self-medicate with alcohol when they were bad; it didn't matter the day as long as he could drink.

It's like this: I would rather go through the bad days with the one I love as opposed to not being with him at all. I was hoping for a new beginning as husband and wife, and in a few months, he was going to legally adopt my daughter. Maybe this would help bring our whole family closer. My daughter would be happy to have him as her dad. Life is full of good and bad, but in those tough times is when you see what you're really made of as a couple and as a person. You hold one another's hand and go through it together. You never let the one you love go through anything alone; you always give your support.

We left for our honeymoon. We drove with no particular destination, just driving to wherever we ended up, because we didn't have the money to go anywhere special at that time. It didn't really matter what we did, just that we were starting our life as husband and wife; being together was all that mattered, at least to me. I thought to myself, *he wouldn't have married me if he wasn't in love with me with all his heart, so here we go together from this day forward for the rest of our lives as Mr. and Mrs. I am so happy to be his wife!*

September 24, 2004

It's been over a year since I last wrote in my journal ....Well life went on kind of the same way good times and bad times. As the kids started getting older more issues would arise with them, and it is difficult to parent with an ex (his) and her new spouse when nobody agrees, so that caused a lot of stressful times as always. We still had our moments of togetherness too, but they seemed to start getting further apart as his drinking started to increase as time went by.

Also; there was a big issue with his oldest daughter and her failing a year of college and lying to us about it. They had a terrible argument and my husband wanted to ground her and she felt she was too old for that and she wanted to go out of town that weekend to visit her Aunt's and he told her if she didn't like it she could move out and that is exactly what she did. That weekend she moved out, she was nineteen years old and the grand baby was four years old; she moved in with her boyfriend and his family. That was just a few months ago during mid-summer of "2004".

*There was a big problem I wanted to write about that happened last
week. Saturday my husband was gone for about twelve hours. He took
off on an old motorcycle, and he didn't even tell me he was leaving.
We didn't really talk again until Monday. He got home early from
work, so we sat down and talked. He told me he took some money out
of the bank account that we didn't have to spend. He said he went
with his brother. He rode a motorcycle that had bad tires, and if he
took a turn that was too sharp, he knew the bike couldn't handle it.
Then he said that if he went off a curve and crashed off a cliff, he
figured he wouldn't feel the pain he feels now!*

*Telling someone you'd rather be dead is just a horrible thing! I
couldn't believe what I heard him say. Hoping he would just fly off
the side of a mountain? What the hell is wrong with him? He has
a family, a wife, kids—I mean, what is it? If I could put him in
a rehab program right this minute, then I would do it so he could
get better. Sadly, he is the only one who has that control. I know he
doesn't really want to die; he just doesn't have the coping skills to
deal with the tough times that life sometimes deals us. The way he
copes is by running, but at some point, you have to stop running,
turn around, and walk toward your problems. Face them head-on
and put the effort into changing things and you will see that it isn't
always as bad as you make it by running.*

*He has these delusional thoughts that we would all be better off
without him, but we wouldn't. We would all be devastated. What
a terrible thing to say to someone! I would be lost without my love,
without my husband, the kids without their father. That is just
his guilt talking and not having the emotional skills to handle it.
This man is the love of my life. I would be distraught if anything
ever happened to him; he would take my heart with him. I think
depression and alcohol go hand in hand. He should have gone into
intense therapy or rehab many years ago, but he just stuffs everything
inside, thinking if he doesn't talk about it or associate a feeling with it,*

then it doesn't exist. He is doing so much harm to himself and others by believing this is healthy or even holds any truth.

After some serious thought, I took off my rings and set them on the table. I told him that I don't want to be responsible for causing so much pain and misery for him. If he would rather take the risk of ending his own life, then it wasn't fair to me to go through life feeling such guilt for something that wouldn't have been my choice, and all because, truth be told, he is an alcoholic. He took his ring off and set it next to mine for a few minutes, and then he put it back on and he said, "I am still married. You do what you want," and he left to go to the bar again.

He called about three times. I didn't answer the phone. I needed to breathe (I should have answered; I know he is hurting and we needed each other). Then he got a hold of our daughter, and he told her he wouldn't be coming home because he was drunk and I probably wouldn't go get him. She started crying when she told me what he said, so I consoled her and loved her until she was okay.

Then I called him and asked him what the hell he was thinking by calling our ten-year-old little girl and hurting her like that. He said he was just being honest with her. I said, "No, you were playing games through her, and it is so wrong!" At about midnight I got another phone call to go pick him up so he and his brother wouldn't get into a physical confrontation. Since this has happened before, I did go and pick him up. I felt such a sense of guilt, I wanted him to be home safe. I was wrong taking my rings off. I should have never done that. Threats are so counterproductive. I needed to be more loving and try to find a different way to understand and communicate with him. He is already having a hard time with himself, not realizing he is an alcoholic. I didn't need to make him feel like he was even more alone. I should have hugged him, said "I love you," and let him know we would get through things together. After all, he is my husband and I his wife, and I cherish him with all my heart. I would do anything in this world for him. I always put him first, but he doesn't do the same thing for me. I just need a sign from him. I guess I would just like to know what I mean to his heart.

Over the years I have heard him say things like that a few times. Like if he were dead, it would be easier and everyone would be happier. It is a terrible thought because none of us would be happier; his family loves him. He is the love of my life; he is my person to grow old with, to take my last breath with. I would be lost without him. If something happened, I would be devastated and heartbroken!

My husband runs from anything bad. He doesn't like confrontation, but what he doesn't realize is that problems follow you wherever you go until you face these issues. He is a good man, with a good heart. I know he loves me, and I know he suffers from alcoholism. I just wish *he* knew, so he could get healthy and we could live our lives without addiction controlling them and find a new beginning to be happier than we have ever been because we love the hell out of each other. We really do!

Before we got together, he tried to hurt himself by mixing alcohol and pills; it was a cry for attention, a cry for help. This was due to an infidelity situation with his ex. He had to go to the hospital and have his stomach pumped. Thank goodness he didn't die. Death isn't the answer; help is. Treatment, living life and finding support, is the answer!

Look how every time we have an argument, the way he deals with it is by running, leaving, and going to drink. He is very introverted and I am not. I let most things out; it eats you up inside if you don't. Maybe it does look like I nag and complain a lot and maybe I do, but you know what? I would rather get it out and try to resolve our issues than to pretend like they don't exist, because they do exist and pouring liquor all over them doesn't help—you just ignite a bigger fire!

We have all argued and called each other names. Maybe you started the argument; maybe your spouse started it. Whatever the case may be, the simple truth is this: words hurt, negative actions hurt, and they have consequences. Sometimes there is so much emotional damage that you cause a wound, and that wound eventually heals and it scars. Even once it has scarred over, you never forget the story behind how you got that scar. I have always said that words mean nothing if your actions don't follow.

October 19, 2004

I asked him if he wants a divorce; he said no. We argued a little. I said, "I need you to work on our marriage," and he said, "No. I don't know how to give anymore or how to try." Nothing more to give? Seriously, did he really just say that he has no idea how to give anymore? It is just an excuse for him to be lazy and not put in the extra effort. It would cut into his drinking time. Nothing is more important than that! Well, he better figure it out!
Always, always, always it's about him and what he wants or needs, not about him showing love every day to his wife, just what I can do for him! Does it matter that I am not shown love every day?

October 26, 2004

The past week has been good up until now. All weekend we played darts together, we cuddled, we didn't argue, we even read a book together about marriage. It was great! We laughed, had fun, and talked; we were us again the way it should be every day. It was pretty awesome to feel that close again.
Times like this when we are all family, they touch my heart, but not all days can be like this with an alcoholic. Many days you just never know what to expect because the broken promises keep coming,

I know he means to keep his word, but for whatever reason, he just can't seem to do it. I know one day soon he will be able to keep promises. I have faith in him! I mean, I know he will always be an alcoholic, but he can live a sober life. I will never give up on him. At some point he will be able to express to me what I have meant to him all these years, and then I will know the depth of his love. I can't wait for that day!

His ex called and asked if the kids could do something that we agreed a long time ago we would discuss together before we let them do it. He just decided to let them do something he told me he wouldn't be allowing. I said, "Why didn't you talk to me first instead of making that decision yourself when we decided to do it together?" He said because he changed his mind, and that he was thinking about us but the only thing we would be doing this weekend is ending our relationship. Here come the threats again! Seriously, this constant bull crap about just ending things when things get tough is getting old. Let's just talk like adults. Oh yeah, I forget I seem to be dealing with a grown man who has teenage tendencies. I just want to scream, "Grow the hell up! What is wrong with you?"

I know it is the alcoholism, but some days you want to rip your damn hair out of total frustration! He yelled at me the whole time. He told me I opened my big mouth for the last time and I screwed everything up. I simply said I was upset he doesn't discuss things with me; I am just told what's going to happen, and that isn't right. We are sharing the responsibilities of raising the kids and being husband and wife. You don't just do what you want. It doesn't work that way. You talk to one another and remember to keep that line of communication open. I guess because I am a stepparent, I don't deserve the same respect.

I knew better than to think it was okay to speak my mind, because it never is. He was out of line the way he talked to me, or I should say, yelled at me. He always leaves me home. What do I keep doing wrong, and why do I feel like it is my fault? I don't want him to leave me home and run. I want him to stop and care to turn around and run to me and take me in his arms and hug me. I want him to say, "I love you; I am sorry." I want him to take my hand and take me with him, let me know he won't leave, do things differently. I don't trust that I can be who I really am with him anymore.

I guess I am in the wrong because I am not their mother. I really don't have a say. I am just a stepparent, and I don't count when it comes to decisions; I have no voice here. I am expected to raise them, take care of them, and support them, but I can't tell them what to do, and then when I don't tell them what to do, I get the third degree, so no matter which way I go about things, I will always get the shit end of the stick. This alcohol is just tearing us apart. I don't have any rights. Well, guess what? If you don't like it, raise them yourself. After all, they are your children! Get off the booze; be a husband and a father. I am so proud of my daughter. She is getting good grades in school, and she is doing so great in dance class. My daughter, her being happy and raising her the right way, has always been the most important thing to me. It doesn't mean I am a perfect parent. I make my share of mistakes, believe me, but I do believe in balance, structure, and discipline. We will be friends later in life, but right now I have a child to raise.

This life with him is turning into a nightmare, and I don't understand how he doesn't see that his drinking is a huge problem! Yes, I do. It is called D-E-N-I-A-L!

January 23, 2005

We will be starting counseling tomorrow. We have trouble communicating, which can cause us to argue. I am hoping this will help give us the tools we need to learn how to do it in a healthy way. As long as he is willing to take in information and work on us, we may be okay and have a chance at a great life. All he seems interested in is drinking. I feel him all the time, and how can I describe this?

It is like he is imprisoned inside of himself, like being trapped inside of a glass bottle of alcohol, and there is nothing to hold onto in there almost like your drowning. It is just a slick, straight wall with no options but to drink your way out.

To save yourself you have to be willing to pour out that bottle, smash it, walk away, and face your demons head-on or you will never be free. I know it isn't that simple, but what I mean is when he is ready and the time comes to stop, he will let me know, and I will hold out my hand and he will take it (I hope). I will go through it with him side by side. I will never leave him alone. I know it is his battle, but he doesn't have to do it alone. He can't do it alone. I will love him every step of the way. I know we all get lost at different times, but we will always find each other, never give up, and keep the faith. Never stop believing; there is always hope!

February 12, 2005

We had a great day today. We dropped the girls off at their grandfather's house. We went up to the lake to clean a client's house. We went to lunch and a movie. We spent the day alone together. It was much needed, and everything was amazing. We held hands, laughed, and talked. I miss him being like that; I miss us being like that. If we had more days like these, things would be nice at home. We are close, just not as close as we want to be all the time. Life gets in the way sometimes with kids and jobs, bills, family, and so on.

When we feel like this, life is good, we are in love, and all is right with our world. We are happy, but this disease is always just around the corner lurking, ready to pounce on your good days and crush them as though they never even existed and create havoc once again. He can choose to stop these days, though, if he would just do something about it and get some help, but first he has to be able to admit he has a problem. So far besides moments of those thoughts, he isn't there yet.

March 12, 2005

I don't understand what has changed so much with our relationship. We used to be so happy and in love, and now it seems like it is a challenge just to get through the day together sometimes. I know what has me upset and sad (for good reason). I don't know what his problem is. Actually I do, it is the alcoholism, but since he can't put his finger on it, he doesn't understand what's happening and all he can do is blame me for it. But I know he will get it one day. If I were to turn my head and not say a word about his drinking that would be like a slice of heaven for him, but no such luck, honey. I want you to live a long healthy life, so I will be on your ass about your drinking until something gives. Some get lucky; blended families go smoothly and they all love each other. Others, well, quite simply, it is like a train wreck. I don't want to be together because it is comfortable. I want it to be for love and friendship. I need him to be my best friend, my biggest supporter, my protector, my rock, my husband. Why can't he see that's all I want? More importantly, he may not be capable of providing that on an emotional level because of his addiction, at least not completely, not right now. Seems to me that in his eyes, he found the type of woman he always wanted in me. I take care of him, our family, and everything else, but he doesn't want to really put himself out there and be the aggressor. He is glad to receive, but does not give freely unless given to first. I always have to be the strong one, so where do I go when I need to fall apart, when I feel weak? If he isn't working on himself or on us and I have stopped, then we just fade away into what we used to be instead of what we could be.

March 13, 2005

If I had one wish that would come true, it would be this ...
I wish that my husband understood me, had respect for me, and loved me for the woman I am. I wish he loved me more than anything. I

wish he wasn't so selfish. I wish he knew how to feel compassion for me. I wish he adored me, cherished me, shouted from the rooftops that I am the most beautiful loving woman who has his heart and I am the only one for him. I get those things in moments, but not continuously. I know if he didn't drink so much, it would be better, wouldn't it? I said to him after breakfast, "Would you please unload and load the dishwasher for me?" He said, "Why?" I said, "Because yesterday I did three loads of dishes and eight loads of laundry, and I asked you for some help." He rolled his eyes and looked away.

I swear it's like I was asking him to give me a kidney right then and there! He threw such a fit about it so I just asked the girls if they would please help me. They are so good about that. Thank goodness for my little girls!

June 30, 2005

Another attempt at sobriety has failed, so far this month he went on all out binges on the 10th, 11th, 12th, and on the 13th he was gone for 24 hours. We were both on vacation this week and from the 14th to the 17th we had three great days together.

It felt like we rekindled our love and it was a new beginning for us. Then we had a little disagreement and he grabbed his keys to run and leave again and I didn't want him to go, so I picked up my plastic cup with soda and threw it across the room at him, it didn't hit him I just wanted to get his attention! Boy was that a terrible idea, he got so angry with me that he told me to pack all my shit get out of the house and take my animals with me! I apologized for throwing something and explained I wasn't trying to hit him I just wanted him to stop. He said you got my attention all right; now I want a divorce. I said are you serious? I said I was sorry please don't leave. He grabbed a can of soda and as I was walking away into the bedroom he throttled that can at the wall just by my head, he threw it with such force it exploded everywhere and sounded like a bomb went off. Clearly this was way out of control and none of this should have happened. As usual though I was home hurting and crying, and worrying while he was at the bar getting drunk, this is so damn dysfunctional I tried to make it right but he wouldn't let me.

September 9, 2005

Things keep getting better—I say sarcastically. Now his son has been in jail for five weeks—and he is fourteen years old! I am very concerned. The trouble just will not stop. What's even worse about this situation is I warned my husband this spring that something terrible was going to happen with his son. I could feel it. I could see him crying out for help, but no one wanted to listen to me because I am always wrong and I have no clue what I am talking about. Now the kid's in jail! I wish my husband could see that his drinking is not the answer; he needs to get help to be sober and clean and take over with his son. It is so heartbreaking to see kids go through stuff like this. I never thought my life would be like this! It can only get better, right? I hate it when we argue. I love him like crazy. I just want to be close to hug him, kiss him, to be laughing and talking. The fighting hurts me and bothers me. I am sure he doesn't feel good about it either. When will enough be enough? Will he ever see that he has a serious problem? Will it ever matter that he is destroying our family? Will he ever see that this is really starting to affect all the kids because he isn't capable of being present most of the time?
The older the kids get, the bigger the problems will get. Would it even matter to him if I was no longer a part of his life? It makes me sad because when he is good we are so good. We are happy and loving, and just when I feel like this is turning around, he goes right back to being selfish, verbally abusive, and abandoning me. I don't understand! I

love him. I am here for him. He tells me he is lucky to have me for a wife and how I take such good care of him and our family—and the next minute he is telling me how awful I am when I have done nothing wrong. Alcoholism sucks!

This is a hard life path that I have chosen—was it the wrong one? Sometimes I think yes, and other times I think no. Stay patient, be positive, and keep faith! I love him. I shouldn't walk away. This man is my husband. He is my heart. No matter how dark this storm gets, I will weather it with him for us because I know the sun will shine through once again and it will be brighter than ever. When we get to the other side, we can say we made it and know how strong our love is and what we have been through. That isn't something you walk away from, not now, not ever. You hold on tight and find ways to be grateful. I do find the silver lining and stay optimistic most of the time, but I do have those days where I just get down. Don't we all? It's normal. It is all part of life. I just have to make sure I get back up!

Chapter 6

There are countless victims that this disease of alcoholism affects. It is truly a baffling disease! Families are destroyed by it, friendships are ruined because of it, people lose their jobs, lives are completely changed, and no one seems to suffer more than the spouses, children, and families of the alcoholics, who are victims of their behaviors day in and day out—month after month and year after year. The alcoholic suffers a great deal, but when he or she isn't even aware of the destruction he or she is causing, it is hard for alcoholism to have a deep impact on him or her as an individual. I know there are thousands and thousands of people out there who suffer from this disease, and the only way to get it under control is through treatment. I am not just talking about meetings; I mean intense treatment centers/rehab as well if needed.

I know firsthand that my husband has made so many promises of slowing down or keeping his drinking under control or just flat out not drinking at all, but he cannot keep those promises for very long because the hold that alcohol has over the alcoholic is so much stronger than the alcoholic is—that is, until the alcoholic is willing to admit that he or she truly has no control over the addiction! This disease is pure evil and takes so many lives. We all hear about it in the news when it is someone famous, but what about the countless faces every day that we don't know by name, like your parents, your spouse, your neighbor, your children, your friends? Addiction of any kind does not discriminate; it affects any age, race, or sex. These distinctions don't matter! It is not something my husband can do on his own. He needs help to deal with the triggers that keep him going back to the bottle, and until you deal with your demons, you will never be free of the addiction holding you prisoner, which essentially is in your own mind!

I know the empty promises will keep coming, and all they do is get my hopes up when a week goes by without a drink, then a month without a drink, then three months. I become so hopeful, but can't figure out why things still are not better at home or emotionally between us. And then suddenly *wham,* there he goes on another binge, and we are back to square one. The reason things don't get better is because such alcoholics are now what is considered a "dry drunk." A dry drunk is someone who has given up drinking, but has not made any internal or emotional changes; essentially, dry drunks are sober, but not living a truly sober life. I didn't understand it at first either, but it really does make sense once you take the time and educate yourself to see that sobriety isn't just about putting down the bottle; it is about cleaning your emotional house from the inside out.

October 3, 2005

I know that being the child of an alcoholic parent raises your chances of having a substance problem, but when both the parents have a drinking problem, you really have to watch your children. I feel like his son has been shouting out for attention for years, but no one has taken the time to notice. I have noticed but, no one wants to listen to me. I am apparently just the mean one, the insignificant adult here. I couldn't possibly know what I am talking about. Maybe if they opened their eyes a little, they would see I am not mean, I care very much, but now he is going to start getting into real trouble so they will have to pay attention to him. This is all so sad because he has already been to a detention facility, and I just feel like he needs his parents to step up and give him structure, guidance, and discipline. God, does this kid need discipline! I try to help and make a difference, but I am the stepparent. I will always be in the wrong trying to give guidance. This kid needs to have a chance, so there isn't much I can do except protect my daughter and keep raising her with what I believe is right and pray the negative doesn't affect her. Maybe one day my husband will see what I have been trying to do—simply help, simply care about a family that we are all supposed to be a part of.

October 9, 2005

This is a tough time for our marriage because the kids are getting older and there are serious problems here. Our issues are intensified, and I don't know if we will get through this together if we aren't on the same team. He says he wants to have his son live with us, but first of all, if we can't communicate, that isn't a good idea. If he can't stay out of the bar and stop drinking, what the hell good would it do to bring his son into our home if he is gone half the time? He won't allow me to do anything with him, so he would be worse off than he is now. I don't know why he doesn't put the bottle down and be a dad to all his kids. I don't know why he doesn't put the bottle down, stop running away from our issues, and turn around and be a good husband. He has me, his wife, who loves him so very much, and he just pisses it away like it's nothing. How am I supposed to feel? What do I do with that? He rarely says, "I love you" or "I am proud of you" to the kids, and that just hurts me for them. I have to remind him, or I'll ask him, "When is the last time you said, 'I love you,' to the kids?" His response is usually, "I don't know." That answers the question in itself, doesn't it?

October 28, 2005

When we first got married in "2003" we went to counseling for eight months. Seems like newlyweds shouldn't have a need for it but with him being an alcoholic and our families being blended we needed the right tools to communicate without causing harm to one another. I shared with my husband that I wanted to get back into counseling for myself since he won't go with me, and he freaked out, saying he is a little worried when his wife tells him she wants to go to therapy. Are you serious? He feels therapy doesn't really help. It's a way to not support me, to make me feel like there is something wrong with me. I don't understand him. I mean, why the hell would I of all people want to go to counseling? Ummmm, so I don't lose my frigging mind here? Really, I just need someone who will listen to me, someone that I can talk with and I can work on resolving my own feelings and issues. He doesn't understand what him being an alcoholic is doing to me, what damage his behaviors have caused. He doesn't have the capability most of the time to be there in the way he should be. Sometimes, though, he is just amazing, and it is so easy to get lost in my love for him. But sadly, his presence never lasts very long.

He wanted to talk about it, so we started talking. I trusted him. I was pouring my heart out. I was digging deep down, hoping he would feel my pain and how much I am hurting, how much I need him and to feel his love. Is it too much for him to reach out and hug his wife and tell me whatever I need, he is here for me? Nope, no such luck. We had stopped at a park and sat and talked in the parking lot. So because he became angry with me he drove home dropped me off, then left and went to the bar.

Please, ask me again why I feel the need to be in therapy—because I just poured my soul out reaching for my husband, and all he can do is make me feel like shit and leave to go drink. Yeah, I am the crazy one! Gosh, I can't imagine why I would want or need to go talk to someone who can give me the professional knowledge I clearly need to understand and cope with my husband.

Today was fun. I caught my husband in a lie! He said he went to his brother's house because a friend of his brother had passed away. I didn't believe him, so I checked his cell phone and his brother never called him and he didn't call his brother until two hours after leaving home. I straight up asked him if he lied to me, and he said, "It's easier for me to lie to you than to hear your bullshit." Isn't that just great? My husband feels it is okay to lie to my face if it benefits him, if it gets him to where he wants to be. He could sell a damn ice cube to an Eskimo! What a joke. So he is going to lie about someone dying just to get out of the house to go drink. Now please try and convince me again, tell me you don't have a serious drinking problem when you lie about a life being lost so you can go get drunk. My heart hurts for my husband because he is so sick. It breaks my heart. This will inevitably kill him.

December 4, 2005

It has been awhile since I wrote an entry, but today he is angry with me, so he had to leave for thirteen hours to go hang out at a bar drinking himself into a frenzy to clear his mind. How is that for irony? He called me to say he was too drunk to drive home and to go get him. I said, "You got yourself into that mess; now you can get yourself out of it!" I have rescued him so many times over the years, but sometimes I just can't do it. I thought maybe he would learn from it.
I would love my journaling to be happy, joyous writing, but my life is difficult right now. This is not how I pictured my life being. I want so much more! Truth be told, in asking other women about their journaling, most of us journal to get our feelings out, mainly when we need to vent where we feel safe. There isn't a better place to me than a blank piece of paper to spew my anger, hurt, and heartache, because no one can tell me that I shouldn't feel that way.

January 2, 2006

It's a new year, and thank goodness for that. Last year was a hard rough year, with a lot of heartache. Let's catch up on the last few days ... On New Year's Eve, my husband and I got into an argument because he accused me of being the type of woman who does bait and switch, pretending to be something I'm not. Me of all people, the woman who is too honest for her own good! I don't think so. If anyone did a "bait and switch" as he calls it, he did by pretending that he was an honest, upstanding, protective man. He said the first year and a half we were together I showed him I loved him so I got him hook, line, and sinker. He is being ridiculous. I love him so very much. If he just opened his eyes and got off the bottle, he would be able to see in every way how much I actually do show I love him. So because I had major surgery and I had to focus on myself for a while to recover, he got angry because I wasn't focused on and giving all to him—you can't get any more selfish than that! Let's talk about how I needed him during that difficult time. Isn't that what a husband and wife should do—be there in one another's time of need?

He got angry and left about four thirty in the afternoon, and he didn't come home till about four o'clock in the morning. So he brought the New Year in sitting at a bar while I was home alone. All I can say is here we go again. Happy Friggin' New Year. How many years do I have to be alone for holidays because he sits in denial about how bad his drinking problem really is?

He tells me the next day that he was talking to some woman at the bar who was having problems with her husband. (Wow, that makes me feel so much better. Misery loves company?) Then about another woman who was flirting with him. He said people at the bar told him to watch out for her because she is married but goes to bars looking for men. What man comes home to tell his wife about these philandering women who were hitting on him when he is already having trust issues at home with his wife? Feels like a control thing to make me feel more insecure! He insists that he is proud of himself because he tells me he has never cheated on me and will never cheat, he has no desire to; that when he leaves, it isn't about that, and he loves me too much; no woman could ever make him want to cheat because I am the only woman for him.

It would be nice to believe, but words are just words without actions. Yet he doesn't come home some nights and sleep in our bed, so where is he? Then I hear about these skanky bar flies that could care less if they are married or if you are! So tell me again how much you love me and how you "slept in your car again." I really want to believe he would never be unfaithful, but the insecurities that his actions of drinking have brought leave a whole world of imagination open to anything happening in my mind. He is oblivious as to what this is doing to the kids. He isn't a good role model, and it makes me very sad for them, for all of us as a family.

January 4, 2006

Another day in marital hell! I don't think this is what marriage is supposed to be like—or any healthy relationship for that matter— but I have to remember I am with an alcoholic. He isn't thinking rationally! Our arguments are usually about the kids these days. He wants me to take care of everything he isn't doing with his kids, but I can't tell them what to do and I have to run it by him first. Well, how the hell does that work? See, he doesn't think rationally! That doesn't even make sense.

Ummm, no, if you don't like it, then you should be here spending time with them and be a part of raising them. It isn't fair to me that I have limitations with the kids. I am the only parent taking care of them. Then when I don't say something to them, he will say, "Why didn't you take care of this with the kids?" Either way I am screwed! He tells me to back off and I need to keep my mouth shut. When I say something to him about being a more present parent, he gets mad. People don't always like to hear the truth. I have a hard time keeping my mouth shut anyway. I am a powerhouse at times, and words come very easily to me. I communicate well, but sometimes I should keep my mouth shut. Let's just say I don't always bite my tongue when I should. I can't win with him. I will always be to blame for something in his eyes until he gets some help for his addiction and can get his life together. Until then, I just take the beat downs and do the best I can with the kids and for our family.

January 5, 2006

As if things couldn't get any worse, they do! He asked me a random question about the kids. I answered honestly, and he got angry; I can't be honest unless he likes my answer. Could someone give me a damn rule book on the right things to say to this man? Because this is just insane! He said that he doesn't have to look far for reasons to hate me; he said he wishes right now he could tell me he cheated on me so he could hurt me (what a great, thoughtful man) but he said he can't because he hasn't cheated. I told him he is a POS for saying that to me (what a terrible thing to say to my husband! I am just as guilty sometimes for saying hurtful things), and how dare he try and hurt me in such a cruel way, telling me he hates me and wishing he could tell me he was unfaithful! He is a sick, sick man to have such destructive malicious thoughts just to hurt me.

He jumped off the bed and walked toward me angrily and started pushing me with his chest and said, "Don't you ever call me a piece of shit again." I said, "Only a man with a cold heart would say something so cruel to the woman he loves." I said, "You can't possibly care about me or love me because a good man wouldn't have been in a bar on New Year's Eve flirting with other women. He would be home with the woman he loves, doing whatever it took to work things out; and he sure as hell wouldn't have come home bragging about these women just to hurt his wife!"

I told him when the kids leave; I want him to leave too. He said, "Good luck paying for everything and having the vehicle repossessed!" I simply asked him to leave and go cool off, but he takes it to a whole different level of threats and control! Then he starts threatening to let all the rescue cats out and says he will give me a reason to hate him! I have a selfish, self-centered, split-personality, alcoholic husband who doesn't naturally help other people. I am so completely lost and devastated right now. I can't fathom some of the things he has said to me; they are cruel and heartless. What happened to this amazing, beautiful kindred spirit I connected with years ago? What happened to my best friend, my soul mate? He is so lost in the world of addiction. He needs help to get healthy, and I pray that day comes soon, before he loses his life to it. What have I done to deserve to be treated with such disrespect and disregard for my heart? I love him and have always stood by him. Why would he want to make me cry and abandon me so often? I don't get it. What am I doing so wrong?

January 7, 2006

Looks like we may be getting a divorce. It is a very long and excruciatingly painful story, but he is tired of me not making an effort to do certain things, and I am tired of putting my all into the whole family and not being appreciated. He says that he has a switch, and he turns it off and shuts down completely; he gets mean and nasty and says things just to hurt me. Says it has always been his way of fighting. I was so desperate to get my husband's attention that the only thing I could think of was to say what I did, that I wanted a divorce. I really don't want a divorce. I spoke out of anger. I just wanted to stun him into realizing what he has been doing and how serious things have gotten. In my mind I was hoping for some movie scene, like having him rush to me and say, "I love you so much. I have been such a selfish fool hurting you like this for so long. I am so sorry. Please don't leave me. I don't want to live without you. I promise to get help for my drinking, and if I have to work hard every day to make up for what I have done to you, I will do whatever it takes." Yes, it is so cheesy I know, but really it is a nice thought, don't you think?

I have been crying and trying to get him to hear my heartache for so long that I just became desperate for any hope. Whatever happens, I need things to change. I want to feel loved and supported by my husband; I need security. He couldn't even be civil with me. All I got was him cussing at me and being mean. All I can say is I hope my husband comes to see his mistakes with me and chooses to change. I love him. I want to be able to reconcile. Marriage means everything to me, but only if he wants to make changes in the way he treats me, talks to me, and gets help for his drinking.

January 20, 2006

So here it is 8:00 p.m. Friday night, and let me tell you where my husband is. Well of course, the bar. Where else would he be? Certainly not at home because in his words, "The kids don't need me." I guess neither do I? He doesn't realize how much we do need him! The girls are only eleven and his son is fourteen, but when he is out drinking, he needs me to be here to take care of the kids. He takes total advantage of the woman I am. He knows I would not leave them. He knows I have a big heart, and I am not walking out on our family. He does not deserve me. I deserve to be with a good kindhearted loving man who wants to put me first, one who will spoil me and adore me, be my best friend, my biggest supporter. What the hell am I doing hoping he will change? It isn't happening! Sometimes I feel like it is me that is hopeless. He plays these mind games with me, and I am really pissed off right now. I believe things happen for a reason, and I have to believe that my life will turn out the way it is supposed to, with all I want in some way someday. I love being married, but I hate the way my marriage is.

This morning my husband said to me, "What do you do for me that I can't do for myself?" Like dishes, laundry, shopping, bill paying, raising the kids, cleaning the house, working, and so on. Hell, if he can do it himself, why doesn't he? He doesn't do any one of those damn things. I said, "You can do everything I do, but the point is you don't, and you don't appreciate that I do it for you, for us!" I don't get how he can hurt me with such force and not turn around and run to me and make it right, to hold me, wipe my tears, to really have remorse and be the man who loves me as much as I do him!

I remember one night he was so drunk. We had gone out. He usually drinks beer, but that night he drank the hard stuff, and he was so unbelievably mean to me. We got home and he was angry about something, but nothing happened. We weren't even arguing. I think the alcohol just set him off. He was calling me nasty names. Next thing I knew I was sitting on the edge of the bed and he suddenly kicks right above my head, touching the hair on the top of my head with his foot, and broke a mirror that was on the wall. As it shattered all over me, the shards of glass cut my arm in a few places as he continued to yell at me. I had my cell phone and asked him to stop. I begged him to stop. I was scared. I was calling the police. I had dialed 91, but I don't know why I didn't push that last 1. I just didn't; I couldn't do that to him. I suppose it was because I wanted to believe he really wouldn't hurt me. I was scared. I didn't know what was happening, but thankfully shortly after that, he passed out.

I just sat there looking at him (after he passed out) with tears in my eyes, feeling so hurt, so alone, wondering what happened to this beautiful man I met. When did the demons take over his soul, and how much pain would he have to suffer and cause before he was willing to admit he had no control over anything in his life anymore? Sometimes he will start an argument for no reason, so he can leave to go drink and blame me for his behavior. Abuse is abuse, no matter the form it is in, and this is emotional abuse!

Through the years, we have spent a lot of time together doing fun things with family and alone. Everything like going to the shelter to look at animals, going out to eat, going to the movies, taking a walk, talking, laughing, playing games, rescuing animals, cleaning the yard, fixing our home. I mean, in between there are glimpses of closeness, togetherness, forever, fun, such a deep intense love. But being an alcoholic he can't stay present for very long because the enticing draw of the alcohol (at least for my husband) has such a strong hold that he gets lost in the obsession of it; before you know it, he is off on his next binge. It doesn't matter if things are good at home or bad, he will do whatever it takes, even if it means starting a fight, so he can run to where he finds comfort. Sadly, that is in the bottom of a bottle.

Chapter 7

Imagine this: every time he is out really late or overnight, it makes me physically and emotionally sick. Even if I do get upset and we argue or if I raise my voice, it still doesn't give him the right to treat me this way, to stay out for a ridiculous amount of hours or not come home at all at night, to just leave me to take care of all the kids because he can't stay out of the bar long enough to be present in our life together. As I lie in bed, most of the time I can't sleep; I toss and turn because I never know if he will ever walk through the door again to come home to our family.

I care what happens to him. I just want my husband to be home with me and love me as much as I love him, for him to want to work at this and take better care of himself and better care of us. To just love our family! The abandonment, neglect, and rejection I have felt from my husband is nothing short of heart-wrenching, to say the least. I will jump up a dozen times in a night and look out the window; each time it isn't him, I sigh and go back to bed. Sometimes tears will roll down my face, and in that moment I say, "God, please make sure he is safe. Look out for him; don't let him hurt himself or anyone else. Help him get home safe." I feel like I did something wrong to be treated so badly.

It is agonizing wondering why he isn't answering his phone. Has he gambled away all our money again? Is he dead? Is he hurt and suffering? Is he in jail? Is he with another woman? Could I have done something so he wouldn't have gone out drinking? What can I do to make sure he comes home at night? All I really want is for my husband to be home, go to bed with me every night, hold me, and be totally present in our life. Why can't he do that? I have allowed him to make me doubt my own self-worth. Because of his drinking problem, he has to make others feel worse than he does. Meanwhile I sit home and pray for him that he is okay and safe, but who prays for me?

I feel ashamed, and I haven't done anything. Why do I carry his shame as if it is my own? If I talk to friends or family, they will look at me differently. They will feel sorry for me, blame me, maybe even be angry I haven't left, and that isn't what I need. I have called the hospitals and police stations time and time again looking for him, to see if he has been arrested or if he has been injured. I have spent nights driving around town going to the bars, looking in every parking lot for his car.

One day I had all the kids with me and I found his car, so I drove the kids home and went back to the bar. When I walked in, he was sitting down, and this woman was about in his lap. I will tell you what. I blazed through that door, and with a very loud voice I said, "Why aren't you home with your wife and kids? Who is this bitch, and why is she practically in your lap?" Man, that woman ran out of the bar (probably a good thing at that time), and do you know, he took me outside and said, "Go home now. You have embarrassed me. I will come home when I feel like it." I couldn't believe his response! He was only concerned with himself, not me, not the kids, but what the other drunks thought of him. Really, we should be at home in bed curled up together watching a movie or in the living room with the kids playing a game or something like that. Not sitting in a bar with a woman who is not your wife! I want to be his first choice. I want my best friend to be my husband, to be supported, to communicate, to feel secure, to be taken care of. If I am sick, he would take care of me, he would help me achieve my dreams, he would be my biggest fan, he would be my biggest protector and not allow anyone to hurt me, and most of all, he wouldn't hurt me, leave me, lie to me. He would love me for all that I am and all that I am not. As I have done for him all these years. I need to know I have a safe place to fall apart. As a woman who is married, I have never felt more alone or sad in my life. I have made excuses for his drinking, lying to the kids about him working late, to my family, to his family, to my friends, and most of all, I have lied to myself. That isn't okay; none of it has been okay. I keep waiting for a change, for a miracle. I love this man with all my heart, and he couldn't care less about me, or so it seems. But I know he loves me; he just doesn't have the capability to show me consistently. What does that say about me? What does that say about him?

I didn't realize that by going to the bar to have fun, even to just play pool, or buying him beer at the store, or lying to people about his drinking, or picking him up when he was too drunk to drive home, making excuses, it is all enabling him. I became part of the problem! To stop enabling just means you are saying that their behavior is not acceptable so you don't buy them alcohol, you won't go with them to bars, and so on. You love them, but you have to have boundaries. That is really tough to do; it is hard to not take care of them when we are needed. I know there are thousands of women, men, and other family members and friends who feel the same way I do, embarrassed and alone, looking for validation that it isn't you. We all go through tough times and we all need support, so I believe that is what I am doing. I am going through the tough times with the person I love because that is the way I feel it should be. That isn't to say that I am right; it is just my belief.

February 13, 2006

Today I went to my first Al-Anon meeting, and let me tell you why I decided to make myself finally go. I can't feel any more alone at this point if I tried. I just need some validation that I am not crazy and other people are going through similar situations. I didn't say anything. I just listened to everyone else talk. I almost got up and left a few times. I sat there while my eyes filled with tears waiting to pour down my cheeks, and I thought how the hell did I end up here? How did I end up in this situation, in this life feeling like no one is caring about me and feeling so alone when I should feel so loved and happy? Will I be like one of these people who have been going through this and feeling this way for years and years, only to sit here and still be this sad and lonely thirty years from now? This was very sobering to me. I wasn't thrilled with this meeting. I just wasn't comfortable. It depressed me even more.

My husband was pissed off at me for going to a meeting. He treated me like I did something wrong. Why do you suppose that is? Does he feel threatened in some way?

February 14, 2006

To sum up a long story, we went out Saturday night. We sent all the kids to the grandparents. He seemed irritated with me all night for some reason; we weren't fighting, so I don't know what his deal is. We went to dinner, and then of course, we ended up at a few bars to play shuffleboard and pool. The first bar we went to, the smoke was so thick I couldn't breathe. He started getting mad that I was complaining. Well okay, I will just sit here and keep inhaling this secondhand smoke so you can keep downing the alcohol—not happening! He kept saying, "You don't love me anymore." I said, "Yes I do." He kept saying it over and over again. I just didn't say anything else. Now over the course of this night, he drank about fifteen beers or so. I lost track.

When we got home, he said, "How long were we at the bars?" I said, "About two and a half or three hours. Why?" He said, "Now do you see how I can stay there for so many hours?" I said, "No, actually I can't, because between choking on the smoke and some of the people that came in acting like idiots, I couldn't wait to get home!" To me the people that go in to drink themselves into a coma are ridiculous; someone who is married, has kids, and leaves them home for their own selfish reasons so they can go out to drink for hours and hours is just crazy to me.

He got upset with me and said mean things (I have to remember he is drunk). He continued with I can go to hell and he hates me, and then he started saying stuff under his breath after I walk out of the room. That kind of stuff just gets under my skin, so I did what you shouldn't do when someone is drunk: I walked back in, and I was trying not to fight, but this drunk asshole had me so pissed off I couldn't keep my mouth shut. If he was going to call me names, I told him to say it to my face, so he started with, "You're a bitch." Then he had the audacity to say that I was a loser! I said, "I am a loser, me, I am a loser? How the hell do you figure that?" I said, "I am not the one who constantly leaves his wife and kids at home to go out and get stinking-ass drunk or gamble my paycheck away, not knowing how I am going to pay my mortgage next week, and leave my wife to clean up my mess." He said the worst part was having had to look at my face all night! Ouch! That really hurt; that was cruel.

I turned around, got in bed, and curled up in a ball, crying myself to sleep. Verbal abuse is never okay, and to say those things to your wife, drunk or not, makes you a horrible person.

So he woke up Sunday, with no apology of course, just blamed me for how much he drank and continues to drink, so he wanted to talk about the end of our relationship. We started getting into it a little bit, and I said, "who the hell do you think you are talking to me like that, calling me a loser when I take care of all the kids and everything else because you're too busy getting fucking drunk anytime you feel like it and not giving a shit about how you treat the rest of us?" It is always the same fight, though: he blames me and makes excuses for himself.

Maybe it would be the best for everyone to just end this nightmare and start over. I don't want another man, though; I want my husband. I love this man so much. I just want to feel like he loves me all the time, not just here and there, and I want him to stop using the end of our relationship as a threat for control. Sometimes I would like to slap the shit out of him, I swear!

I want to be married to him. I like being with one person and building our life together. I know my husband is a good man. (I know for some of you that will read this may be thinking, *this woman is crazy*. Keep reading to the end; you won't be disappointed.) I know he needs help. I know he doesn't think he has a problem, but he needs an intense treatment program to help him begin the journey to be sober. He can't even take care of himself, so I can't expect him to take care of me, and I want to be taken care of sometimes.

I don't want anyone to feel like they are alone in this, because I am here to tell you that I understand all too well how you feel. I know your loneliness, your pain, your sadness. I have gone through this for twelve and a half years; it has been a long painful journey! It took me a long time to realize that it would be okay to talk to my close friends and family; they wanted to be there for me. I didn't have to be alone. When I told my therapist about wanting to write a book about being the wife of an alcoholic and wanting to insert my journal writings through the years, she said she thought it was a wonderful idea because, as I said before, there is a lot of material out there for alcoholics and treatments for getting them sober, but not much for wives of alcoholics. I know for me it has been a very lonely process. I will share my most intimate journaled thoughts with complete strangers, friends, and family. I know that it is not only cathartic for me and my soul, but if I can help one woman, one couple, one family, it will all be worth it. How many times have you felt like you were utterly alone in this life? How many times have you felt so embarrassed that you didn't want to call and talk or tell anyone?

Maybe even the person reading this is an alcoholic, and you can identify with some of these situations or behaviors in yourself. Maybe this will help you to see that you really don't have to go through this alone. There are people in your life who want to be there for you; they are just waiting for you to open up to them. Know you don't have to give up and walk away. There is help and hope. We are all human beings, and we all just want to be understood and loved.

Some may think I don't understand what it is like to drink or do drugs, but in fact, I know all too well. This is my own personal experience with drugs and alcohol. I did have addictive behaviors for several years. I started in eighth grade; we would skip school, go to a friend's, and smoke pot. Well, the summer between ending eighth grade and starting my first year of high school, I drank so much and smoked so much pot, I don't even know how I survived all of these situations I got myself into.

One time I stole my father's car keys. We all got in and drove his car across the highway. I didn't even know how the hell to drive. I went right into a ditch, which we thought was friggin' hilarious because we were so damn high (thank God we weren't killed or hurt someone else). There were days that I drank so much or smoked so much, I blacked out. One time I woke up in my brother's closet, and I have no idea how the hell I even got there I wasn't even home when I was drinking.

I was asked one time if I wanted to snort some powder. Well let's rephrase that into I felt really pressured! I was told it was crank, but who knows what it was? I went along with it because my friend did it. I was up for three damn days; I couldn't sleep. I was thirteen years old, and I felt sicker than hell. That is something I only did once. I never ever did it again, but it still didn't stop me from getting drunk and high every single day.

Meanwhile, my family life was going to hell. I was a terrible kid. I stole money from my parents. I caused them so much grief and heartache. I got into a lot of trouble. I caused trouble. I couldn't stand to be around my family; I didn't want much of anything to do with them. A few of us girls skipped school one day and went to some guy's house. We played quarters with straight vodka in a coffee mug. Now I ask you what the *hell* were we thinking—a coffee mug and *vodka?* Fourteen years old? Oh my goodness, what a lost young teenager I was! So I proceeded to get completely shit-faced, so much so I had to go lie down in this guy's parents' bed, where I found this enormous, and I mean gigantic, bowl of mixed nuts. I laughed so hard. I was so amused at the giant-sized bowl. It was like a giant lived there. Everyone laughed with me because, well, we were clearly very stupid kids. I ate so many nuts I threw up everywhere, and I mean everywhere, including all over myself. It was like the exorcist in there! So my friends threw me in the shower with my clothes on to get me cleaned up because we had to take the city bus back to our school bus so we could get home. I was so drunk I couldn't stand up by myself. It was such a bad situation, and I have no clue how I really got home that day. It was all a blur after that.

I remember one night in particular that was so scary. My friends and I were so high or drunk, probably both, but my friend was running alongside of another friend's car when next thing we saw was she somehow got stuck and was drug on the ground with her shorts on. She fell, and the car drove over her. She was just lying there in the street! We took her home to her parents, and here is the messed-up part: we all, including her, lied and said that she had an accident down the ditch on a bike or something like that, but we weren't telling them the truth. We knew they didn't believe us. They took her to the hospital. She was pretty messed up, with broken ribs and terrible road rash for a while, but that didn't stop us from partying. We rocked on!

My friends started progressing toward acid and shooting up. That scared the living crap out of me to watch, but I never did it. I was never going to put a needle in my arm, and I never did. Well, one day while skipping school and walking around high as a kite, we were picked up by the police and brought back to school. Now picture this: I am so high everything is a joke, and I didn't know police cars locked from the inside, so when I tried to open the door and I couldn't, I started freaking out so bad, jumping around like a monkey in a cage, kicking the car door. I am thinking, *this cop has no idea I am high; I am too sly for that and I cover it up well.* Seriously, what a moron I was. Of course he knew. I looked like a lunatic in the back of this cop car freaking out and laughing trying to get out.

My parents were called, and my mother came down. I had over fifty truancies. I have no idea how it got to that point, but I failed every class. I failed my first year of high school, and here is the best part: I was kicked out of school for the rest of the year for skipping so much. Reality was about to set in here! My father wanted to kill me, and after chasing me down the hall, yelling at me and throwing a pinecone at me, I am pretty sure if I didn't lock myself in my room at that time, he would have. They were so hurt, disgusted, and disappointed in me and probably blaming themselves for not knowing what was going on behind their backs. I used to hide peppermint schnapps in the back of my dresser.

I was so out of control at one point that my mother drove me down in the middle of the night to juvenile hall and said she had enough. I remember I threw myself down in the parking lot on the ground. I cried. I grabbed onto her leg and begged her not to lock me up. We had family visiting from back east staying at the house with us (my mom's sister). How shitty was that for me to behave that way and ruin everything for everyone!

I became pregnant at fifteen years old. I was just a baby myself. I lived a terrible existence for about two and a half years. I am so grateful that the experience didn't kill me, but it sure taught me some very hard life lessons, which have stuck with me to this very day. It wasn't my parents' fault. They were great parents, very loving. They raised me right. It was me, it was me feeling a need to fit in with people that I thought cared about me, so I did what they did. At that time in my life, I was a follower, not a leader. I wasn't strong enough, but now I have the ability to be a powerhouse of leadership.

To start my sophomore year off right, I stopped hanging out with my old friends. I mean I walked away completely. I didn't drink or smoke pot. I stopped everything. I made a decision for myself at sixteen years old that I was starting over to make new friends and try to make up for the year of high school I completely failed. That was it for me! I did drink sometimes after that, but not like that. I never did anything like that ever again. I was done experimenting. I was done with it ruining my life. I needed to make up to my family for the way I treated them and behaved. I was just awful, but I had learned my lesson early on in life. I am so grateful that I could share that with my daughter and stepchildren because I prayed they wouldn't take the wrong path. (Unfortunately my stepson did go down that dark path)

So you see, I had my run at a very young age with drinking and drugs. It was not a pretty sight, but I am so grateful for the early-on life lessons because it gave me a unique ability to find myself and who I was and what I wanted, without having any clouded judgment about it. I wanted to share my own personal experience with everyone so you know that I am not coming from a judgmental place or one of criticism, but rather one of understanding and compassion because I too have experienced life with substance abuse.

April 18, 2006

I woke up to find a receipt for money withdrawn from our bank account with a note written on it that said, "Bad habits. I don't need a text message. I know I blew it again." Well hey; as long as you know it, we are good? What the hell is that about? We just got through discussing how we have to really watch our money. I just lost a job that brought in a lot of extra money a month. I am still working, but that was another job that really helped us out, so he goes out and takes money for drinking and gambling, and it's just like a casual "hey, it's a bad habit, I know."

I wanted to get the girls a stuffed animal for Easter, and I got the third degree from him because the girls have plenty at home and he said it would be a waste of money. To me it isn't a waste of money when it would bring a smile to their faces; no one smiles when he is out drinking. We don't sit around and say, "Oh good, he is out blowing money again by drinking and gambling. How happy does that make us!" His daughter said to me that when he came home he smelled really bad.

I know that I shouldn't let his words get to me because it is his defense to try and purposefully hurt me and cause insecurities, but I can't help it. They hurt, and nothing about it makes me feel secure.

I know it is easy for someone to judge and say, "This is her own fault for staying; she should have left a long time ago." However, unless you have walked a day in my shoes and know what my feelings are, what my fears are, and what life is like every day for me and my family, it really isn't right to judge me or anyone else for that matter. Who is to say that the person reading this would do anything different, and who is to say he or she wouldn't? Who is to say that another man would be better? Who's to say he wouldn't? He could be far worse. What I mean is, who is to say that I am not exactly where I am supposed to be at this time in my life, and who is to say that I won't leave at some point because I am not where I am supposed to be? Maybe I am here to help him get better because I am the only one who has had the courage, strength, and love to stand up and call him on his bullshit; everyone else has just turned the other way and hasn't really looked at it as a serious addiction problem with serious consequences.

The truth is, I love my husband, and I believe in the sanctity of marriage. I don't believe in leaving when things get tough. Sometimes you have to ride it out to see the rainbow at the end of a terrible storm. Not everyone would have stayed in my situation and others may have, but I stayed because somewhere inside me, I have faith and hope that my husband is lost inside the evil demon that holds his true self hostage, which is alcoholism. I may find at some point that he is exactly who he has been and nothing more than the man I have known all these years: one who has been selfish, hurtful, and at times vindictive, but I may also find that he is the man I thought he was always capable of being, the one that I see from time to time, someone who is loving, compassionate, my best friend, kind, and a great husband that adores me. I wouldn't leave my husband if he had cancer and was sick in that way, and alcoholism is a disease. It is a sickness. I wasn't going to leave him; I love him too much. He is my person!

At times I have thought about it, but I have never wanted to really leave. I just wanted things to be better, for him to be attentive, the man I first met. I know he is in there, and one day I know he will be on the road to recovery from this terrible disease.

April 22, 2006

Every time the girls try and watch TV in the living room, he walks in, takes the remote, and changes the channel, even if they are in the middle of a show. They say, "Dad, please." He says, "Sorry," and they walk to their room sad. He is so rude and disrespectful to them. What is the reason for that type of behavior toward your two young daughters? Does it make him feel like a big tough guy? Because to me it is like taking candy from a baby; it makes you a cold person. His son wants to watch something, and that is different. It is crap. He separates them. He treats his son different than he treats the girls he favors him and it isn't right. He is oblivious as to what he does to these kids. He will lose the girls, and his relationship with them will forever be damaged. They feel he is unfair. He just plows through them like they don't matter because, he says, the TV was his Christmas present and he is the man; he should be able to do what he wants in his house. Somehow he seems to believe he is superior to the rest of us. He is selfish and inconsiderate to the girls' feelings.
He does the same thing to me. He will come in the bedroom, take the remote, and change the channel even if I am watching something. I know it sounds so petty. I just want to pick up the TV, take it outside, smash the damn thing, and say, "There you go; you're the man of the house. There's your damn TV."
This is the same man who I have caught urinating in the yard! Who in the hell does that? I mean as a grown man, what the hell are you thinking? Why would you piss in our yard instead of walking in the house and using, oh, I don't know, the bathroom like a normal person? He told me it was easier because when he was outside in his shed pounding down the alcohol, he would just pee right there so he could continue drinking and not be far from the alcohol. Wow, something to be really proud of. Maybe all our kids will learn to use our yard as a friggin' urinal—how disgusting!

That is how the alcoholic mind functions: anything to make it easier, to not let anything interrupt your drinking.

This is for all the women out there, or anyone for that matter, who can relate, for anyone who feels alone and feels too ashamed or embarrassed to share their stories with anyone else. You are not alone. I understand; I know how you feel. I feel your pain, your disappointment, your heartache. I know I am just one story in a world of thousands upon thousands, and some are far worse than anything I have ever been through, but to open up my personal rawest of emotions to those whom I may touch and bring hope to, then it will have all been worth the exposure. Hell, I got to a point where I wasn't showering for two or three days at a time. I just didn't care. I was so numb, I didn't care if the house was messy, laundry piled up, not cooking much; I didn't care what I looked like. I hear you. It is okay.

We get depressed and down on ourselves for something that has never been our fault. We can't help but feel like it is, because we are told year after year that it is our fault, because the alcoholic can't take accountability. Alcoholics usually put blame on someone else besides themselves, and we come to believe the lies we are told. My husband would say things to me like, "If you were a better wife" or "If you did this or that," and even when I would try so hard and do those things and show him what he wanted, I was still treated the same because that wasn't the problem. I wasn't the problem. The disease of alcoholism is the problem. It wasn't that I wasn't a good enough wife, that I didn't cook enough or clean enough, it was because he was sick and so wrapped up in this disease that he didn't realize he was crushing the very essence of my spirit. I am a damn good wife. I have always taken good care of my husband and my family.

It took me many countless years to realize that this isn't my fault. How he chooses to deal with arguments, finances, his job, kids, family—that is all him, and as much as he always wants to blame me or anyone else, I know we all make choices for ourselves. If he chooses to drink himself till he feels it makes the pain go away, then it is his choice. That is something I struggle with, though. I can say it, but to convince myself that it isn't me is a tough one. Even though I feel like he has reached bottom many times, he hasn't reached his own personal bottom yet, and maybe he never will; but someday he might, and then it will be a real wakeup call. Until then, hold on, because it is a roller-coaster ride of blame, shame, anger, resentment, disappointment, and loneliness.

The financial burden is another huge part of this because the whole family suffers at the hands of his addiction. At least for my husband, gambling has been an issue, and mixed with the alcohol, no good comes from that!

May 7, 2006

Whenever he wants to be mean, he says things to me that aren't true. I mean, he accuses me of things that couldn't be further from the truth, calls me names, and tells me to pack my stuff, all to cause insecurity. It's like some type of power control trip for him I guess.

Our daughter's cat got out a few days ago, and she has been a strictly indoor kitty. Our daughter was very upset and scared, so she asked him if he would help get her cat, and he said to her that he was too busy to go under the house to play with cats. Yep, he is too busy doing alcohol, curling up with the bottle. How mean can you be when your little girl comes to you upset to help her, and you can't be bothered because you're too busy drinking? What a jerk!

Then he said if I even thought of having someone else come out to help get the cat, he would throw all my rescue cats out of the house. This always frightens me and gives him a leg up on me because I won't leave the house fearing whenever he threatened to throw out the animals that he would really do it and I couldn't risk that. I felt almost imprisoned because if I left, who knew what he was capable of doing? That is a terrible feeling to have. I said, "No, you won't," and he said, "We will see." How could he even have a thought like that, to take my animals and just throw them outside? I mean, what thrill would it give him to cause me such heartache? He helped rescue most of them—why be that way?

I said, "You can't ever have a healthy disagreement, can you? You always have to threaten to do mean things, call names, and such." He said, "You don't know when to shut the fu** up and stop!" I started to say something else, and he got so angry he jumped up out of bed at me, grabbed my arm, and put his hand over my mouth. He squeezed my arm and my face so tight! Then he got right up in my face. I was up against the wall. He said in such an angry tone, "You just don't know when to shut the fuck up." I could feel his hot breath on my face; he was that close! He left a red mark on my face from grabbing me so hard. I had never been so afraid of him. I thought he was going to beat the hell out of me; he was so out of control with his anger!

This triggered an emotion for me. It sent me back to when I was sixteen and in a physically abusive relationship. Why hurt me when all I have done is love you? I stood there, shocked and crying that the one man that would never treat me that way just put his hands on me. I pushed him in the middle of his chest and yelled at him through tears, "Don't you ever fucking put your hands on me again. Get away from me, you physically abusive jerk." I went into the bathroom. He followed. I kept trying to shut the door, telling him to get out. He was saying over and over again that he wasn't abusive.

Just then one of the kids came in and said he needed to come outside right now because they were scared about something. He walked out so I locked the door. I was shaking and crying. I couldn't believe he could do that to me! He couldn't control his anger. I am his wife, the one he is supposed to protect with his life. How could he hurt me like that?

I didn't talk to him for three days after that, and I slept on the couch. When we did talk, he blamed me because I wouldn't shut up. Even if I couldn't stop talking, that gave him no right to put his hands on me! Sometimes my mouth should have a filter, but it doesn't. I can be a hothead and have a potty mouth, but I apologize when I am wrong or out of line and I right my wrongs—or do my best to make amends for what I feel wasn't right. Why can't he do the same thing? No matter what, though, no one has the right to ever put their hands on anybody to try and punish them. I don't want to hurt people. It doesn't make me feel good. I don't get that about him; he is hurtful to people he loves, but just leaves it. Yeah, it's my fault you couldn't control your temper and you put your hands on me? Then he said he couldn't apologize because I would never forgive him anyway. He wasn't really sorry. It was just another excuse to not take accountability for what he had done, so what good would an apology really be anyway?

June 29, 2006

I had to go in for outpatient surgery to remove a little nodule under my eye.

My husband said he would try and show up, but no surprise, he didn't show up; he said it was because of work, but this is the same man I have seen leave work early to go drink at the bar, but he couldn't be there for his wife for even a half hour when I needed him. Why doesn't he understand I just want him by my side? Why doesn't he appreciate how much I love him and all I have done for him?

The nurse said that her husband would be all over her; she would actually have to tell him to go away, and the same with her sons. I said, "I will never know what that feels like." She said, "I am sorry." I said, "Me too." She probably thought I was pathetic. I know I did. My daughter took good care of me; thank goodness for her. I know she looks out for me.

July 25, 2006

Here is my all-time low, and I mean this is beyond embarrassing for me to admit! I can't believe I am even going to write this down, but one day I can look back, and I am sure to beat myself up over how stupid I was.

My dearest friend and I were talking the other day. She asked me if he could be cheating on me due to the way he has been behaving. I have been sick thinking about it. I used to be able to say no way would he ever do that to me, but now I am not so sure. He doesn't seem to really think about anyone but himself. He doesn't come home at night sometimes, so yeah, I suppose it could be a possibility. I pray it is just me feeling insecure because of his behavior when he drinks. He hasn't shown any concern for the destruction he has already caused. My heart was pounding. I was so anxious I finally took a Xanax to calm down and help me sleep. The last time I looked at the clock it was 2:36 a.m., and he still wasn't home.

When I got up, the kids weren't up yet. I saw he was sleeping on the couch, so I woke him up to come in the room before the kids saw him. See how I try and protect them so they won't know what is really happening with their dad? When he got out of the bathroom, I took a deep breath, and through tears I said to him that I needed to smell him to see if he had been with another woman. Talk about completely and utterly humiliated! I said, "I need to know if you have been unfaithful." Right then and there I broke down. I fell to the floor on my knees and started crying uncontrollably until I couldn't catch my breath. I said it shouldn't be like this; this is so wrong! I have never been so ashamed of myself in my life. I have never felt so sick. This was definitely not right. No woman should ever have to do that or feel she needs to check her man to smell if he cheated. What the hell am I doing here? What has happened to me? Is my self-worth really worth all of this?

He came right to me and held me; he swore to me that he has never and would never cheat on me. I mean, he really seemed to feel awful that he caused me to feel that way, that I felt I had no other choice than to check him. It made him stop and think about how he was behaving. I was surprised. He comforted me for a long time, and we talked about it. He realizes that his not coming home at night and the excessive drinking have caused serious doubts in my mind, and why wouldn't they? I have never felt like a bigger idiot than I did in that moment. Is he telling me the truth, or is he lying? I know he cheated on his ex-wife and she cheated on him, but he swears to me that he did it to get revenge on her for her cheating first. Regardless, it is still wrong!

I got up and hugged him. I said, "Thank you for understanding." He said, "You're welcome." I said, "I love you. I don't want to lose you." He said he didn't want to lose me either. He promised to be better and not do things to hurt me.

A male friend of mine told me when he was young and dumb, he cheated all the time. He was telling me about how when he was living with someone, he would tell her that he was going to a buddy's house to work on a car when really he was out cheating. Then on his way home, he would stop off and get under the hood of his vehicle to make sure he had grease on his hands, and then stop at the gas station and put some gas on himself so it would cover up the scent of another woman. He was very young, but that is my point: you never know when someone is lying or telling the truth, and look at the lengths some people go to and get away with it. We are supposed to be able to trust the people in our lives to be true to us, but that isn't always the case. That is very sad to me. As the kids grew up, the problems became bigger and created more problems for everyone. The biggest thing is if you separate your kids and treat one differently, you create a hostile environment. If you are your child's friend instead of his or her parent, you aren't showing your child boundaries and how to have respect. When I was growing up, my parents were consistent with my brother and me; we had consequences for our actions. I was a wild child between the ages of I would say twelve to sixteen; these had to be the worst years for my parents. I can look back now and see how awful I was and what I put my poor parents through. My mom especially tried to be there for me, but all I did was lie and go behind their backs.

My point is that as parents we learn along the way because every child is different; we have to guide them and show them right from wrong and know when to move out of the way to let them spread their wings and make their own mistakes, which have their own consequences, and other times we have to protect them. We never know how anyone is going to turn out and we don't know what every situation will be, but we do our best to go with our instincts and to do what's right morally and have values. My husband has tried to be the best parent he can at this time. I mean he has tried to get his ex to delegate consequences to their son whenever he was at her house but it seemed to always be a battle with her. It also doesn't help that my husband is harsh on him one minute and the next its do whatever you want.

My husband knows all about my daughter's biological father and what happened with him, so why wouldn't he want to be a better dad for her, because after all he adopted her and she is his daughter too? Does alcoholism really have blinders so thick you really cannot see the destruction that is staring you right in the face? The answer is yes, because it is hard to see anything for what it really is if you are not sober.

Chapter 8

August 13, 2006

Yesterday we dropped the girls off at one of their friend's house for a pool party. As soon as we left my husband said "what are we going to do"? I said I didn't know. He said "do you even want to be married to me anymore"? I said "yes of course I do but I am not happy". I said you constantly go to the bars, you go on binges, you talk mean to me, I feel unloved, unappreciated and taken for granted.
And every time you promise me you'll stop you do it again.
He said "will you give me a chance to change"? I said like what? He said "your right, I need to control my temper, he said I won't go to the bars unless you are with me. I guess I gave him a strange look because he said "what is that look for"? I said I can't take you at your word anymore, "seeing is believing". He said "please give me a chance to change things", I said "OK". He told me that I am beautiful and how much he misses me, he apologized for everything. It has been a while since he has taken the time to compliment me. He was very attentive towards me all day. He made me feel so loved and cared about. It feels like for the first time in years he really understands the hurt he has been causing to our marriage. I hope this lasts because it felt so good to feel important to my husband again.

August 21, 2006

First I need to say that I am so proud of my husband for really putting forth the effort to change some of his bad behaviors. He hasn't gone to the bars like he promised. He has listened to me, and talked with me. He has come down harder on his son who has been getting into so much trouble recently. He has also shown me more affection and attention. At this moment I am so happy, it feels wonderful!
He even went as far as to apologizing to all the kids for disrespecting me in front of them and explaining why that wasn't ok for him to do. This was really amazing!

November 16, 2006

My husband told me that his sister and her boyfriend invited us to go out with them this weekend. Later that evening I said when we go out with them this weekend I don't want to sit around with two guys getting as drunk as they can. (Her boyfriend is also an alcoholic) He automatically got mad at me, he became rude and he said "we will be going out with them and I will drink however much I want and I will not tell him what to do" he said he is a grown man who can make his own decisions to do whatever he wants! Can anyone say selfish......? I even said that I was sorry if it came off that way I just asked him to please not drink so much, but he just wanted to argue so I shut my mouth.

January 25, 2007

Another year and more of the same old crap! I don't understand but I wish I did. It seems like my husband doesn't care if I cry, if I am hurt, he just leaves me to feel bad. Tonight's comment from him was "I wish I could just leave everyone behind and just go away". I ask you again, what the hell is wrong with this man? Alcoholism is like the devil, it sucks the life right out of you. I said if you want to go then pack your bags and leave, people leave their families all the time. He said it's not that easy, I said well you seem to want to leave us pretty bad so go! I sit and wonder what have I done so wrong that my husband doesn't even seem to like me, let alone love me? We have been together almost seven years and it's as though he doesn't even know me, and I sure don't know the man he has turned into, it tears me up inside because I love him so very much.

March 1, 2007

We now know that my stepson is doing drugs. We started checking his text messages and they are all about buying drugs, doing drugs, and selling drugs. Oh lord I knew this was getting worse. He is skipping school all the time, failing all his classes, this is such a mess. My husband's ex tells us that nothing works to stop her son so she just isn't going to do anything. Well that makes absolutely no sense. She babies him way too much it is so aggravating, she needs to be harder on him he may appreciate her discipline when he is an adult. She will be sorry someday that she didn't put forth serious consequences for this kid or maybe she won't, that will be on her conscience.

April 30, 2007

Seems as though journaling is my best friend lately well for many years now. I was trying to have a conversation tonight with my husband about a few things. I was kind and heartfelt. As per usual he doesn't have the heart or patience to discuss anything with me so I am always left wounded, and I am the only one or so it seems.

June 4, 2007

So our daughter has her first boyfriend, she has been crushing on this kid all year. I just hope she gets to enjoy her young life I don't want it to be full of heartaches and disappointment's. My baby, she is so sensitive yet rough at the same time, I know it sounds like a strange combo but she makes it work. She is doing so well in school I love watching her grow up, what an amazing process it has been being a mom. She will accomplish so much in life she is so intelligent and driven, sometimes moody, I love her so much I could not be a prouder parent!

June 17, 2007

Having your own cleaning business can really suck sometimes! I am grateful for the work but you have to work around the schedules of others which means at times you work weekends and nights as well as all week long. To start off; we pulled into the alley in the back of the salon we were going to clean and there was a car blocking part of the road and a garbage can on the other side. My husband said "I can get around it" I said "well I can't, it's too close together". He said "well I could do it if I was driving". I said "whatever". Once we parked he looked at me like he wanted to talk and I said I don't want to talk right now I have work to do! He said "I don't give a fuck what you have to do" I said "you better watch the way you speak to me"! He said "fuck you"! I became silent I wasn't going to have this fight. A couple times he asked if I was ready to talk, I said no that I wasn't. On the way home he said "are you not going to talk to me"? Then he said something and my response was 'the next time you want to accuse me of treating you like crap you better stop and take a good look at yourself first because you're a hypocrite"! I don't cuss at you or call you names but you cuss at your wife and you tell me to "fuck off" you treat me like shit!

So he is arguing with me all the way home playing the poor victim, because of course it is somehow my fault that he can't control his temper. If I hadn't made him so angry he wouldn't have cussed at me. I said if you are angry with me find another way to express that because cussing at me is not ok, his response "deal with it"! See my husband can be a very cold person and one who takes no responsibility for the hurt he inflicts upon others, mainly me.

July 19, 2007

We attempted to get away for a three day vacation with the girls. This was a nightmare......it started out where the girls and I wanted to get a hotel room and my husband wanted to camp in the tent trailer. Of course we ended up doing what he wanted. He got mad at us every day for something, and before we even left we were all excited to go we were anxious and he got mad at us because he said "we didn't understand what it takes to get the trailer ready to go" well excuse us for being happy! We went to a small water park we found but it was awful we didn't really enjoy it. Then we had no place to shower, and no electricity I had to use the water park showers to wash my hair etc. we tried in between to lighten the mood and have some fun. We did go to the Jelly Belly Factory on the way home, we did the tour to see how they make jelly beans and the girls were so bored and miserable. For whatever reason this was just a bad trip.
My husband wanted to find this lake to camp at but he had no idea where it was but insisted instead of getting directions it was only fifteen minutes down the road. Well after two hours of driving down a twisty pitch black road the girls started to get freaked out it was late at night, we were all tired and hungry, and he clearly had no sense of direction. Finally after stopping at two different bars he got directions and we found it, but not before the girls got really scared.

Our daughter started crying saying "dad we just want to go home", and my step daughter on the verge of tears, they begged their dad to turn around and go to a hotel. He didn't care he was mean and then he yelled at them to "knock it off" and told our daughter to quit crying! I was so pissed off! The next morning his daughter said she stopped herself from crying because her dad would have gotten angrier at her after the way he was with her sister; she said she didn't want to say anything. How sad is that? Your child can't express themselves openly because you yelled at one for having natural feelings of being scared and crying and the other has to hide it from you fearful of your anger!

December 18, 2007

Finally a good day! We took the girls to a professional football game this weekend. I wanted to take my good friend and my daughter, but my friend didn't want to go because it wasn't her team playing, so our girls went with us. We had a blast watching the tailgaters before the game, all decked out in their football gear; we took pictures with some of them. We laughed, cheered, talked—what an amazing day! I would like to take my father one year. I think he would enjoy the hell out of it. What a great family weekend; this is the way things should always be. This is what family is about—togetherness no matter where you are. These days when we are close, laughing, and loving, I wish time could stand still and these moments would last forever!

December 23, 2007

My daughter wasn't feeling so good today, so her younger sister told her to lie down for a few minutes. We were getting ready to go Christmas shopping. I said we should stay home, but she said, "No, I will be okay." After a while she got up, and I was doing her hair for her and her sister was sitting on the edge of the tub. We were all talking, and my

*daughter turned toward us; she was sheet-white. She said, "I can't see."
I was waving my hand in front of her face saying, "Can you see my
hand?" No response. She turned back to the mirror, and the top half of
her body just collapsed onto the counter. I picked her up and called her
name. She took one step out of the bathroom. Her eyes were fluttering,
and her whole body just collapsed. I caught her in my arms. I started
yelling her name, but there was no response. I was freaking out!
I told her sister to run outside and get her dad before he left and to call
for an ambulance. He ran back in the house and had her lay down
and elevated her legs up higher than her heart until the paramedics
arrived. I was so scared about what was happening. What was going
on with my baby? She finally started coming to. I said, "Honey, We
called for an ambulance they are on the way. When the paramedics
arrived they came in and checked her heart. They did an EKG,
checked all her vitals, and checked her blood for diabetes, and so
on. I was so scared! I didn't know what happened, but I have never
seen someone turn so pale before. We are going to the doctor's in a
few days to check this out to make sure she is okay and there isn't
something more going on. She said right before she passed out that she
got a really severe headache and that our voices sounded so loud; that
must have been so scary for her to feel that way, not knowing what
was happening. The EMTs said she just passed out and they couldn't
explain why, but they assured me everything checked out okay. They
said to make sure to take her to her doctor, but a hospital visit wasn't
necessary. She still wanted to go Christmas shopping about an hour
later, I was skeptical about that but we went and everything was fine.*

December 29, 2007

*I didn't write anything for Christmas, which means it was another
bad year again and not something I cared to remember. The effect
that my husband's drinking has had on our family as a whole is bad*

enough every day, but the holidays are supposed to be about family, giving, and good times but with an alcoholic it is anything but good times. It has taken a toll on me emotionally and physically, I can't imagine what it has done to his body and mind.

I took my daughter to the doctor's, and they said that she is anemic and has an iron deficiency. The doctor said he wants her to take a multivitamin with iron, and that should take care of the problem. They will recheck her blood in a few weeks and see if the vitamins help.

It doesn't seem like it could be as simple as that. I am so grateful it is something easy that can be taken care of and she doesn't have any major health problems. Since she had open-heart surgery as an infant, I sometimes worry more when I don't need to, but that is part of being a mom, I think.

January 31, 2008

My mom and her husband were in town visiting. We had so much fun while they were here. We went to a friend's house to play games and eat. We had fun laughing; it is so nice when we are all together. The kids would hang out and play games too or watch movies. I wish they lived here. She has lived so far away for so long, and my daughter is growing up so fast; it would be nice for her to have her grandma close. On the surface, everything looked fine; you couldn't tell we had problems because we laughed, smiled, held hands, and kissed. We went places together, and those moments are genuine; underneath it all, we truly love one another. I mean, it isn't always bad. We do have good times together and with the family, but our good times together should be happening so much more. He is so busy being an alcoholic he doesn't see much else, and his drinking over the years has become worse. I miss having my mom around. It would be nice having more of my family closer here with us.

This is a letter I wrote in my journal on **February 5, 2008** ... just for me.

To My Husband,
I love you with every breath I take. I need you to do the same for me!
I want you to be the man who always stands by me, protects me, and
supports me. I want to have a happy family for our daughter to enjoy
every day with. Watch her grow through life's experiences and enjoy
that with you. Why can't you see the toll this has taken on me, on us,
on our daughter, and on our family as a whole? I am so desperate
to feel loved by you, for you to be strong. I can't lean on you, I can't
depend on you, and right now you are the type of husband who sees
his wife on the floor crying and steps over her, leaving her in pain
so you can run to your next binge. Your soul has become dark. You
have no remorse for the damage you have created, and until you
find yourself and maybe lose everything, you will never know how to
appreciate anything. With all my heart I want you to be healthy and
alive again to get the help you need because right now you are dying
a slow miserable death and you're taking me with you. I am going to
be a young widow mourning the loss of the love of my life if you don't
stop drinking. Please stop; you are killing yourself! You're missing our
life together and all the blessings we have been given. Please, God,
help my husband to find himself. Help him find you before it's too
late and he loses his life, which will just take mine.
Love, Your Wife ... XOXOXOX

This letter is full of sadness, hopes, and dreams of the love I wish I could feel and have from my husband; at one time I did have such a love, and from time to time I still do. I also hear the hope that somehow he can be saved.

How many of you have felt the exact same way? Does this sound similar to your life? I am sure there are things you can pick out, and you will hear yourself say, "I hear those exact words. I have those same thoughts and feelings." I am sure there are so many of you out there who can relate on some level to these feelings of hope, despair, and sadness; you feel lost. Ultimately I believe we all want love and acceptance from our significant other, and those who have an alcoholic in their life, you sacrifice who you are, what your wants and needs are, just to make it through the day sometimes. Then you have those days that are wonderful. Your alcoholic is sober and seems to be able to have conversations and laugh with you and empathize with you, and in that moment, even if it is just a moment in time, you feel like you have broken through. The alcoholic is present; he or she gets it and understands. But as quick as you feel like things will be okay and you hold on with dear life to the possibility that this time things will be different, he or she changes, and in a blink of an eye, all hope is lost once again, and you go back to just getting by the best way you have learned how. The tolerable, the unbearable, you become numb and get through your days doing what you have to just to survive. The wishes, hopes, and dreams are once again shattered, and the cycle continues of your life with an alcoholic.

March 7, 2008

My husband has recently decided that he is going to buy some drums and become a drummer; he says he wants to be a "rock star." Okay, I am all for living out your dreams, but here is my issue with that scenario: bands usually play in bars and he has a serious drinking problem, soooooo I feel that type of environment for him would be so toxic that he will never have a chance to stop drinking and get help for himself. Things will continue to get worse along with his health, and then what?

I will wait and see how this pans out first, if he joins a band or what happens; maybe this will fade on its own, and if not and it is what he really feels like he wants to do, I will support him, but not while he is drunk and playing in bars, being gone all the time, not coming home at night—that has to stop. I have a bad feeling about this. I will be his biggest fan, his greatest support, but he has got to do this sober. He wouldn't be worth a damn doing it drunk anyway.

May 20, 2008

So, I didn't get anywhere with the diet I started. I don't have a lot of willpower or drive to do much of anything. I am pretty sure it's called depression, and I have a thyroid problem so that doesn't help me much. What I am doing with food is medicating myself, like he does with alcohol. Food is my comfort. It doesn't have to be a lot of food, just the wrong foods, that in the moment make me feel good—I suppose maybe much like a drink does for an alcoholic! I don't eat the right way or always eat the right foods, and I don't want to exercise, so there goes that right down the drain. I feel like I failed again.…
I didn't fail; it just isn't the right time to be doing this! I need to accept myself and love myself no matter what size I may be because that doesn't change my heart or the person I am and always have been. He just doesn't know how to love me. I mean, sometimes he is wonderful at it, but he doesn't know how to put forth that effort every day because he suffers from alcoholism; he is sick. I do understand it is the alcohol that prevents him from being anything like that, so I am limiting myself in what I am getting out of life with him because I have chosen to sacrifice myself for the hopes that this man I love will one day "get it" and will beat this addiction, and then underneath all of that, there will be a different man, a better man, a man that people can look up to instead of looking down at in disappointment. The heart I fell in love with!

July 11, 2008

We have been in couples counseling for almost four months now, and it seemed to be helping, but then we hit a bump in the road. He is constantly on me about finances; he wants me to account for every penny spent. I have been doing the bills for eight years. I know where and how everything is done. Maybe if he stopped drinking and gambling, there would be more damn money in the bank—the nerve! We hardly talk, and we don't have any meaningful conversations because he is always drunk or it's too overwhelming for him, and on the rare occasion when we do have them, it isn't consistent. He doesn't know how to have healthy conversation. He is always defensive about everything, and it is beyond frustrating. He doesn't have the coping skills to handle life's real issues. His resolution is alcohol; that makes everything better in his eyes. Handle it drunk, and everything is good.

August 2, 2008

Yesterday his son overdosed on heroine at the very young age of sixteen! Sixteen, people, sixteen! From what we were told, the paramedics had to revive him—such a sad situation. I mean, we could have been going to my stepson's funeral; this has got to stop. I wish I could just do something. I wish I could take over just for a moment. The problem here is they just baby him; they won't see things for what they really are, and when I try and shed some light on the truth, well, it always causes an argument. I wish my husband at the very least would listen to me. I am not saying it would change anything with his son, but what if it did? His son is clearly crying out for help; why can't they see that? It's because they can't see past their own addictions. They won't hear anyone else. They perceive it in a bad way instead of in a loving way.
My husband doesn't understand he is not his son's friend; he is his father, and it is his responsibility to do what it takes to help this kid.

Later in life, there can be friendship; right now you have to be their voice of reason. That isn't to say that he hasn't tried things, because together we have tried many things, made many phone calls and many other attempts, but all while fighting his mom because she wants to baby him. We are trying to be part of the solution, not the problem. My stepson's mom just looks at it as I am not their mother, so it isn't my business. But it is my business. I may be a stepparent, but I am still trying to do what is best for the kid here, and that in itself should have put the four of us parents on the same side many times, but it has just been a battle year after year. No matter how I feel about my stepchildren's mom, I always taught the kids to talk to her with respect, and I have never tried to take the place of their mother. I just tried to care and help. What if it gave this kid a chance to have a different life path than the one he is on now, which is self- destruction? He is going to kill himself; he is lucky he didn't lose his life yesterday. The way that this is handled also affects our girls. It will show them what to expect. If it is handled wrong, it will send them the wrong message, and I don't want this for any of them. Will I ever have a voice here? Probably not, what have I brought my daughter into? All I can do is teach her the lessons I feel she should take away from this. I hope someday she understands and knows I never set out to do anything that would make her unhappy or hurt her. I feel like I have failed her in some ways, but I have always loved her and made sure she was my priority. I hope someone steps in and forces my husband to put his son in a treatment program now while he is young and before he moves on to heavier drug use. This is going to get bad; I can feel it! The kid almost lost his life. People, wake up. Let's do something right now while this is happening.

From August 2008, things became progressively worse with my husband's son. The arguments seemed to become more heated. The difficulties it caused in our marriage was damaging, and my journaling became mostly about the kids. I do not feel comfortable dragging them into those years of nothing but daily heartache. I don't want them to feel like they were to blame for anything, so I have chosen to skip those years and move forward to 2011. However I will share some significant moments that did occur during that time. My husband and I had times when we were very bonded and close and others we were not. His drinking started to become more frequent it wasn't just the weekends anymore. During this time we also took my husband's ex to court for full custody of his daughter. We learned she was sneaking out of her mom's house a lot; she also took her mom's vehicle driving when she didn't have a license. She was going to parties, so at this point we felt she needed a serious change. We were awarded full custody and we made the decision to have her change high schools as well so she could go to school with her sister. She seemed to do better, her grades improved. She did not sneak out of our house because in her words "she knew I would catch her because I hear everything". My stepson dropped out of school and was deep into drugs and in and out of jail; we didn't see him very often. The kids were growing up, and driving, they didn't want to spend much time with us. We did things as a family still, we would go out to eat, see a movie, and play games. My mom and her husband finally moved back here to live I think in 2008 or 2009. It has been so nice to have her here. To sum things up life went on with him drinking more often, no more visitation with his son, we gained full custody of his daughter, my cleaning business went under when the economy went downhill, just life really day by day. One day things were good the next they were awful.

February 19, 2011

Our marriage is still not in a good place, but we stay together just the same. It isn't that I don't care anymore. It is that I feel so beaten up by this life with him. He is an alcoholic and progressively getting worse. He refuses to stop drinking. He tells me he can stop anytime he wants, but the truth is he can't. I mean, he can stop drinking for a period of time, but he is just a "dry drunk" during that time; he acts the same without his liquid courage. We have had many struggles and many rough years; we aren't very close anymore. With the things we have dealt with over the years, we should be so close.

Our dog has been battling breast cancer for the past two years, and it has come back again for the third time. She just had her third surgery in January, and on February 4 she started chemotherapy, which we have to drive her to another state for. Her oncologist is so awesome. She just had her second treatment, and she handled it really well. The doctor said she gives her six months to a year tops before she is gone. We sat there in disbelief, saying there is no way! She said the cancer is so aggressive this time that if she makes six months, she would be surprised. Our dog is so full of life still; there is no way I would give up on her. She is our family, and a family sticks together and fights things like this head-on. Our dog is a beautiful Rottweiler/mastiff mix; she is just over ten years old. My husband got her for me for my birthday in 2000; we had been together eight months. We have had her since she was just six weeks old. We pull together for her; it is good that we can still find a way to come together. If we can still find a way to be close, then not all is lost, but we have to work at it and realize that our love is a blessing, but he needs help first and foremost for his drinking. The chemotherapy and testing is going to be expensive for her. I took out two credit cards. It will cost about $10,000, but I would give up everything for our dog to be healthy and cancer-free. I don't care what people say, animals are not just pets; they are part of our family. They are "fur babies"; they are living breathing beings like you and I, and they deserve the same respect. Animals love unconditionally. I wish people would learn from their pets, because our world would be a much more loving place to be.

February 20, 2011

*I don't know why after all these years I keep trying and hoping for
a different outcome, but I guess I haven't lost all faith yet; there is
still a tiny shred that I hold onto. I opened up and went very deep
emotionally and gently with him, but somehow he makes it always
about him, and I mean everything! He has been saying that his
drinking isn't the problem. I told him that for me it is the problem.
He insists that isn't what causes the problems; it's me that causes our
issues.*

*I said, "You think your drinking hasn't affected me/us over the years,
so let me share this with you. All those countless nights over the
past eleven years that I stayed up wondering where you were, if you
were hurt, in jail, cheating, in the hospital, just ran off and were
never coming home, lost all our money ... every headlight I saw,
I would jump up for hours upon hours looking, hoping it was you
coming home safe, pulling into the driveway. You didn't answer any
phone calls from me. You never cared what was happening at home;
you never gave it a second thought whenever I was sick or the kids
were sick; you weren't here for us. Then let's not forget there were
several times you would leave, saying things like you were going to
kill yourself by drinking so much and drive off a cliff, or you're not
important to anyone so who cares if you die, or maybe you will never
come back home. All these things are emotionally abusive, and to
play with someone's mind and emotions in such a malicious way,
it is terrible! I would become physically sick from this, so sick to my
stomach it would be twisted in knots and cause cramps, headaches,
nausea, severe anxiety, which would cause fast heart palpitations!*

*"In those few seconds it crossed my mind wondering if you really hurt
yourself, would the pain stop? I wouldn't have to sit and wonder
anymore, but of course not because I would never want anything bad
to happen to you, but you always made me feel like things were my*

fault, so this would leave me feeling for the rest of my life like your death was my fault! What a terrible thing to leave someone with!"
I was trying to show him that saying things like that to someone is selfish, because if he did hurt himself, I know it wouldn't be my fault, but how do you not feel like it is you when someone has blamed you for so long you start believing it yourself? He said he knows how it feels because his ex said something similar to him like she would rather be dead than to be with him, but if he knows how it makes me feel, why the hell would he want to inflict that on me or the kids?

March 21, 2011

I can't take it anymore. I need someone to talk to and help me sort things out, so I found another therapist I really like. I just started; we will see how it goes. Our couples counseling ended up like it always does, we got into an argument he said "fuck it" and doesn't show up for our appointment with me. So then I am left sitting there looking like an idiot whose husband doesn't care to show up, that's always how the end of therapy has gone for us, me being alone and we never go back. We have gone through this I believe four other times. It is so embarrassing but at the same time for me so heartbreaking!
My dad had a freak thing happen this weekend. When we were out we all went to moms to eat and play games, he said one of his eyes was blurry, he said he could see white dots. He went to the eye doctor the next day, and they sent him to a specialist, and now he is legally blind in his right eye. They said that a piece of calcium broke off from his carotid artery and went to his eye instead of his brain, which would have caused a stroke. Wow he is so lucky that it didn't cause a stroke that could have cost him his life.
My father has been diagnosed with primary progressive MS, and his health has gone downhill for the past six years. He can't walk on his own anymore, and really he should be in a wheelchair because his

legs are so weak, he falls often, even with his walker. It is so hard to watch your parent's age.

He also had to have a bump taken off his forehead; it was skin cancer. He has had a lot of that over the years, nothing deadly; thank goodness, but still countless surgeries. My poor dad can't catch a break. I just want him to be happy and healthy, without all these health issues.

August 3, 2011

So much has been going on; I don't know where to begin. Therapy has been going great, I like her ways of explaining things to me and getting deep down into my life so I can work on unraveling and resolving my feelings. I am happy I made the decision to talk to someone it is very helpful and insightful! Now let's move to the issue with a friend. A man she had been dating for about three or four months broke up with her, and she just lost it; she couldn't even go to work. She had trouble just getting out of bed to function. I understand heartache, but the way she was reacting, we were really concerned. I think she had an emotional breakdown.

Back on July 17, my husband and I went to her house around ten thirty at night because the son of one of her friends was there; he called me and said she was talking about killing herself and her former boyfriend. I had to go help her. See, that's my thing, I have to try and save people. We had been friends for sixteen years, and our daughters grew up together; she was family. I went upstairs to talk to her. She was a mess and had been drinking like she does every night. It made me so sad. She is also an alcoholic. I tried to comfort her and talk to her, but she was convinced that the only person who could help her would be the guy who broke up with her or she wanted to kill herself. At one point she grabbed my arms, and she said to me, "If you were really my best friend, you would go home and let me kill myself."

She even said, "If my family loved me, they would let me die." I was going through enough with my own life, but I have always put others first and take on their stuff too, especially her. I said, "No. I am your friend, and I care about you. I am going to prevent you from hurting yourself, and I hope you can forgive me one day for what is about to happen here." I said, "Come downstairs."

I told my husband while I talked to her to call the police and get help over there. The police and an ambulance showed up. Needless to say, she was really pissed off and argued with the police, but finally she agreed to go to the hospital in the ambulance for an evaluation. I rode in the ambulance with her. I was so stressed out and so worried for her and for her kids to see her that way.

Two days later I took her to her doctor's, and the doctor wanted her to voluntarily go into an inpatient rehab center. She was freaking out in the office, crying, rocking back and forth, and saying that if this guy just came back to her she would be fine. It was just heartbreaking; she definitely was having a nervous breakdown. Really all she ever wanted was to be loved by a man. She was always so sad when relationships she had ended, so I can relate to how she felt. I think everyone can. What is better than to feel loved and enjoy life with someone special who takes the time to make you smile every day? She drinks every day and my husband is a binge drinker, but at the end of the day, they are both alcoholics, so the only difference is their drinking style, not the disease.

Later that weekend her other best friend called me and was worried about her because now she was talking about starving herself, and as the week went on, she got worse. She did stop eating and started drinking more. We didn't know what else to do' she was clearly on a path of self–destruction. When her friend called me, she told me that our friend's parents were in town and that she thought we should let her parents know what was happening with her. They didn't even know she drinks, let alone is an alcoholic. She always hid her alcohol

when they stayed with her, and she wouldn't drink until they left;
then she would resume when they were gone. They are very religious
people, so I think she never let them know she drank because she
would feel judged by them.

I was outside talking to my friend while the other friends and my
husband were inside telling her parents everything. They were so
shocked. We felt so bad doing that (and it was her poor dad's birthday),
but we were worried for her safety and her life, and we thought her
parents could admit her if they wanted to but no one else could.

We knew going in that our friendship may be over at that point, but
I would do it all over again if I had a choice, because a friend never
leaves you even in your darkest moments. Friends do what they need
to do to help you even if it means walking away. That is what I had
to do at this point in my life, as hurtful as it was and as much as I
needed a friend. I knew she couldn't be that friend for me. I knew
she was an alcoholic, and until she got help for herself, that wasn't
going to change, and I couldn't do it anymore. I couldn't be the only
one committed and giving to our friendship with a clear mind, so I
walked away.

October 27, 2011

Today one of my favorite rescues passed away and went to the Rainbow
Bridge. We rescued her and her litter of kittens six years ago. She was
the sweetest cat. She was silky gray. She had such a beautiful gentle
presence about her. She was diagnosed in May with kidney disease,
and I knew yesterday would be her last day. She took her last breath
in my arms at two thirty this morning. She was my shadow. She
followed me everywhere I went. You could hear the little pitter patter
of her paws on the wood floor.

It has been a rough few months for me trying to get used to not having
my former friend in my life anymore. We did everything together:

holidays, football games, lunches, dinners, game nights, birthdays.
We talked just about every single day. It's just so sad it couldn't be
different. Maybe one day it will be different. Only time will tell! I
was always there for her, but on the occasion I needed her, it was too
much trouble for her to be there for me. I mean, we had many good
times, but what was missing is that she couldn't be someone I could
count on because of her alcoholism. I also found out after, that even
though she has been there with me and has seen firsthand how my
husband is when he is drunk, she gossiped about me, saying that I
should just let him drink and party and I always tried to have him
on a short leash.

I remember she was supposed to help throw me a party for my fortieth
birthday. I ended up calling most of the people myself. She was
supposed to help my mom make food and do other stuff, but she
didn't. It was just a mess. She has always been more concerned with
herself and what guy was in her life at the moment than she is about
anyone else. She knew my sadness and still didn't seem to care much.
She seemed to make it less than what it was, but then again, she is
an alcoholic, so of course she will see things her own way. I realize,
though, that she too doesn't think rationally and so the cycle continues,
even in friendships.

One time she was chasing my husband up and down the street in
front of a bar downtown around one o'clock in the morning, trying
to get him to get in the vehicle while I was driving. They were both so
drunk. He was being such a jerk that night; it was so embarrassing!
Another night she came to stay the night with me. We were just
watching movies and hanging out. He came home, and he turned
out the lights while we were watching TV in the front room. He was
standing in the dark just staring at us, and he wouldn't respond when
I asked what he was doing. Then he went into the laundry room and
hid behind the door. He freaked us out a little bit because he was so
drunk. Well, his behavior scared me a bit, that is for sure. Then he

was going to leave, and I mean, drive his car, so she said he couldn't drive and that I couldn't let him go. I said, "You can't tell him what to do when he is like this. Go ahead and try." She went out and talked to him, and she got him to go pass out in the other room and go to bed. I don't know why he chose to listen to her, but he did. At least I didn't have to worry about where he was going to be that night; I knew he was safe.

A friend of mine asked me what the Rainbow Bridge is because he didn't know about it, so for those of you that don't know about the Rainbow Bridge, there is a beautiful poem that someone wrote about a place our pets go when they pass away.

Rainbow Bridge Poem

Just this side of heaven is a place called the Rainbow Bridge. When an animal dies that has been especially close to someone here, that pet goes to the Rainbow Bridge. There are meadows and hills for all our special friends so they can run and play together. There is plenty of food, water, and sunshine, and our friends are warm and comfortable. All of the animals who had been ill and old are restored to health and vigor; those who were hurt or maimed are made whole and strong again, just as we remembered them in our dreams of days and times gone by.

The animals are happy and content, except for one small thing; they miss someone very special to them, who had to be left behind. They all run and play together, but the day comes when one suddenly stops and looks into the distance. The bright eyes are intent; the eager body quivers. Suddenly he begins to break away from the group, flying over the green grass, his legs carrying him faster. *You* have been spotted, and when you and your special friend finally meet again, you cling together in joyous reunion, never to be parted again. The happy kisses rain upon your face; your hands again caress the beloved head, and you look once more into the trusting eyes of your pet, so long gone from your life but never absent from your heart.

Then you cross the Rainbow Bridge together ...

Chapter 9

November 5, 2011

My husband went to a meeting for work yesterday and stayed overnight out of town because of the road conditions, but here's the thing: they were clear, the road conditions were fine.

Anyway, he got home this morning and asked if I wanted to go to breakfast. I said, "Sure, but I also need to get some work clothes and return something at the store." He said, "I will go with you. I'd like to spend time with you." I'm thinking okay, this is good, odd but good, and then he reminded me that he was going to a memorial at a bar with his brother at 2:00 p.m.

By the time we got through running around, he was running late and asked if I could just drop him at his brother's and then I could pick him up around four thirty. He isn't usually that nice to me; it's like he was trying to make me feel better about something he had done or was going to do. It made me feel like I was being set up so when he did get drunk, I wouldn't get so upset. Maybe this would be okay, though. I would pick him up in a few hours, and maybe he wouldn't be drinking this time. It is a memorial but it is at a bar. Okay, let's just hope he doesn't drink; give him the benefit of the doubt that he will be good.

I sent a message around four thirty asking how things were going. He called me back and said things got started late, at four o'clock, and he would be eating there, so give him a few more hours. He called about seven forty-five. He was drunk. I said, "I need to come get you now." He said, "Well, they are playing music, so I'm going to stay." I said, "I have to work early, so have your brother bring you home." He said, "He has been drinking too much also, so I'll just stay at his place"... and there it is!

I knew it wasn't going to be as easy as what he had told me, but I was just dumb enough to get sucked in again, hoping it would be different this time. It was never about spending time with me. It was about making me "think" he was spending time with me when what he was really doing was trying to make it okay *for himself. I know my husband; he already knew what he was going to do before he even left. If he really wanted to spend time with me, he would be home with me, plain and simple!*

November 6, 2011

I have no words for the heartache I feel, the devastation that has been caused, and the emptiness where my spirit once was. You'd think I would have learned by now that I can't fix or save anyone. I guess when I feel needed and wanted, I get in deep and feel I will be given the same love and help in return when I need it. I want so desperately for him to get the help he needs, for something to wake him up and make him see he has a serious drinking problem, that he is an alcoholic no matter how much he tries to deny it. No matter how much he blames me for his drinking, it isn't my fault.

Please, God, I just want him to get caught for driving while under the influence before he hurts himself or someone else, before we lose everything we have due to his poor choices and bad decisions. I know that may sound awful, but the truth of the matter is it may be the best thing that could happen to him, because right now he thinks he is invincible; to him there are no consequences for drinking. I mean, it would be terrible for him to get a DUI, but maybe it is what he needs: to be slapped in the face, to shake his world up. I don't know what it will take at this point; maybe nothing will help. He needs to be stopped, and it won't happen until fate intervenes or his health declines. How awful would that be? I mean, how can he have so little respect for his own life and those he shares life with?

December 13, 2011

This makes two years in a row he hasn't been around for my birthday. This year was classic. He couldn't be there because it was more important for him to go try out for a band, and a boy band at that. Yes, I said he missed his wife's birthday to go try out for a band he found on an Internet ad. Even worse is they were a bunch of young kids, and it wasn't the music he even liked to play. Well, that was so worth it! Why as his wife am I worth so little to him? Why does it not matter that my heart aches? Why don't I deserve special surprises on my birthday?

He shouldn't have missed my birthday. I am his wife. He should be spoiling me and making it a good day for me. No matter what! I can't begin to express the sadness I feel. I don't want to feel disposable; I want to feel cherished and adored by the man I love. How can he not feel bad about missing my birthday again (two years in a row) or ruining it by drinking?

Sometimes we are so good when we are together, and those are the moments I cherish and wish would last forever. One day they will. One day we will be amazing again, but it isn't going to be today. Maybe not tomorrow, but someday it may happen, and for my birthday the gestures I would love will happen, and they will be from my husband's heart, because as much as he pisses me off, call me crazy, but I love him! As close as I come at times to feeling like I should give up, I won't give up on him. I won't walk away because in those moments, something says, "Don't give up. Hold on. It will all be worth it," so I listen and believe with all my heart that we are worth it, that he is worth it and he will prove himself to me. Today, though, I am disappointed in his behavior and the selfishness that he feels is somehow justified. It isn't justified; it is really sad and sick. Sometimes he is the most loving passionate person with me, and other times he is Jekyll and Hyde—that's really the only way to explain it. Our dog is on hospice care. She is so close to the end of her life, and all he can think about is himself. I need him here; our dog needs him here. He will regret not being here one day. I am with her every day that I can be. If I don't work, I am home with her, just loving her and making sure she is doing okay, not in any pain.

I am all for him wanting to play in a band, but this whole situation isn't even right; you have to have your priorities straight. He is just running in circles and can't find a way to stop. Do you know how shameful it is for me to sit with my mom, her husband, my daughter and stepdaughter, seeing the way they look at me sitting all alone, no husband for my birthday, because something else was more important to him, and for the second year in a row, we were in the same restaurant celebrating my birthday with the same husband not present because he is too damn selfish to put his wife first on her own birthday. I am sure they are all a bit upset with him for hurting me like that and not being there. After all, he is my husband; he should want to do nice things for me. What can I really say to them? Not much at all about his behavior. I excused myself to go to the bathroom, and I sat in there and I started to cry because I was devastated that my husband wouldn't be with me on my birthday. The loneliness I feel just breaks my heart in ways I can't begin to express.

When friends ask, "What did your husband do for you?" I put my head down in shame, like I have done something wrong, but it isn't me, it is him! One friend said, "You can't keep living your life like this. You deserve to be treated with love, kindness, and admiration, someone who is there for you. This guy, he just isn't doing what's right, and at some point you will have to make a choice. You should be spoiled on your birthday. He should want to be with you. You're his wife. You have such a good heart. You deserve all you wish for, and he should make that come true for you." Such a sweet thought. As I sat there with my friend, the tears started coming, because he was right: my husband should be giving more than he is. I know it is ultimately my choice, but is it unreasonable to love my husband even though he is a selfish man? Yes, I heard myself as I said those words, and it does sound insane. Maybe I am crazy, believing and having any hope that he will be anything more than who he is right now, but is it so crazy for a wife to want so much more from the man she loves with all her heart? I know the man my husband truly is inside. I know who he is in his heart. He isn't this image of the man who stands before me today, the one who is mean, selfish, and egotistical—that is the disease talking. I see the person he can't because he is too clouded with alcohol, but someday, I believe that there is hope and he will beat this; he will get better! I have spent many birthdays & many New Years alone, not to mention the countless nights I have gone to bed alone and woke up alone. I want to be his everything. When will it be my turn to be cared for?

December 16, 2011

We talked a little this morning, and get this, he said that I should have gone out of my way on my birthday *to make* him *feel special; like I wanted him there with me ... did he really just say that to me? Are you kidding me right now? Wow, he has some nerve. Unbelievable is all I can say at this point! Just totally unbelievable! He should go out of his way being my husband, making me,* his *wife, feel special on her birthday and apologize for being such an* ass. *He came home from work this afternoon, got ready, and left without saying a word to me. Our dog is dying from cancer, but hey, it's all about him. What a selfish, selfish, man! Here is my Christmas wish ... that our dog doesn't suffer.*

I would love for it to snow one more time so she could play in it with me; she loves to catch snowballs, but I know she is weak. She has slowed down and sleeps a lot. I feel her time is getting close, and it hurts my heart. I can't imagine waking up every day without my dog; she is such a big part of this family. Two years ago when the house was broken into, I couldn't hear her barking. I thought for sure they killed her or stole her. I walked in with the police with their guns drawn. It was scary. We went from room to room opening the doors; we finally found her locked in another room. I cried. I dropped to my knees and hugged her. I was so grateful we found her. Everything else could be replaced, but not our dog.

My baby girl is out of town this year, and for the first time won't be with me for Christmas. It makes me feel so sad.... The night before my daughter left, she sat on the floor in my room with our dog. She cried and cried and loved on her; it was so sad. She said, "If she isn't here when I get home, I don't want to leave without saying good-bye to her." I had to wipe away my tears; my daughter grew up with our dog. Truth is, I didn't want my daughter to go out of town. I was against it and said absolutely no at first, but things have been so bad here with her dad and me that I thought she deserved to have a once-in-a-lifetime opportunity to go and she could have fun and be happy. She would celebrate Christmas on the East Coast this year. I will miss her more than anything. I have never been away from my daughter for any holiday, but sometimes we have to put others' happiness before our own, so I gave that gift to my daughter even though it broke my heart. Have a blast, honey; Mom will miss you so much! Keep her safe, keep her safe....

I don't know why I am still holding out for hope with him. I haven't had any sight of it changing; what do I hope will happen? I will tell you, I am hoping and praying for a miracle, and if I believe hard enough and long enough, it will come true. It just has to! He will be able to stop drinking one day and begin to recover so we can be healthy; I have faith in that, and I believe with all my heart it can happen. I mean, there have been moments of fun and happiness, moments of clarity for him when he does feel bad and knows he has done wrong, but they are only moments, they don't last long. As I said before, I wouldn't leave him if he had cancer or some other illness and needed treatment to get better; he is sick from alcoholism, and the more I educate myself about it, the more I understand it, and the more I am convinced that getting help will be his only saving grace. Something tells me to stay, to not give up hope—is this what it means when you truly love someone: you are there no matter what? Yes, that is exactly what it means for me. There is a reason why we have not left one another. We have a strong bond that even though it seems lost; it still holds us together in ways we can only feel. I often try and really think hard about why I am still here with a man who seems to only have interest in himself and not his family.

I talk to my friends, but there are many times I don't bother them because the conversation feels like a hamster on a wheel; it just keeps going around and around the same thing all the time. At times I have self-pity; other times I am angry at myself, and many times I am angry at him, and over the years I have become so bitter and I resent him. The resentment is agonizing. I feel ashamed and humiliated, and very, very lonely.

My friends have never made me feel like I am bothering them or like I am foolish for staying; they just try and understand. They are here for me, caring about what I am going through and what happens to me. I know my husband is not concerned with how anything is affecting me at this point because he can't see past his next binge. The binges have grown closer together. His alcoholism is out of control so much that I am surprised he hasn't killed himself, and that terrifies me.

December 22, 2011

Today he called and asked me how much money he can use for Christmas shopping. I thought, that is great; he wants to give. I asked who it was for. He got angry and hung up on me. Whatever, Mr. Attitude, see you when you get home; can't wait for that to happen.

The reason I asked is because I have always done all the shopping for the holidays and birthdays. He never really wanted to do much except buy his one special present and that was it. He already bought the girls their gifts, so I told him I didn't want anything because I don't think it is right to buy each other gifts and pretend just because it is a holiday.

I thought I would try and be nice, so when he got home, I said, "Would X amount of money work for you? Who do you need it for?" I couldn't believe what he said, and I quote, "There is a sale at a music store, and they have something I want." I said, "So all of this is just because you want to buy yourself something?" He said, "Yes." I said, "How much is this thing you want?" "Oh, like $250.00." Really? Are you kidding me? How selfish can you be right now? I mean, not even a gift to surprise me or for anyone else.

I wonder what makes him feel like he is entitled to do or get whatever he wants anytime he feels the need. Christmas is the time of year to give to others, those less fortunate, not for yourself. I am so disappointed in him; words escape me at this point. I mean seriously, our dog is dying, our daughter is on the East Coast, my first holiday without her, our marriage sucks, you ruined my birthday, and all you can think about is yourself? What is wrong with him as a human being, and more so, what the hell is wrong with me that I am still here spending one more day under the same roof as this person? Oh yeah, and he quit counseling again. Do you know how embarrassing that is for me? I show up for an appointment, and my husband doesn't. Talk about uncomfortable! It looks like I am the only one who cares; it looks like I am with a man who doesn't care if our relationship works or not because he just leaves, and this has happened like three or four other times. He isn't committed to anything. Fuck this!

Our dog went to the vet for a checkup last week, and they told us that when she starts to have a nosebleed that is when we know there isn't much time left. Now I understand what they meant. I sat on her bed tonight for hours because her nose was bleeding. I sat there crying while cleaning it up with tissues until it stopped, and all the while, my husband was out getting drunk. He came home to see me on the floor crying and our dog just lying on me not looking so good, with a stack of bloody tissues. He stood in the doorway just staring. He was drunk again. He never asked what happened. How can a person be so cold? He should have walked in and got on the floor with us.

She deserved more love from him than that. She followed him everywhere, and although she was supposed to be my dog, she ended up being his shadow; but when she got sick, she turned to me, almost as if she knew that I would take care of her and be with her till the end. We became so bonded she was always near me.

During this time, my closest and dearest friend and her husband came up and stayed for a few days with my mom and her husband. She said she knew she needed to be here for me so they made it happen. Who could ask for a better friend than that? She has MS and so does my father.

While they were here, I witnessed her having seizures. It was terrifying for me and so sad to watch. I just wanted to be there for her and make it go away. I sat on the floor with her husband and my mom for over an hour while she was having little seizures, coming in and out of consciousness. This woman is a one-of-a-kind beautiful person. Who wouldn't be grateful to have someone that loving and kind in their lives?

Where was my husband, you ask, while all this was happening? Well, he was sitting on the couch watching TV. I guess I didn't need any comforting watching my best friend go through this, and her husband didn't need any support either.

At one point I left the room for a minute, ran to the living room, and started crying; my mom was hugging me. She was there for me; she always has been. My husband saw what was happening, and he still couldn't reach out to me. He didn't come and sit down with us on the floor; he didn't show any regard for my friend. It just made me feel very sad for him as a person that he could be that closed off and not show any kindness for someone else during what would obviously be a difficult time.

She has been my sister, my friend, my therapist, my confidante, my biggest supporter, my rock. Without her, I don't have any idea where I would be today. She knows how to handle me when I call her screaming. She knows what to do when I call her and I am crying so hard I can't breathe. Without her to talk with, I would be so lost. She has been there for me through every good and bad time in my life. If there are angels that walk this earth, which I believe there are, she is one of them. She is one of the most selfless people I have ever been blessed to know and have in my life.

December 25, 2011

Christmas sucked this year! Hands down the worst holiday ever, and I mean ever! Don't get me wrong, I love my family. Things with my husband have gotten to the point where we act like things are okay, but let's be real; no one believes the act anymore. They know things aren't good; you can cut the damn tension with a knife. My daughter is thousands of miles away, my first Christmas without her, and sometimes I feel like I just want to smack the crap out of him to wake his ass up to the destruction he has caused in our lives. I was so happy to be able to spend the holiday with my childhood friend. We laughed and took silly pictures. Even if for just a moment, she took the time to be with me in my time of need, and for that I will always be grateful to her. To make things worse, I hate pretending to be something I am not. I mean, my husband and I are not close and have serious issues, but let's go out and buy gifts for each other. I don't think so. I don't feel comfortable with that. I would rather give no material gifts and work on us and our marriage; that would be a true gift, but that's just how I feel. That would be the ultimate gift to me: to feel his love. This year was full of great sadness. With every passing day, I see our dog slipping away, and now it is so close I can feel it.

I love to decorate and bake treats for people, but this year we didn't even have a Christmas tree. Seriously, me, no tree, no decorations. You know things were bad if I of all people didn't decorate. I did nothing. Things were very depressing. My daughter wasn't here for Christmas, my dog was dying, my marriage is a huge mess, my dad's health isn't the best, and neither is my mom's, so Merry Christmas wasn't so merry this year.

December 28, 2011

Our dog passed away today around six in the evening. I can't believe she is gone. Oh my God, what am I going to do without her? My heart is hurting. I can't lose her, not now, no, no! The past year with her going through chemotherapy, having her third surgery, she has been a brave, strong, courageous girl, who up until the last month of her life had a great quality of life. Then she started slowing down, and the last month they put her on hospice care. She rested her head in my lap, sat right against me when she knew I was upset. I talked to her, and she looked at me like she really listened. She was an amazing dog. Heaven received a beautiful majestic angel tonight, and I know she will always watch over us and protect us.

I am in my room. I can't hear her breathing. It feels weird not having her here, not seeing her on her bed. What am I going to do? It hurts so bad. She is part of our family, part of my heart! We had to tell my daughter that she is gone; she was on the subway when my husband told her. She was so upset and heartbroken, like the rest of us. I am emotionally exhausted; I am devastated.

I know you're no longer in pain, your cancer is gone, and you're playing with all the other fur angels that have gone before you. I will forever miss you. I love you. Your paw prints will forever be on my heart. I don't want to say good-bye, so I will say "until we meet again. You will never be forgotten."

January 1, 2012

Before I get to last night, let's quickly go through the past year. Our dog went through her third cancer surgery, then chemotherapy treatments, and sadly passed away. My rescue cat passed away two months and one day earlier than that from kidney disease. I also lost two other feral rescues to kidney disease. RIP, sweet babies. Heaven now has more beautiful fur angels watching over us. My truck keeps breaking down, so with animal bills and the truck, we're talking an extra $15,000 at least added to our already mounting debt. Our marriage is just a mess, and he doesn't try to help us.

A former friend of sixteen years and I stopped being friends. I watched my dearest friend have seizures and saw how this disease has really affected her. My dad's health is not good. He was just in the hospital again for falling. My daughter wasn't here for Christmas for the first time. My husband's son was sent to prison. My mom and her husband had some issues with property in another state. My brother and his wife had some legal issues, and they lost one of their cats to kidney disease. To top it all off, my husband made a commitment to our counselor that he would go for six months, only to quit after the seventh session. He went for two months, and he promised her no drinking as well, but last night he broke that promise.

Surprise, surprise … he is drunk on another binge. He came home drunk, stinking like smoke from the bars; another New Year's Eve with me being all alone. I wonder how many New Year's Eves I have brought in by myself even though I am married. Has he ever thought I am alone in all of this? Has he ever thought about how much I need him?

I wasn't able to write it the other night, but this is what happened with our dog. We took her out to go potty and her paw curled under her. I straightened it out for her. She took one step and collapsed in the front yard. She couldn't get up; she just lay there, looking at us. I sat down with her. I said, "Is it time?" It was time. We talked to her, and she gave us the look that said she was ready, she was tired. She never got back up after that.

I called the vet, and they were waiting for us with a stretcher. We were both on the floor with her. I was holding her, telling her it was okay for her to go. We love her so much. We are beyond heartbroken. Even with all that was happening with us, we still are able to pull together; we do have a strong love. Next thing I knew, she was gone. I could no longer feel her breathing as I lay on the floor cuddling my dog, hugging her so tight, wishing she was still here. I felt her heart beat for the last time, and my tears started falling so hard. She was still warm. My heart was broken. I didn't want to get up and let her go. I just wanted to lie there holding her, and I did just that.

In the car my husband and I cried and held each other. We were beside ourselves with grief. We can always come together. She was our baby, and now she is gone.

What I can't quite wrap my head around is how do you spend so many years with someone and not have any regard for how they feel? How many times can you watch your wife cry and just walk away? How many countless nights can you stay somewhere else and wonder why your wife doesn't trust you? How many chances can one person give to another person? How much can you love someone and be taken for granted before you realize and believe that you deserve something so much more than the life you are living with the person you are living it with?

I ask myself these questions and so many more so often, and some days I think I have the answers, but just when I feel confident I have figured it out, I question my own answers and ponder once again. Each day I get stronger; even in my moments of weakness, there is strength. Every day is a lesson, and I have the opportunity to follow what I believe to be right for me for that day. We all do.

Chapter 10

January 4, 2012

I got the mail today. Something told me to look at my husband's statement for one of the bills. On December 23, there was some type of jewelry he purchased, but here's the thing: I never received any jewelry. I asked him about it, and he said he returned it, but it didn't show that on the statement and he couldn't show me a receipt. The alcoholic has the inability to tell the truth. He tells you his truth, and that is what he believes to be true. Something sounds awfully strange to me. He says he can't explain it but it's not what I think, but if it isn't what I think, why is it that he can't seem to find the words to explain it? What is going on here? Is he having an affair? Did he give this jewelry to someone else? He said he returned it because I decided we should only give each other one small gift. He said he thought, well screw it. Then I am not giving this to her! *This very well may be my fault. Maybe he did buy me something he wanted to give me, but because I am so bitter, I said one simple gift to each other. I guess he could be telling me the truth; I'm just not sure. He has told me so many lies; I don't know what to believe anymore.*

My daughter will be home in a few hours. I can't wait. She has been gone for ten days. I miss her so much!

January 12, 2012

It sucks walking around day in and day out feeling like my husband could be unfaithful to me, yet he has not done one damn thing to convince me otherwise. I just want to know the truth. If he hasn't been unfaithful, then let me know without a doubt. Clear all the misconceptions up so I don't have to keep wondering about it and we can move forward.

I have given him a million second chances, and yet he constantly tests my trust. Why? Look at all the things he does: he hides his wallet, he has put passwords on his computer and phone, he says he bought jewelry for me but can't explain that whole "weird situation," he doesn't care or ask what is going on with the truck, he left me alone and ruined my birthday and did the same for New Year's Eve. None of this is good. It's all shitty, but most of all, he doesn't seem to care about the destruction he is causing.

January 14, 2012

Today is my mom's birthday. She has been sick the past week and a half, very unusual for my mother. I am a little concerned about her because she is kind of weak. She says she is slowly feeling better, but I don't really believe her. I think she just doesn't want me to worry about her.

I attempt to have a heartfelt conversation with my husband. You'd think after twelve years I would know better, but I keep trying. No one will ever be able to say that I don't try. All he could do was blame me for this, that, and the other thing, and then he left; because why would he stay home and try and make things right with his wife when he can just go get drunk and be numb?

He came home around three o'clock in the morning so stinking-ass drunk that he had to make himself throw up. I mean really, are you kidding me? How many times do people have to make themselves throw up year after year, so sick poisoning their bodies with alcohol, before they realize there is a serious problem? When your gag reflex no longer works right because you have shoved your fingers down your throat so much, that to me is a big problem. Instead of being a stand-up man, he makes himself a victim (poor him), then behaves badly and destructively and expects sympathy. I say to him while crying terribly that abandoning me all these years to go drink has destroyed me and hurt me so deeply, but he refuses to change or acknowledge that he has a drinking problem, so he will not get help for himself.

As I lay in bed at three o'clock this morning listening to my husband shoving his fingers down his throat for what seems to be the thousandth time, gagging because he poisoned himself with alcohol again, I thought maybe I feel I don't deserve any better. Maybe I feel he needs me in some way. Is this what my life is supposed to be like?

I shouldn't be awake at three o'clock in the morning having such intense thoughts. Is it any wonder why I don't sleep well? I am so grateful for my friends and family. Without them keeping my head up, I don't know what I would become. I couldn't imagine going through this without one person to trust or talk to, and I did it for a long time. My family has been supportive of both my husband and I through the years. Even with all the devastation he has caused, they are still here for him. That to me in shows what an amazing family I have.

January 17, 2012

Today was full of finding out that he continues to hide things from me. He was giving his daughter money for something that he lied to me about. She became rude with me, and I was not nice in return. It isn't about giving his daughter money; it is about the secrets and the lies. It was a bad day, and then he started comparing the kids and pulling his twisted bullshit mind games; it was a totally messed-up day. I need to go to sleep. I just can't fight anymore to be loved. No one should have to fight this hard to feel loved; this isn't right. He either loves me or he doesn't.

February 6, 2012

My husband is back to his old drinking ways again; he never stops for long.

We keep trying to do things together sometimes, but I am so resentful and sad and he just wants to do whatever he wants with no backlash from me, so it just ends up not good most of the time, which is very sad. Throughout most of our relationship, we have done things together: playing darts, pool, shuffleboard, going over to a friend's to play games and eat, going to football games, going to the movies, taking a drive, going to the lake, celebrating birthdays and holidays, whatever the case may be. Even during difficult times we would still go places together; we just couldn't connect for some reason. It breaks my heart because I am where I want to be, where I know I belong. Even if I say during the bad times I don't, I do; his heart is my home. He said something about giving someone money on the phone, so I asked him not to because we are in huge debt ourselves. We barely make our own bills every month. We can't be handing out money we do not have. He starts with I need to get back out in the workforce full-time and pull my share of the load. I said, "Plenty of men are the main financial providers of their families, and so are many women; they are proud of that. You happen to be ours." He said, "Those woman take care of their husbands," implying that I don't take care of mine.

I am the only one who has taken care of him all these years; he has always come first. What is wrong with this man? How can he not see that he hasn't been much of a husband who doesn't take care of his wife? How? Then he gets pissed off of course because hey, it's just another excuse to continue drinking, so he had his daughter drive him to the bar and drop him off, so now he is making her an enabler. I asked her not to take her dad to the bars or pick him up. She said it's not her place to tell him he can't go; she said I can't control him. I said, "You can't control him, but you can control what you do. You are enabling him and helping him to get drunk. You should just say no." But she will cater to her dad, and it makes me sad because she knows he is an alcoholic, but she turns her head like the rest do.

I am in this alone! I feel like it has been nothing but heartache for me to help him raise his kids. I have mainly been treated with disrespect. I am not a perfect parent by any means, but I have always taken care and protected all the kids. I took the time all these years to be there when he wasn't. I put them all first, and I came last. I paid attention to things that were being neglected with them, and I am the one they treated like shit. Go figure! They have no idea how much they hurt me all these years; they don't seem to care how I feel anyway. This is how it has been for me ...

It was one of the grandkids' birthday party a few years ago, and my husband didn't want to go because it was more important for him to be drunk and sleep under a bridge downtown, and yes, I am totally serious. So I went to the party with my girls, doing the right thing for our granddaughter, yet I was barely keeping it together, wanting to break down in tears, but I hid my pain for the sake of the kids. And do you know that everyone was worried and sad for him? They didn't give a shit about what it did to me or to our younger daughters, just concerned for him because once again it had to be all my fault, it couldn't possibly be this perfect man that they hold so high on a pedestal. See, all these years, he has used me as a shield for his family, because he didn't want to tell them the truth or let them know what was really going on with him, so he threw me under the bus with the kids, with his whole family, and because of that behavior I feel most of his family has disliked me for a long time. Hey, if someone doesn't like me, they don't like me, but don't use gossip and lies as your reason for not liking me; at least know me first, and then if you don't like me, that's your choice. It was terrible for me and even worse for my daughter to feel like everyone in his family was against her mom, yet I never did one thing I was ever accused of, not one. I have cried about that so much over the years.

It was very hurtful to me, and countless times I asked my husband to fix it, to make it right, so they knew the truth, but that would have meant he would have to be held accountable, so he never made it right for me. I take that back. He did finally make something right and came clean with his older sister and told her the truth. I just wanted them to love me and my daughter, to be part of their family, for them to know that I wasn't the terrible person I was made out to be, that I have always been there for the kids and have tried to get my husband to always do the right thing, but I was gossiped about, and it broke my heart.

February 9, 2012

I went for my annual mammogram Monday. Today is Thursday. I received a phone call to schedule follow-up tests because they found a spot. Holy shit, seriously, not again! Like I am not stressed out enough or dealing with enough in my life at this moment. I can't deal with something like this right now. I am so overloaded emotionally as it is. I just threw my hands up to it all. My mom is going with me, but I am definitely scared. I pray and pray it's not cancer—oh please! No matter what, I am a strong woman, and I can get through anything. I have my family and friends to help me if need be.

I came home and told my daughter; I cried, freaked out a bit. I think I am entitled to do that. When my husband came home, I told him what was going on. He gave me a quick hug, and went out to play his drums. Not the reaction I was hoping for, but what can I say? He seemed concerned but didn't show much emotion. I think he is afraid again. He went through cancer with me once before and how is he going to react given our current situation with one another? Then again, empathy and compassion are great tools. Sometimes we have a reason to change our behaviors. There are things that make us open our eyes to all we can lose. Why not my husband?

About an hour later, I asked him if he would mind going to get me some comfort food. I really wanted pizza from my favorite place. He said he had his drum set all apart; he was making excuses not to go. I said, "Never mind; it's fine." I just wanted him to care that I was scared, but that didn't seem important to him. Taking care of his drums, now that was more important than what I was feeling in that moment. Not that pizza would fix anything, but I didn't want to cook, and mainly I just wanted him to care for me and do something nice.

I sent my dearest friend a message and told her that he wouldn't go get pizza for me because he was too busy with his drums to be bothered, and I found that to be hurtful. I was just complaining; she is safe for me to vent to. She called my daughter and asked where my favorite pizza place was; my daughter told her that they didn't deliver out where we live (which is why I asked him to go get it). So my best friend, who lives out of state, called the pizza place, talked to the manager, ordered my favorite pizza, and talked him into delivering out here because she paid them extra money. I am the luckiest person that I have a friend who cares so much about me. She went out of her way to get pizza delivered just because I was having a really scary day—who does that? Something so simple meant so much to me.

Seems as though every opportunity he has to step up to the plate and make a choice to do the right thing or a nice thing, he just turns away.

February 11, 2012

My husband won some tickets to go see a tribute band, so he invited our daughter and her boyfriend to go with us. Things were fine until I heard him on the phone say we should be there, so I asked what that was about. He said it was for our granddaughter's birthday party on Sunday. I said, "I assumed we wouldn't be going because you have band practice and you missed your wife's birthday for band stuff. I thought for sure you wouldn't go to her party either." He said, "What did you do, take a bitch pill?" I realize what I said may have come off as rude, but I didn't have a rude tone. Oh, who am I kidding? It pissed me off because of what he did to me on my birthday. I was just being honest asking a question, and yes, reminding him that he missed my birthday. I wanted him to feel bad for that. After all, I am his wife. That one was my fault. I was just calling him out on something, and it wasn't nice of me.

He is drinking again; there is one consistency I can always count on. I can't talk to him about anything. He is my husband; he is supposed to be my best friend. It isn't like that now. I am so unhappy. I haven't felt constant joy with him in a long time, and I know without help he will never change. It will continue to get worse. I know I will lose my husband at a young age to his drinking, and that scares the crap out of me and makes me feel so defeated. I feel so worthless. What am I doing wrong that my husband wouldn't want to protect me, his wife? Most men protect those they love. Why not mine?

February 20, 2012

To play catch-up: the past two weeks since my mammogram have been crazy, filled with doctor appointments. The doctor said there is a small spot about the size of a BB; he doesn't seem too concerned, but I have to go for an MRI this week and then go from there. So far I had a standard mammogram, then a diagnostic mammogram, then an ultrasound, and now an MRI. I feel nervous and scared; it could be breast cancer.

My husband and my mom went to the first appointment with me. I am having all these tests and waiting to see what's happening, so I had a little emotional breakdown last Monday. I threw my cup of tea on the floor. I yelled and cried at my husband, and then I ran to the laundry room and sat on the floor just bawling my eyes out. I said I was done and that was it with our relationship, that I couldn't do it anymore. I freaked out. I have been so stressed out. I couldn't take anymore; I was emotionally bankrupt. I needed him to come to me and hold me, love me, give me something to hold onto, show me some kindness and understanding for what I was dealing with. I was scared! He came in and just stood in the doorway. I mean, tell me you understand that I am scared, reassure me you're here for me, and let me know it is okay that I freaked out. Instead, he argued with me and left me there to cry all alone, and then he walked out and slammed the door.

I got up, called my dearest friend, and finished crying. Thank goodness for her and her warmth. She is so kind and never judges me. Let's face it, I would be easy to judge with everything that has happened, but she doesn't; she accepts me no matter what.

I know I said our relationship was done, but we have said that before to each other in arguments, which isn't right; it is so wrong for us to do that to one another, but he just walked away from me, knowing I am waiting to hear if I have cancer. Our relationship is terrible. Our dog died less than two months ago. You'd think this would be a time for a little compassion, a hug, a touch. Words of comfort would have been all I needed. I needed him. I wanted him. Why doesn't he see that? I know I pushed him away by using a threat. I just got so overwhelmed, I blurted it out; I didn't think. I mean, in 2001 I went through adrenal cancer. Could you just show some concern for me? No such luck for this girl. I know I freaked out, but given what our life has been like, don't I deserve a little room to "lose it" at times? I have been there with him through every drunken episode.

Two days after that happened, my husband informed me that he pulled everything out of the 401-K and made an offer on a house for himself without telling me. Are you fucking kidding me? Right now? Seriously this is happening? Christ, how could he do this to me? To us? With everything we are going through, how could he be so cruel and selfish? Trying to buy a house for himself—this is just incredible. Who the hell does something like that?

He didn't tell me until after he closed the account and put all the money into his own personal bank account, and they told him he prequalified for the house. He said when I broke down on Monday, he panicked, went and emptied the 401-K, and thought, shit, I better find a place to live! *How did he expect me, his wife, to react to him taking a large chunk of money out without my knowledge, and then trying to buy a house behind my back? How deceitful is that? What about me? He was just going to leave and buy a house because I had a breakdown because life has been handing me some tough situations lately, including my parents' health issues, and all he could think about is how quick he could just bail on us? So this is how he deals with life's serious issues—he runs!*

I had to leave the house for a while. I was crying so hard I couldn't see. I couldn't breathe. I was hurting so bad, and boy, was I pissed. I went to the park around the corner. I was sitting in my truck, banging on my steering wheel, crying so hard that my eyes were burning. I didn't know what to do with myself. I was heading into a serious panic attack, so I called the one person I knew would know what to do and how to help me. I called my dearest friend and told her everything. It took a while, but she calmed me down and just let me talk. She sat there on the phone and listened while I cried, but she couldn't believe what he did, that he could be capable of doing that to me. She herself was speechless, and I was numb. I didn't speak to him for two days.

He asked me to leave a door open for him so he could prove himself to me again! So I did just that. I told him I would give him the opportunity to prove himself.

For almost a week, things were okay, and then today he was supposed to go see the lender about signing papers for this house. He said he panicked and did that, because if I kicked him out, he would have a place to live, and if we worked things out, it could be an investment for us. This house was a huge piece of crap and needed way too much work; he asked me to bring my mom and her husband over to check it out. He wanted to know what her husband thought; he said it was not worth the money.

So since we weren't getting the house and I didn't trust him, I asked him to put the money in a joint account so we both had to sign before anyone took money out. He refused. I said, "That is not fair. That is our money, and a joint account would show trust on both our parts because it would take two signatures to get any money out." He said he didn't trust me, and I said, "I haven't done anything to lose trust. You betrayed me, not the other way around." I got so pissed off. I felt like he was playing games with me, so I got out of the car and walked downtown to a casino. I called and asked my daughter to come get me. I asked him to write me a check for half of the money because if we were to split up, that would happen anyway. Instead of coming home and having a conversation with me like adults, he went and got drunk; that is his answer for everything. To make matters worse, he has access to a lot of money that he could blow, which has happened so many times before.

March 16, 2012

It started raining pretty heavy, and my lazy husband just sat on the couch while I went around with buckets and towels to all the leaks in the roof. What man can sit there while his damn house leaks? Men take pride in their home. Why not him? Why is this happening? Why doesn't he care about anything? Why does he have to be an alcoholic? Why, why? I can't get him to help with anything around this house; he won't lift a finger unless it is for a drink or his drums. Everything else he doesn't give a shit about. There is broken glass all over the backyard, and he won't help me pick it up. When I do ask for his help, he won't do a damn thing, and frankly I am sick of it. I am the only one who has been doing yard work every week, trying to keep this place up, but there are things I just don't know how to do and don't have the money for. What a sad, sad life!

March 25, 2012

Another day, another week, another month with no change from my husband. The only thing he is interested in is playing his drums and drinking. I still keep trying; I sometimes wonder what is wrong with me. Is it hope, loyalty, commitment? Am I friggin' nuts? What is it? It is such a lonely existence. My husband doesn't pay attention to me. I want friendship. I want to be adored. Is it so wrong for me to want to feel that way? I dream about it. For my husband to want to spend time with me the woman he loves, to be the shoulder she needs to cry on, the friend she needs to listen, the one to hold her, the one to lift her up when she is down. Inside every woman there is a little girl who still wants a fairy-tale happy ending. Being lonely is such a big part of being the wife of an alcoholic. I am sure any of you who are reading and are the husband of an alcoholic, you feel lonely too. I only know how I feel as a wife.
I don't know what I am going to do when my daughter moves out. My whole world will change. Then what? I am so proud of her. Being a mom is hands down the best person I could have been; it has been so much fun. I have learned that unconditional love does exist; I give it, and I want it given to me. It doesn't mean that person doesn't

make mistakes or have flaws. It means you love them in spite of all that, and you accept the good with the bad, the happy and the sad. To me it means that my life wouldn't be as full and complete if they weren't in it.

Speaking of adoring, my very first boyfriend felt that way about me. Yes, I was a young teenager, but we met up again when we were about twenty-six years old, and by that time he had become so addicted to drugs and, I believe, alcohol. He met my daughter, and we hung out a few times just as friends. He was one of those people who had such a good heart. He was so kind, but he was so caught up in the world of addiction. I will never forget this conversation we had because we talked about dating, but I knew it wouldn't be a good situation. I didn't want to be around that stuff; that is why I stopped being friends with them when I was younger. He said to me, "You will always be my first love, but you and your daughter deserve a life that I am not capable of giving you, and I want you to be happy" He knew it would be best to walk away even as my friend, and that is exactly what he did.

I found out years later when I ran into his cousin that he was in his early thirties when he lost his life to his disease of addiction. I never felt so sad. I couldn't believe it. I had never had to really deal with death, and it was my first boyfriend. I called my husband and talked to him. When he found out, he was very kind and supportive. I was surprised. He was very loving and talked to me about it for a while. I found his mom and gave my condolences, and she sent me a photo of him and also one of him and I when we were thirteen years old. My husband put them in a frame for me. That's the man I love! I know he is in there. That is why I don't give up. One day he will break the cycle. I have to have hope, hold onto faith. Nothing is ever as hopeless as it seems if you just believe.

As I sit and write this, I realize that although addiction isn't in my family, somehow it seems to me that I have had relationships with several addicts, and I am not sure I understand why. Maybe because the first people I ever really hung around and cared about were all addicts.

As I look back on the past few months alone, it seems as though I have just been hit by a freight train with a cargo full of *bad luck*. I don't think my husband means to be this type of person that lies, betrays, drinks, is mean, selfish, and so on. But he is so caught up in the evil world of alcoholism that he doesn't know any better. He is just a big mess spiraling out of control.

When I try and talk to my husband, all he can do is blame me or whoever else because he doesn't see himself for the type of person he has become. When he has stopped drinking before and things didn't change between us, he got the attitude of "screw it, I am going to drink because see, it isn't my drinking after all; we still have problems, and it's you." I would tell him that he is a "dry drunk" so we have no opportunity to change the cycle of our relationship because the substance is gone but all the triggers and behaviors are still there because he hasn't made any internal changes emotionally or spiritually; without help through therapy or abuse substance programs, he will never be able to grasp on his own the damage he has done to his own body and mind.

I didn't quite understand how alcoholics could hold down jobs and take in new information but relationships are a different part of the brain. Wow, this gets more complicated, but the damage it does is just incredibly sad. Alcohol does and can kill you; you can poison yourself and destroy your body so much and in such a way that you can damage your liver, pancreas, brain, heart, and every other organ. Once you learn that, I think how can you not stop? Sadly, not all do stop, but there is help out there. I hope everyone will seek it out because it may seem impossible now to not have that drink or drug every day, but it is possible. All it takes is something as simple as going to a meeting, walking through the doors, and just listening.

March 30, 2012

My therapist offered to have my husband come in and do a few sessions with me so she could help us with some communication tools. Today we went to counseling, and she was trying to teach us how to do damage control, but I don't think he gets it. More importantly, he doesn't want to.

We drove separately, and when we left, he sent me a text message saying he needed some time so he was going over to his brother's house to hang out. I knew that meant he was going to get drunk. He called around five o'clock in the morning. I said I didn't want to hear it and hung up. He got home around eight o'clock. He said he was at his brother's for a while and then he went to the casino and gambled all night, then slept in his car. Awesome, sounds like a fun life, doesn't it? I think he is a liar. He has been doing nothing but hiding things from me, lying to me, wasting his money, pissing it away. For hell's sake, we are in debt; give me the money so I can do something useful with it like pay bills instead of going to every damn concert that comes to town and drinking like you're a friggin' college kid. Grow the hell up! I realize I am the one who tries to smooth things over to try and make things better, but I am tired of being the only one.

April 3, 2012

Yesterday was my baby girl's eighteenth birthday. We took her, her friends and the family out to dinner for seafood. We had fun. We laughed; it was so good to laugh like that. I am excited to see how her future unfolds. She is such a smart, beautiful, kind person, with a bit of an attitude, but she is my daughter and I love her. No matter what she decides to do, I know she will be successful. Before Christmas we started filling out college papers and scholarship forms. She was doing essays. It is a lot of work, but she is focused on going to college and having a career so she can be comfortable and support herself.

It has been such a pleasure to have her as my daughter. What a wonderful journey being a mom and going through the years together has been! We had a tough go of things for a while, and she scared the hell out of me having open-heart surgery at seven weeks old and almost dying, but we came through everything together. We have a strong mother-daughter relationship, and I hope it gets better as the years go by.

I keep trying to talk to him because I care about our girls, and well, as usual, I am not supposed to feel anything that he doesn't agree with or like. If it is going to bother him, I shouldn't speak. I just want them to be happy and have a good start in life. We all make our own choices, but as parents it is our job to teach them as best we can. When they spread their wings, we pray they don't fall because they are our children, no matter what age, and we love them. He is such a selfish person and has raised his kids in the same way.

I know my husband suffers from alcoholism. I miss my love so very much. I actually ache from it, just thinking of how lost he is. I'm going to bed alone again. I can't take this day anymore or this life. I need him to save himself; I can't do it for him, although I wish I could.

April 7, 2012

As long as I don't talk to him about anything important and I don't voice my feelings or opinions about anything, then things are okay; we don't argue. But what kind of relationship is that? This is the other thing I thought about ... I feel like I am a broken spirit. I am stuck where I am right now because I have allowed him to do the damage he has done to me. I wasn't like this until he started bingeing, staying out all night, not coming home to sleep, not caring how he has destroyed me, but that has been for the past, what, eleven years. I blamed him for doing this to me, but I realize I was also guilty because it was me that allowed him to continue to treat me this way. It became my fault. I believed, or I wanted so badly to believe, that he would love me enough to see the hurt and devastation he caused and he would want *to change because I would mean more than his next binge. Sadly that wasn't and hasn't been the case. Maybe it never will be, or just maybe, if I hold onto hope, it will happen one day.*

April 11, 2012

Today we are completely broke. I have zero dollars in the bank, no money to get gas, no money for food, nothing. So I asked him if I could have $20 for gas. I know he has all that money hidden someplace, and he can't part with $20 for his wife.

He has a yearly conference for work that is at one of the hotels in town a few minutes away from our house, and he informed me that he would be spending Friday night there in a room. I said, "I don't feel it is necessary. You can come home; it doesn't end late." He said to me that he would come home when he wanted to come home. He has some nerve! He has been running all over the place, rarely home, always drunk, at concerts, stays out all night, lies, and hides things. I think that the last thing my husband should be doing is staying the night in a hotel room, leaving his wife's mind to the unimaginable, which has already been on my mind anyway. I wish I could run away.

April 15, 2012

I was informed by a family member that my husband is one of the big reasons why his family seems to have an issue with me. I have been his excuse for not dealing with his family. I heard he has been saying

*things like I don't let him be with his family, I am too controlling,
and so on, but here is the interesting twist on that: his family does not
know he has used me as his shield for years so he didn't have to deal
with them. Maybe it wouldn't matter to them. However, it matters
to me!*

*Early on there were lies spread about me that pertained to his kids:
that I kept him from his kids and did all these terrible things that
were never even true. People assumed the worst of me, and he never
corrected them because now he didn't have to take any accountability,
which is typical for an alcoholic, so any type of family function that
came up, if he didn't want to go, he would say, "She doesn't want to
go, and I have to stay with my wife," when the truth of the matter is
I didn't know about most of these events until well after the fact or
even years later. It was all such crap. I have asked him for years to
fix this and correct it because the way I had been treated was wrong.
Sounds to me like instead of him being a strong man and standing up
to his family and telling them what he really thinks, he used me as a
reason to not deal with these issues, so in return I am thrown under
the bus and betrayed by him once again.*

*Of course the only thing people are going to think is it must be poor
him, he is a victim of that bitch, or no wonder why he drinks so much.
People have no idea what it is like living with my husband; family
or not, they have no idea. Like ostriches, they bury their heads in the
sand about his alcoholism; no one but me will call him on it. No one
thinks it is serious. I know how serious it really is. I can't reach out
to them; they don't understand and wouldn't be there for me. Am I
the only one who cares that his health has gone to shit? He is just a
mess. He is out of control. He is headed for something really bad to
happen, and soon it could be a DUI or it could be he hurts himself or
someone else; maybe he will poison himself enough with alcohol and
he dies, and then maybe someone will listen. Then the problem will
get the attention it should have had.*

I am so sick to my stomach with all the bullshit that goes on, the heartache and pain I have been put through, and my daughter—the terrible heartache she must feel! Seems to me he has played both sides so he didn't have to take any responsibility for anything; he is too chicken shit to face his own damn issues, so he used me as a pawn in his mind games, and over the years, he helped create needless pain for me. Why do that to me? I have been so damn good to this man. That's it! No more hiding things or not telling this person and that person. I am going to talk to him right now. I have had it this time. Enough is enough. Now I am really pissed off....

Turns out he is really pissed off too, but not at me. He said I am the one who has been lied to, because he never said any of those things about me that I was told he did say. He said that is why he doesn't go around his family much, because of stuff like this. He said he has never said anything like that about me.

I hope he is telling me the truth. I want to believe him, I really do. I told him I wanted him to take care of this and fix it this time. I need him to come clean and tell them the truth. I am so tired of hurting in every direction that life has thrown at me. I need him to do it for me.

April 18, 2012

We went to another counseling session together. It was a bit emotional today.

We left there and went straight over to his sister's for him to straighten out all the BS and gossip! He came clean with his sister and told her what he had done all these years, letting everyone believe it was me. Once in a while he has moments of clarity and does the right thing. Today he is in a moment of clarity. He is correcting what has happened and letting people know the truth and clearing my name so to speak! Today I am proud of the man he is, one that is stepping up and standing with his wife.

Yesterday morning I was sitting at the table poking at my breakfast not really eating, and a tear rolled down my cheek. He said, "What's wrong?" I said, "Do you really need to ask?" I told him that I just hoped we would be like one big family, we would all be loved and happy, but he said that is why he hasn't bothered with his family most of his life. So those are his issues. I have encouraged and asked him to talk to them for himself, but he has no interest so I just leave it alone. It makes me sad, though, for him because I think it could be easily resolved, and then he wouldn't carry the hurt feelings around anymore and he could finally let go.

He went to work, but of course he didn't come home. Now after just saying how sorry he was for others treating me poorly, he goes and does the same thing. Isn't that a hypocrite? Why couldn't he just come home? I was feeling close to him. I don't understand why he keeps hurting me. Why?

Around midnight, I got a phone call from him. He was slurring his words. I couldn't understand him, but what I did understand was he was so drunk; he was in a parking garage and felt sick. So being the woman I am and not wanting anything bad to happen, I went against my better judgment, and once again I enabled his behavior when I should have just left him to figure it out for himself. I went and rescued him, and what's worse is our girls got up and went with me because someone else had to drive his car home.

When we found him, he was passed out in the front seat, doors unlocked, wallet, phone, and keys just lying there. He is so lucky that someone didn't see him, open the door, and kill him or rob him. These are things he doesn't think about, but as his wife I do, and it scares the hell out of me sometimes the big risks he takes with his life. I opened the door, and the smell was just disgusting. There was a strong odor of booze that rushed out of the car. It took me a few times to wake him up, but when I finally did, I asked him to get in the backseat. He started being a jerk. He said, "Don't you tell me what to do." He refused to move. I said, "We can't drive you home if you don't get out of the driver's seat. If you don't want to move, then we will leave you here and go back home. It's your choice." He finally listened.

His daughter drove him home, and my daughter and I were in the other car. She was disgusted, just shaking her head.

I asked him to sleep on the couch because he smelled so bad of booze and smoke. He said, "This is my bed," so I got up and went on the couch myself. I was not having this fight tonight. It is so sad that the girls have to see this and live like this. They have seen him like this for years. What does he think it has done to them? He has all but destroyed our family. He is an alcoholic who is in serious denial about how bad this disease has become and just how out of control his drinking is at this point. I am pretty sure he is drinking every day now, and what started out as just beer or a glass of wine has turned into shots and hard liquor as well. He needs to stop living in the problem and live in the solution; that would be the answer.

My daughter said to me on the way home that he is the biggest reason why she wants to move out. She said, "Mom, this is bullshit. He is supposed to be a role model." She said he hasn't been anything close to a role model for her or any of us for a long time. As her mom, do you know how it hurts my heart to hear her say that about her father? She should be proud, not disappointed, but she is right. That's why it hurts! He was really good when the kids were younger. He was around more. He drank at home, well, outside in his shed, but he was here and we did a lot of things with the kids. When the girls joined dance class, he was there for most of the classes and for their recital, but as they got older and started paying more attention to how much he was drinking, he started drifting into the bars to drink but they were still young. He was away from home more and more until he wouldn't come home at all. She is absolutely right, though. It has been destructive in all our lives.

April 21, 2012

We went to pick up a load of cat food. When I got home, I asked him for his keys so I could get all the cat food out of the car. It was unbelievable: he sat there and watched me and didn't lift one finger to help. I didn't ask for his help, but did I really need to? I unloaded 100 pounds of cat litter into the house and over 350 pounds of cat food. How does a man just watch that and feel good?

Needless to say, we got into an argument. He said, "Why don't you go out and get a real *job, make as much money as I do, and stop getting a free ride?" Are you kidding me? Did this lazy alcoholic just say that to me—his* wife*? It has been far from a* free ride *here, mister! I said, "I bust my ass doing housecleaning. I also work another part-time job doing retail, along with every other thing I do around here. Don't talk to me like that. I do have a real job; I have about a hundred of them. How mean can you be?" He loves to hurt me and make me feel like shit, like somehow it is me. He keeps playing these mind games. But hey, he got to get angry and leave to go drink himself to death again, so kudos to you, buddy. What a joke!*

So many lie's so much selfishness. I often wonder how he goes through his days just doing for himself and not giving to others. How does he keep his stories straight, or does he even care if he messes up? I always find out he is lying. There comes a point in every person's life when your entire world is turned upside down and life as you know it at that very moment is forever changed. Strange to say, but at times people find comfort in some of the worst possible situations because it is what they know and the thought of the unknown, even if it is wonderful, is scary because your life has almost become predictable and routine. Even if it is bad, you know what to expect. Sounds sad and lonely and it is, but there is so much truth to it.

Marriage to me is forever. That is what I have always believed in, but I also know that sometimes you have to walk away for your own sanity. It doesn't mean you don't love that person and it doesn't mean you have to walk away forever; maybe you just need a break to breathe from each other, to see things from a different perspective. Some couples won't make it through things together, and others will. Sometimes we make hasty decisions in a moment of anger, and if you can't take it back, you may regret it for the rest of your life. Never make a decision in anger. Be clearheaded about it before you do anything.

When you are together in the way my husband and I have been for so long, because of his alcoholism, he "just exists here." I am essentially alone, and I have been for a long time. He pops up emotionally and sometimes even puts forth effort for weeks at a time, even a few good months. It is such an odd feeling being in a marriage, or any relationship for that matter, but feeling like you are alone when you are together. Raising the kids alone but there are two parents; it has been an emotionally exhausting journey to say the least.

Every day I learn more about myself and what alcoholism does to someone, to everyone. The definition of an enabler is this … a person who by their actions makes it easier for an addict to continue their self-destructive behavior by rescuing. To enable the individual with the addiction, the mutually dependent person makes excuses and lies for the addict, which enables the addiction to continue.

I for one know I am most definitely guilty of being an enabler because I thought I was helping. The times I went to the bars, the times I bought alcohol for him, the lies, the excuses, picking him up, taking care of him when he was sick—all enabling, and I allowed myself to be put in that position. However, in my own defense, I didn't realize he was an alcoholic until after we were together. I didn't understand that you do not have to drink every day to be an alcoholic. I fell in love with this man who has had my heart from the beginning. I knew we would spend our lives together. We found what makes us complete when we found each other, so good or bad, I had to keep hope that it would find a way to work out.

I have become so bitter and resentful toward him for all the pain he has put me through that my anger is starting to really get hold of me. I stopped going to pick him up. If he would call drunk, I would say, "You got yourself in this situation; you need to find a way to get yourself out." That was me getting healthy. But I wasn't always consistent with that, and I should have been. But then I would have feelings of guilt, like what if something happened to him, what if there was an accident and he hurt himself or someone else. Then I realized that it isn't my fault, it isn't my guilt to carry; it is his, he is responsible for his own actions. But I couldn't change what I felt in my heart, which is the responsibility to take care of him. Easier said than done, that is for sure, and at the end of the day, I couldn't live with myself if something happened to him, so where does that leave me? I know I need to figure out another way to make healthy choices to get better myself, which maybe will help him get better too.

Chapter 11

April 28, 2012

Every time I think he can't do any more damage, he shows me that he can.

Every time I think he couldn't be any more selfish, he shows me he can.

Every time I think I can't hurt anymore, he shows me I can.

Last week, following the therapist's advice, I put all our bills and debt on paper for him to see. I included the house and everything.

Today he came into the bedroom and informed me that he would be getting a motorcycle. He didn't want to talk about it; I was just told. That is not what couples do; they do not *make big purchases without discussing it first. I told him that he* would not *be getting a motorcycle; we have way too much debt right now. But in a few years, when we are in a better place, I would be totally fine with that. He said, "I told you when the girls turned eighteen, I would get a Harley!"*

First of all, I told him, one of the girls just turned eighteen, and the other will be eighteen in a few weeks. Talk about jumping the gun. Can they graduate from high school first? Can we focus on them? Graduation was only like six weeks away. Second, you don't just tell your spouse you will be making a large purchase; you discuss it, and you both have to agree. And third, I told him the therapist suggested that I write out all our debts for him to see, so now clearly is not *a good time to make any purchases, let alone a big one, since we are clearly drowning in debt.*

I told him we are just getting by every month, and if we were to get any newer vehicle, it should be to replace our truck that I drive; it is fourteen years old and has a lot of trouble starting. Every time it goes in the shop, we spend thousands to fix it, or I should say charge thousands to fix it. He said, "You had to have that truck." I said that was our *decision together twelve years ago because of how many kids were here; we couldn't all fit into one small car, so we got a Suburban. I said, "It took your signature to get it; you wanted it too." Just something else he wants to blame me for!*

I asked him if he thinks he is an alcoholic, and he said, "No." I said, "You're in denial. There is no justifying buying a motorcycle at this time." He said he doesn't have many more years left, and he wants to be happy. Whatever that means? See, it is the material things that he thinks can bring him happiness, but he isn't truly happy. He is not happy at all no matter how many things he buys, and the sooner he figures that out, the better. It is just like drinking. It's just a cover to hide behind something so you don't have to face the reality of anything happening in your life. It's all about him, what he wants, what he needs. I am not going to struggle any more than we already are so he can have a motorcycle.

Our life is a mess. I am miserable, he is miserable, I am with a man who is selfish and an alcoholic, and he is verbally abusive. I don't know which way is up or down anymore. I just wanted to share a life with him, to be loved every day, to laugh and be happy. What is wrong with him? Why does he have to be so mean? Why does he have to be like this? We started out so strong, so good, so in love; he needs to be reminded of that and be grateful.

I don't know when we stopped being us, but I sure do miss it. You know how depressed you are when you stop taking showers or giving a shit about what you look like. I have no energy. I just feel sad and defeated, so I put on a phony smile for those who believe everything is fine; they can't see the truth. They don't know me!

I just withdrew and was isolated from everyone most of the time. I became so lonely and overwhelmingly sad, wondering if this was all my life would ever be, and I questioned if I deserved anything more. I know I have a good heart. I am kind and loyal, but look where it has gotten me. Okay, tomorrow will be better. For now it is okay to have a bad day. I can't beat myself up for that, but I sure am good at it.

May 2, 2012

So, a few days ago he came to me and said he wanted a motorcycle. I explained rationally that I just wrote out all our bills and debt; he could clearly see the amount we bring in every month, what goes out, and what we need, which is way more than what we actually bring home.

Then on Monday, April 30, we go to counseling, and it gets brought up again. The therapist asked what he thought about what I said about how we couldn't afford it right now. He said it made sense and it was logical thinking. Then he proceeded to tell us that earlier that day, while he was at one of the casinos for work, it seems he had an anxiety attack. He said he felt like he was going to pass out. He became shaky. He got sweaty. They called the paramedics to check him and his vitals were okay, so he didn't want to go to the hospital to be checked out.

Usually if something like that happened, he would call me and talk to me about it, let me know what happened, but he doesn't tell me anything anymore. I don't know what happens in my husband's everyday life. That is very heartbreaking to me. I know if I need to talk, I call a friend; I don't bother talking to him because I know how it turns out every time. We are like two ships passing in the night, living in this house together. If we don't argue, then it is just quiet and tense. We go days without speaking a word. Really what I would love to do is have us jump in each other's arms, find our passion again;

*we just don't know how to anymore. The saddest part of all to me is
when we do look at each other at times. It's despair, like you're right
in front of me. Why can't I come to you? Why can't we find our way
back to one another? Why aren't we able to reach out and connect? I
can see the love in his eyes, the longing. Why won't he reach for me?
So last night, May 1, 2012, he came into the room, and he said,
"I bought a motorcycle." I said, "You what? You better tell me that
you're lying to me right now; you better not be serious." He said, "I
can't do that." I said, "Tell me this is a twisted joke. Tell me this is
a frigging joke." He said, "No such luck." Oh man, I went off! I
blew my top. I said, "What the fuck are you thinking?" He was like,
"I don't know. I just wanted it." Holy shit, we can barely afford to
breathe, and you* just wanted it, you just wanted it! *I said, "Where
did you get the money?" He said, "Where do you think? It was from
the money I pulled out of the 401-K."
My daughter took me for a ride because I was so pissed and hurt. I
was shaking. I was bawling my eyes out, screaming, "What the hell
is his problem?" So let's get this straight: three and a half months ago,
he emptied the 401-K without my knowledge, tried to buy a house,
and now bought a motorcycle, all behind my back, and all that time
I was going through test after test to see if I had breast cancer. Wow,
this is too much for one person to handle. What else don't I know?
So much betrayal and sneaking around; this is incredibly selfish. I
think I am actually in shock at the complete disregard and selfishness
toward me. I can't believe this is happening. What has happened to
my husband? When did he become such a terribly hurtful person?
Being out didn't help, so I came back home. I knew he lied about how
much money the bike really was, so I kept asking how much it was.
He kept replying with, "It doesn't matter" so I finally yelled, "It does
matter. How much did you spend?" Here's the kicker to all of this: he
flat out* lied *to my face … he bought the motorcycle on April 27, the
day before he first approached me with, "I want to buy a motorcycle."*

He forgot to mention he already did, *and he kept it hidden at his brother's so I wouldn't know. He lied to me and played bullshit mind games on Saturday, and then again at the therapist's office on Monday, pretending to "discuss" it when all along he was* lying *about it because he already got what he wanted. It was so great to hear all of this tonight and to hear him say he lied to me about all of it!*

No wonder why he is having anxiety attacks: that's what lying and betraying someone does to you. There you have it. My husband has turned into a big liar *and the most selfish person I have ever known. What does that say to me about him as a person, that he can look his wife in the eyes and repeatedly lie? He thinks his behavior the past six months is okay, but he is not a trustworthy person. He has destroyed our family for his own selfish needs.*

I made an appointment for tomorrow to go talk to a divorce attorney to find out what my rights are here.

I have to protect myself. I have to be done with all of this bullshit. He certainly will not protect me, and no one in their right mind would continue to live like this. I am praying for a miracle. I am so sick to my stomach. All he does is get drunk and make poor decisions; he is selfish and dishonest. This heartache is just killing me. My heart palpitations are constant. My anxiety is through the roof. I don't know how he looks at himself in the mirror every day, feeling good about the person he has become. He treats his wife like shit, and he isn't a father to the girls. He is just killing himself every time he takes a drink. How sad. What a waste of a life. You can only take someone down with you for so long before they have had enough and have to change things for their own sanity. I'm done going to counseling with him. I don't want him there anymore. He just sabotages everything. It is a big joke to him. He doesn't take this serious. Now I have to start taking care of me. I believed he was different, and a long time ago maybe he was, but today with his behaviors he isn't someone I would choose to have in my life.

May 7, 2012

What did I do to him that he feels I deserve to be treated this way? Being supportive of him, taking care of him, the kids, the house— this is how I am appreciated: with abandonment, verbal abuse, lies, betrayals, secrets?

Divorces are ugly, and unless you can both be amicable—and I don't think he could ever be fair—this would be very costly for us both financially and emotionally. We would have to sell things and lose things. What a mess! Why does it have to be this way? Oh how I wish he would snap out of this and be a kind loving man, the one he promised me to be! I am overwhelmed and exhausted at the heartache and devastation his actions have caused.

I sat outside the attorney's office, bawling my eyes out before my appointment. I couldn't go in. I called my friend. She calmed me down and said, "You don't have to do anything. This is just for your knowledge. You don't have to leave him if you don't want to; you just need to know if he leaves you, what your rights are." I knew she was right because I still wasn't ready to leave, but I had hoped if I shared with him that I went to talk to an attorney, he would see how serious this is and it would snap him out of whatever this was and he would want to go get help. Well that was not a fun appointment to talk to an attorney. I just can't see how this is the right thing to do, this is not what I want but what will it take for him to see his destructive behaviors? When I told him I saw an attorney today it seemed to get his attention, I gave him her business card so he knew I was serious and I prayed that would be all it was going to take to change things for us. He made a twisted comment a few days ago: he said to me that unless he is hurting me, I don't notice him. That isn't true, but what does that mean? He's setting out to hurt me to be noticed? If that is the case, he needs serious help.

He is in a downward spiral of destruction, and anyone caught up in it, he will take down with him.

May 11, 2012

How can he be emotionally invested? His mind isn't functioning properly; it is clouded from the alcohol. You have no idea how heartbreaking that is for me; to feel like the one you're with; the one you want to love you so much doesn't really care at all. It is devastating.

Tonight my husband came home from work, changed, didn't say a word to me, and left so he could go play with his motorcycle. His drinking is soooooo out of control. He said he is spending hundreds and hundreds on alcohol a month—like that is something to be proud of.

I wish I could commit his ass to a rehab inpatient program so he couldn't leave until he detoxed his body and got the help he desperately needs. Even then it wouldn't change anything until he is ready for a change himself. I just want us to have a chance together at a sober life, to be happy in love, and healthy.

I try to just concentrate on my animal rescuing; it is one thing that brings me great joy. Lately, though, it is hard to even feel joy about that. Don't get me wrong, I love animals. I am very passionate about them. I think I am more brokenhearted than I care to admit to myself or anyone else.

May 12, 2012

After he was gone all day, he came home around ten o'clock. At the same time as he pulled up on his bike, we heard loud police sirens going, and we thought he had finally been pulled over for drinking and driving.

So when he came in the house, our daughter and he had a little argument because she said she was worried it was him being pulled over. He tried to shush her when she was talking, and she said, "No, you don't shush me! Do you know how many times over the years I have had to come and get you when you were drunk?" He said,

"So sorry to burden you. That's what people who care about you are supposed to do when someone is drunk." She said, "Yeah, that is fine, but you have been doing this since I was a little girl."

Then he and I got into it. He said I am mean, I hold grudges, and I'm a bitch. He said all of this in front of our daughter, so she jumped in and she said, "Oh hell no, don't you talk that way to my mom." He said, "Good-night!" She said, "I am not going anywhere. You don't talk to your wife like that. You're being really rude right now." He said, "You only hear her side." She said, "No, I have listened to you and stood up for you so many times over the years. You treat me different than the rest of the kids. Why did you even adopt me if you didn't want me?" At this point she was very emotional; she had tears in her eyes. You could tell she was so hurt.

She was heartbroken. She had been for a while, and I needed to allow her to express herself, while my own heart was breaking for her. The sad thing is he never even noticed through the years that she was hurting. I stood by close enough that if anything happened, I could intervene. I just listened and watched, but I felt this needed to happen; it was a long time coming. She said, "I have felt like this for years, and you never even noticed. I come last to you! I always have! You should be proud of me!" And there it is; here it comes all to the surface. Her emotions have been bottled up far too long. She looked at him, crying deeply, and said, "Have you forgotten I am your daughter too?" Oh my God, there it is, there is the root of the pain. I wanted to run over and rescue her, but I had to stay out of it this time. She got up and started walking to her room crying. She turned around and said, "By the way, do you know I want to move out, mostly because of your drinking? Just so you know." I can't tell you how heartbroken I am for my daughter right now at this moment. I wish I could absorb all the pain and neglect she feels.

I know she is so hurt, and I can't fix it. I can't fix it as her mother. I feel so helpless. He just sat there; he didn't move. I wanted him to go after her, hug her, tell her he loves her, let her break down in his arms, knowing her dad is there for her and she is safe, that he is sorry for hurting her. Please don't leave her alone with her heartache like you have done to me. Please, if only one time to get it, get up, go after her now, get up and go after your daughter, heal her aching heart.

I was thinking all this in my mind, standing there, praying I could somehow project him to do this. That was so messed up for him to talk that way about me in front of her; it's almost like he did it just to hurt her, which if I think about that, it makes me sick and shows his lack of character as a compassionate person. I mean, what parent could see the heartache in his or her child's eyes and not reach out to the child? We are supposed to protect our children. He didn't try and stop her or go after her; he just let her go to her room feeling heartbroken and alone. He is treating her the same way he treats me. It is so wrong. I could never hurt someone so much and just let them walk away without going after them to let them know how sorry I was if I hurt them and how very much they mean to me. Not him. He walks away from everyone, so cold, such an alcoholic. This disease has just about destroyed everything. How long until he sees that?

He is almost making it to where I have no choice but to split up with him before he will see he needs serious help and that his drinking is out of control, he is out of control. I am afraid that he is going to drink himself to death. It is that bad. Truly people have no idea how intense and frequent his drinking has become or the amount of alcohol he pours down his throat every single time he does drink, how intense and volatile this man is at this point.

May 19, 2012

My mom has been in the hospital for the past two days. She started running a high fever of 104 and has been super-exhausted, zero energy, very weak. My mother hates going to the doctor's and even more so the hospital; she is as bad as a young child stomping her feet. I love her; she is so funny. They are doing blood cultures, and they have her on strong antibiotics. They believe it is some type of bacteria that got into her body and caused a staph infection; because she has an artificial valve in her heart, they want to make sure the bacteria doesn't attack it. Her temp is still going up and down, and she gets real shaky when she is cold.

I tried to call my husband two days ago when they were admitting her, but guess what: he didn't answer his phone because he was too busy at the bar getting drunk. He can't stay out of the bar long enough to be connected to his family and his own wife. I have an emergency, and he won't answer his phone; he doesn't care. I go through it alone; that isn't a new concept for me even though I am married.

He got home around one fifteen in the morning. He had a strong smell of alcohol and drove himself home on the motorcycle. How sad that not only do you have no regard for your own life, but obviously you have none for others around you either. I worry every single day about everything that is happening in my life, especially my husband, and to add to my anxiety, he is driving drunk on his motorcycle. That is just fantastic. How long before I get a phone call that he has been seriously injured or killed driving under the influence? There are times when the phone rings I just stare at it because I am so afraid of who will be on the other end. To even have that thought sickens me and hurts my heart deep down; he has no clue the emotional damage he is causing me. To him, he is just having fun, and nothing is more important than that.

May 20, 2012

My friend saw my husband at a concert, went up to him, and said, "What the hell are you doing here? Why aren't you home with your wife? Your mother-in-law is in the hospital." My husband said, "What are you talking about?"

So he called me and was like, "Why didn't you tell me your mom is in the hospital?" I said, "Well, if you would have answered your phone two days ago when she was being admitted, you would have known, but you were too busy getting drunk. I called you several times because I needed you, but you ignored me, it didn't matter. You didn't stop to think for one second it might be an emergency. You don't think about your family."

My friend called me after I talked to my husband. I asked him to keep an eye on my husband and let me know if anything odd happens or if he sees him with another woman. We have been friends since I was about sixteen years old. He has always had my back; he is one of my closest friends. I talked to my friend the next day, and he said he'd told my husband he needs to stop this drinking and get his shit together and yadda, yadda, yadda.

Even after my husband heard about my mom, he still didn't do the right thing and come home. Of course he stayed out; he had to drink. That is more important.

My friend is a very straight-up person. He told my husband exactly what he thought. He said he didn't know if it would help the situation, but maybe something would sink into my husband's head about his drinking hearing it from another person. I seriously doubt it, but it certainly won't hurt anything. I certainly appreciate him just caring enough to say something to my husband in the hopes that he could help us. He tried to help my husband see he has a problem that is clear to others, not just me. One thing I absolutely love about the friends I do have is that they are protective of me. I really like that, because my husband certainly has not protected me from much of anything, so if someone else has my back, I am all for it.

May 24, 2012

Mom is finally being released from the hospital. She is so happy. She has to go and do an intense antibiotic infusion treatment every day for the next six weeks to hopefully kick the bacteria out of her system. I can't believe how sick she was. My mom is never sick. This worried me. She is still so weak; it has really taken a toll on her body.

Once again when something important came up he should have been here for me, but he wasn't. He was too busy out drinking and riding his motorcycle, living life as if he has no family to be concerned about. This life is so secluded, it is like I am hiding in shame, yet I haven't done anything wrong. I carry his guilt. Why is that? I know there are those that may think I am weak, but in fact, I believe that I am strong, choosing to stay and take care of someone like that, trying to make sense of it all, not giving up.

May 27, 2012

Earlier this year when my husband joined a band to be their drummer, there was a woman whom he somehow became Facebook friends with. She reached out to him and asked him if his band would play for free at a fundraiser. Apparently he forgot to mention to me that she showed up a few times to watch the band play at practice, which I knew nothing about; this happened a few months ago. So I admit that I went through his cell phone to see what he is up to, (every time he changed his password I would watch him type it in and try and remember what buttons he pushed and that's how I was able to get into his phone and he didn't know about it) and in his contacts I found an odd name I had never seen before, a "business" name if you will, but I knew it was a cell phone number. At 10:30 p.m. while he was out, I called the phone number, and a woman answered. I knew her name because he had mentioned it to me before, and I simply asked if this was her. She said yes, and I hung up.

I was so sick to my stomach. I couldn't believe it. At that moment I felt like our whole life had been a lie. Once again I thought, can any

man be faithful to me? What the hell am I doing wrong? Am I
unlovable? *I decided that I would talk to him in the morning.*
*When morning came, I asked him if he had this woman's phone
number still. He lied to my face and said, "No." We had a huge
blowout about this woman before when I found out about him not
telling me that she showed up at some practices and a restaurant,
and he lied about some other things so I flipped out. I pulled all his
clothes out of the closet, yelling and crying. I threw all of his clothes in
a pile on the other side of the room on the floor. He just sat there and
watched me. I think in that moment, he knew to let me be. He knew
it looked really bad, as though he was being unfaithful. He swore to
me that it wasn't what it looked like, but that was all he said. He
didn't spend any time trying to convince me or explain; he didn't
really care if I thought he was unfaithful. (He told me this later on.)
He simply didn't care what I thought.*
*Let's go back to asking him about the number. I asked a few more
times, and each and every time he looked me in the eyes and lied. Why
would he lie to me if he isn't hiding something? Why is he doing this
to me? I have been so good to him. I have loved him so much from the
beginning, and he loves me so much that he can look me in the eyes
and lie without hesitation. I am so hurt beyond comprehension; this is
so terrible. I said, "Why are you hiding her number under a business
name?" He answered my question with a question and said, "Am I?"
I finally said, "I know that's her number. If there wasn't anything
going on, you wouldn't have felt the need to lie and hide it from me."
Of course he left, because, well, I am sure he needed to go drink and
calm his nerves; after all, he had just been caught in a huge lie.*
*I called the number several times that day with no luck; she didn't
answer. Maybe he got hold of her first and let her know what happened
and who knows at this point. I finally called her for the last time, and
this time I left her a message. I said, "I don't know exactly how you
know my husband or who you are, and I am sure I don't know the*

*whole story about whatever is going on between you and my husband,
but you will not have any more contact with him. This stops now."
I hung up.*

*My husband tells me it is all in my head, but here is the thing: you
don't lie to your wife when you have nothing to hide. It is not just
in my head; look at all that has happened. This shit is real. Here is
the other thing: no matter what someone's reaction will be, you can't
stand behind a lie and say that is why you have an excuse to lie. You
do not look your wife in the eyes and* lie *repeatedly about another
woman,* ever. *I have asked him to leave, and he refuses to go. I feel so
low that I had to call another woman. That I have to go through his
phone because I am that insecure with our relationship, but look at
how he hides things. That isn't honesty. It is dishonest. I would take
the worst truth over a sugarcoated lie any day.*

*My daughter and I went to see Mom tonight. She is back in the
hospital. She has fluid on her lungs and is having a little trouble
breathing. They said there could be several reasons why there is fluid
on the lungs, but they are getting it cleaned up. I am so grateful that
her husband looks out for her and takes such good care of her. I worry
about my parents, though. Lately their health hasn't been great; they
have both been in and out of the hospital.*

*I won some tickets on the radio to go see a famous psychic at one of
the casinos in town, so my daughter and I went. It was interesting
to watch, and it was nice to have the time together. It was peaceful.*

*My daughter is going to lunch with her former boyfriend. She is
so excited. They have been split up for about a year now, and she
misses him. He is her best friend, the person she talked to about
everything, so going through the past year here without him to talk
to was probably so hard for her. I think they will get back together. I
think they miss each other, and once he gets out of his own way and
realizes that she is his love, they will be fine together. I hope one day
they get married because he is one of those guys that once he grows up*

and realizes what's most important, I know my daughter will be loved beyond her wildest dreams. He will adore her and take good care of her. He isn't the type that cheats or lies. Some of the things they both need to do is well she is angry at times and takes it out on him but she doesn't see that right now. He isn't willing to sacrifice or give a lot to her, things like moving in together, moving out of town when she needs to for school, for college. It may take them several years and dating other people before they come back together but once they do it will be forever and hopefully in between all that they realize their own faults and change things so they can be their best together!

Chapter 12

May 28, 2012

Our dog has been gone for five months today; I miss her so much.
I am such a hopeless romantic, believing so much in true love and soul
mates, living a lifetime with one person and loving them with all your
heart as they would love you the same way and that would be enough.
So now I am reduced to believing that he has been unfaithful. I mean,
what other conclusion can I come to? You don't lie and hide things
from your wife, especially something that has to do with another
woman. Nothing good will ever come from a lie.
I am going outside to plant some wildflower seeds in our dog's
memory. The first ones I planted that came back in a nice satin
pouch with her ashes, well, they were ruined. He ran over my plants
because he was being a jerk. He had to get his drum equipment out
of here because he thought I would do something to them, and he
wasn't paying attention to his surroundings; he destroyed something
precious. I didn't see it until hours after he left. When I went out
to water them, I saw that he ran over the planters with his truck.
They were smashed in pieces. I sat on the ground and cried; it made
me feel so sad. I know he didn't do it on purpose because he loved
our dog, but he is careless with everything and everyone. He doesn't
pay attention to the things around him that are being destroyed by
his actions.

May 30, 2012

I offered my husband an opportunity to come clean and spill the truth about anything and everything he has done. I promised I would listen. I wouldn't judge; I wouldn't leave him. I just wanted the truth because as his wife, I deserved at the very least the absolute truth. I asked him why he lied about this woman's phone number. He kept saying, "I don't know." Then he said, "Because you would get mad." That doesn't even sound logical to me. Because I would get mad? So let's lie and make my wife think I am cheating instead, because that will go over so much better than the truth. I told him that as his wife, I shouldn't be calling another woman to tell her that whatever is going on with my husband is done. That was so humiliating and embarrassing, and above all, very hurtful. My husband stopped and said, "So you do care."

That is what you got out of this that I care? I call and tell another woman to stay the hell away from my husband and to you that is meaningful? That is just wrong! Of course I care if my husband is with another woman. We have been together for over twelve years. I love him, but he turned this talk into something all about him. He disregarded my feelings once again, so I walked out of the room. The past year or so, he has been acting worse than ever, even for him, like pulling out the 401-K money, putting a bid on a house, buying a motorcycle, hiding phone numbers, missing birthdays, drinking excessively and mixing medications with it (I can't believe he hasn't ended up in the hospital), lying, keeping secrets, spending hundreds and thousands of dollars just pissed away on booze and concerts and I am sure gambling and God only knows what else!

After I was done watching my movie, I came in the bedroom and said, "You can go out there now." He said, "I am not going anywhere." I got in bed and left the light on to write. He got annoyed and went into the living room, where he is supposed to be sleeping anyway. I told him I didn't want him anywhere near me right now. He came back in the room a few minutes later and said, "Don't expect me to be quiet in the morning so you can sleep," with a smug look on his face, game on, bitch.

Like I was telling a friend, any good intentions or nice words from him are very short-lived. After only one day of being nice, he is back to this selfish, mean, cold man—thank you, alcoholism. Say what you mean and mean what you say; your actions need to follow your words. Then he turned my leaving a message for this woman into a flipping joke. He even laughed and said, "I think that it's cute that you called her." Just mind games. He doesn't give a shit about me or this family. I made an appointment tomorrow to go talk with a bankruptcy attorney and find out what we can do.

June 4, 2012

Sounds like bankruptcy may be the way to go for a fresh start for us financially, but because we are married, he has to agree and be on board with this; I can't do it without him. Nope, he is going to be difficult. Why would I think that now he would cooperate with what's best? He never has before. Maybe it would be better to just hide like a hermit crab and be alone. I would not leave my daughter here with him like this, and I certainly wouldn't trust him with my animals or my things. Ughhhh, this totally sucks.

June 7, 2012

Okay, enough is enough. He is being irrational. He is making poor choices, so I am making the decision for us. I am done paying the bills. We are claiming bankruptcy. We can rebuild our credit, but the financial burden right now is too much. Sometimes we have to do things we don't really want to do, but it is what is best. My husband said to me the other day that he has ruined everything and that he is ashamed of himself. I told him if he is sincere about that, I will give him two weeks to get himself to a recovery program and into therapy to start working on changing.

So this morning he said to me, "What happens if two weeks goes by and nothing happens?" I said, "I told you that if you're not willing to prove yourself, then you move out!" I just can't understand how he can keep doing these awful hurtful things and not look back and see the devastation he has left in his path. Yes, I can, because I have allowed my husband to walk all over me and take me for granted. I am the dumbass for staying and believing, falling for the empty promises every time that he will change. Maybe instead of wondering what is wrong with him, I should ask myself that same question: what the hell is wrong with me? Am I that broken?

June 11, 2012

Finally, *something good! The girls graduated today.* Yeah, *I am so happy. They are both eighteen, and they did it. Here's the other part of that: I drove to the graduation alone. My husband wanted to drive himself after me, and he showed up late. What the hell is that all about? What is wrong with him? This is all about family today. These are our girls. My baby got an advanced diploma. It was such a proud moment for me to watch her graduate, walking up to the podium, getting her diploma, and throwing her hands in the air with a big smile on her face—priceless.*

We went looking for the girls after to take pictures, and when she saw me and I saw her, we ran up to each other, and she jumped into my arms. It was so sweet. I hugged her so tight. I can't begin to express what a moment like that was for me. My brother and his wife came up for the graduation. It was so awesome to have our family and friends together for such a special occasion. We laughed, we played the Wii, my brother and I were playing the dancing game, and our dad was laughing so hard I thought he was going to pee himself. I haven't laughed like that in so long. It felt great.

I made a special DVD for the girls of all their years growing up together—bittersweet moments. I hoped maybe looking at the girls growing up over the years and our special family moments; it would touch him in a special way realizing what he has. We took a bunch of pictures both at the graduation and at Mom's house for the party. Here is something I noticed, though: neither my husband nor my stepdaughter bothered to include me or take parent pictures with me. How sweet is that? I only spent twelve years raising her, being the best stepmom I could to her, and I am not thought about, just pushed aside as usual—and if my husband cared, he would have noticed. These kids have no idea what I sacrificed and what lengths I went to, to protect them from their dad's alcoholism. In this moment, to feel so insignificant to someone you helped raise from a little girl into an adult, only to be treated like I am nothing. Oh well, what are you going to do? Back to the bankruptcy …

I still couldn't get a straight answer from my husband about it, but I did inform him that I made the choice a week ago to stop paying the bills so we could claim bankruptcy. He said, "Do what you need to do," so I did just that. So yesterday on the way home, since I haven't been "allowed" to discuss it with him, I said, "So the process has been started. I stopped paying the bills like you're supposed to, and some are already late. I wanted to keep you up-to-date on what's happening." Guess what? He doesn't want to claim bankruptcy—a way to screw us again. So now that I spent money for graduation and I can't pay the bills because he told me to do what I needed to do, now he changes things again. Oh the BS—will it ever stop? This is maddening.

Then yesterday he said to me, "I feel like you want to claim bankruptcy to pay your dad back." I said that isn't why, but would that be such a bad thing anyway? He said, "He told us not to pay it back." I said,

*"That doesn't matter. That is way too much to not pay a person back."
My dad had given us a substantial amount of money so we could pay
off all of our credit cards and get out of debt. That was about seven
years ago I do believe. Okay, now, he has crossed a line. I said, "We
owe him a lot of money that he took out of his retirement that he
worked his ass off for years, and he got us out of debt once and we got
back in again." What the hell kind of man is he that he doesn't think
he has to pay his debts back, especially to a man that has been like a
father to him? Then he had the audacity to say to me, "Well, that was
your inheritance." I said, "No, it wasn't. And even if it was, my father
lives off social security. Otherwise he has no money. His health isn't
the best, and after all he has done for you, this is how you're going to
treat him?" That is the most heartless thing I have ever heard you say."
How do you take that much money from someone and feel like you
don't need to pay it back, no matter what they say? It makes me sick! All
the while he takes thousands of dollars and pisses it away on booze; he
feels so entitled that he doesn't have to pay shit back! I am so disgusted
with him. I do not like him at all right now. I can't stand the person
he has turned into. He acts like he is entitled to whatever he feels like,
walks all over everyone to get whatever he wants, and fuck everyone
else. Well, I have news for him. I am about to knock his sorry ass down
off that high horse he feels he is sitting on. I am so pissed off right now.*

June 12, 2012

*Today is my husband's birthday, or should I start calling him the
almighty, your highness? I went to work, and when I came home,
everyone was still here. The girls said they were going to lunch with
their dad for his birthday. My daughter came up to me after everyone
was outside and invited me to go to lunch with them. I asked her if
her dad asked me to go, and she said no, she invited me. I gave her a
hug and said, "Thank you for asking, but it shouldn't be you asking*

me." Even something so simple like that, he could have extended a kind gesture toward me but he didn't.

I may cry now, but the day will come when it starts to hurt less or I just become numb. Maybe the day will come where someone else notices me and cares for me and wants me to know that and wants to be the one who is there for me. The meaner he is toward me just puts me at an even further emotional distance from him. I need to let him go right now. It is just too painful to keep holding on. Please help guide me. Show me what the right thing to do is. I can't bear the loneliness, heartache, and pain anymore being with a man who clearly doesn't love me or want me.

I know my calling in life is to help animals; that is what I am best at. It is my passion, ever since I brought my first animal home when I was ten or eleven years old. I found a dog by my bus stop that had been shot, so I helped him come home with me, and ever since I have been rescuing and helping as many as I can. I know I will never be financially rich by doing what I love, but in my heart, I will be rich with what I love to do. Saving an animal's life makes me happy.

Every time my husband had issues with his ex-wife, he would ask me to do all the paperwork and make phone calls for him, call her, and talk to her. I stood by his side through child support fights, custody battles, and so on. He didn't want to deal with her; he doesn't want to deal with anything. So I did all his dirty work for him with his ex, the kids, the house, the bills, the shopping, my work, the animals—everything, it was always on me. Yet somehow I still turned out to be the bad guy when I did everything in my power to give all I had and with all my heart.

The isolated life you begin to live when you're with an alcoholic is so lonely, and the resentment starts to eat you up from the inside out. You just want someone to notice you and reach out to you, to love you, to save you. You may live in the same house together and be married, but you're not really together anymore. You have stopped dreaming and hoping there could be something more for you out there because, after all, your perception of yourself is just horrible and demeaning. At least for me, it became that way. You feel another person wanting you is just absurd. Then there is all your emotional baggage. Who in their right mind wants to take the time to unpack all that shit? So you find a few good things that you hold onto for dear life and just accept the rest, even if it is bad, because it is what you have come to know as your life.

After all that has happened in my life being with an alcoholic, I have asked myself this question, and you, the readers, may have asked yourselves too, which is, "Why do we stay? What is it that keeps us here? Is it love? Is it loyalty? Is it codependency? Is it the fear that we feel so broken emotionally we feel that no one else will love us? The hope that one day if we wait long enough, they will be capable of loving you the way you always dreamed of? Are they really an alcoholic, or is it just me?" Nobody wants to give up or walk away from someone they love, but at some point, if things don't shift, you will have a choice to make. Even if you stay, it is your choice!

I sit here and think, with all that I have endured in this relationship, I would have serious trust issues with someone new. If they came home late, I would question where and whom they have been with. My husband has left me alone so many nights and days without any resolution as to why. Who in their right mind would want to deal with trust issues like that? It wouldn't be fair to someone else, but then again, I suppose if they loved you, they would try to understand.

June 14, 2012

My dad usually sides with my husband. He thinks I am too moody with my husband (which I certainly am a lot more these days), so it must be my fault somehow. He is about to find out that there is a reason. All these years I have been his daughter, but he has seen my husband, who is mainly mellow and soft-spoken, polite in front of people, and then me, who can be moody, mouthy, and snappy. I am a little spitfire, what can I say? I have a big mouth sometimes. I could use a filter at times, but at least I am always honest. Also, you never know what happens at home. Someone can appear to be the best person when you're out, but behind closed doors, it is a whole different ball game. People forget that they like to judge what they don't know, assume, and gossip, and the next thing you know, you're accused of all these things that you never did in the first place.

I was on the phone with my father, and he started to defend my husband again. I got so upset I said, "Dad, you have no idea what has been happening, so let me tell you this." I just went over some of the big things, like him bingeing and always getting drunk, spending hundreds and thousands on alcohol, not coming home at night or staying gone a few days at a time, taking out the 401-K behind my back, buying a motorcycle behind my back, lying to me about things. I mean, everyone knew that he drank, but the more you keep to yourself, the less people know. They only see what you allow them to see.

As soon as he heard that, he stopped and said, "Oh my goodness, I had no idea what was going on. I owe you an apology." My father speechless never happens, so obviously he was shocked that I was talking about my husband. It couldn't possibly be this guy that everyone knows. He loves my husband and thinks he is a great man (and he is a great man, but a great man that has a serious problem with alcohol). I said, "All these years you thought it was all me. Now you know the reason for my bitterness and what I have been dealing with. I didn't tell you sooner because I didn't want you to stress over it because your health isn't great and it shouldn't be a worry for you." My dad said, "Hearing this really upsets me and pisses me off!" I said, "I have my part in it too, but it was never just me, Dad!" He said, "I need to talk to him, ask him what his problem is, and tell him he needs to get his shit together because you don't deserve that." My dad said he would never find a woman as good as I am to him. I said, "Well, maybe talking to him will help; maybe he will hear you."

I really didn't think it would make a difference, but I thought I have nothing more to lose at this point. I thought that since my husband refers to my father as his best friend and the closest person in his life, who is a father to him, maybe he would listen to his advice and wisdom. Maybe his words of love would get through in some small way.

After my husband went over to my dad's house, my dad called and said he had a long talk with my husband. My dad said he thinks that my husband will change, that it will help. I didn't have the heart to tell him I knew it wouldn't. He said, "You let me know if anything changes."

My husband came home from my dad's and didn't say a word to me, just ignored me. Yep, I knew nothing could change his cold distant heart, not even the tears from someone who has been like a father to him and wants only the best for his daughter. Tell me, where is the compassion from this man?

When my dad checked back a week later to see if any changes were happening, I told him my husband went on another binge. He was so disgusted and sad, he said, "I thought I could help," and he started crying. I said, "Dad, it isn't you. This is something no one can change but him, because he is an alcoholic!" I know my father doesn't totally understand why my husband can't just put down the alcohol and walk away and never go back. It's because he is sick; it is a disease. Many don't get that! I explained to my dad it is much like a cancer; you have to take things one day at a time and step by step. But until my husband feels he needs help and takes that first step, nothing and no one will change his mind.

June 16, 2012

Well, here it is 5:32 a.m. on a Sunday morning as I sit here alone in bed, writing for what seems to be the thousandth time that he didn't come home again last night. Interesting was he asked me just two days ago to give him until July 1 to make some changes. When I asked what changes, he said he wouldn't drink anymore and he would go to meetings, so he is supposed to be working on himself and us. I know without a doubt that he drank last night; that is why he didn't come home. I am nothing to him. I never will be. No one will ever be as important to him as his next drink.

I feel like such a fool staying as long as I have, believing that he could ever change, compromising myself and being the only one to sacrifice, when all he does is run around like he has no one else in his life that he is responsible for. What a slap in the face! I even thought that threatening him with a divorce or a separation would make him realize what he is doing. I foolishly thought that the thought of losing me would hurt him and make him see that something needed to change, that he has a wife that he has hurt beyond what words could ever express, yet I am the dumb one for staying, believing every bullshit empty promise he has ever made to me, that somehow this promise or "attempt" means so much more than the last one. I just want him to keep one damn promise. Why is that so hard for him, why? The cold hard truth is staring me right in the face, and I just don't want to see it, I don't want to hear it. I shouldn't say never because never means no hope and I am all about hope and believing, but I am sort of hoped out right now, and well, my belief is kind of empty.

My friend got me out of the house yesterday with my daughter and her boyfriend. We went to sushi, walked around the mall, and then went to a baseball game. It was good to get out, and I thought since I was coming home late, if he was home first, then he could wonder where I was and what I was doing for once. No such luck because he didn't come home at all that night. I can't even go out, come home late, and have him wonder for a second where I could be, because he doesn't even come home at night; he doesn't even come home.

I just can't quite put into words how I feel, but I know that until you're truly in someone else's shoes, you have no idea what they go through or how they feel or why they do the things they do. When he doesn't come home and doesn't answer his phone, I don't know if he is hurt, in jail, dead, or cheating. Still to this day, every time a car drives down the road, I still get up to see if it is him, and every time it isn't, my heart breaks a little more, wondering why, when you love someone so much, does this happen?

June 23, 2012

Well, he remembered yesterday was our anniversary, but instead of taking the opportunity to, oh, I don't know, buy some flowers and come home, be nice and talk, or take me to dinner, or any kind of thoughtful loving gesture, instead he said because I have been so angry, I didn't deserve anything. Wow, that is so awesome. I am laughing out of pure audacity because I am angry. I deserve nothing? Seriously, could we make that into a card for someone else to enjoy on their anniversary? Holy crap, that is just beyond selfish; it is egotistical. What a sweet heartfelt thing to say to your wife. Then we had an argument, so it was a real shitty anniversary.

Just like my birthdays and every other friggin' holiday lately. Oh yes, and I can't forget that he said I should just forgive him for everything and show him love. You bet, let me get right on that, because I haven't forgiven you a million times before—what a selfish man. He said I am hateful and a man-hater. You know what? Maybe I am right now. He will never take accountability or responsibility for his mistakes because the only reason he does bad things is because I

*"push him to" in his words … And there is the blame and his excuse
for continuing to do what he does best: drink and be drunk. We
have nothing left, just hurt, turned into disappointment, anger, and
resentment. Come on, you see it. He treats you like you're worthless,
he does whatever he wants because he can; start making your own life
changes and do what's best for you. Write, rescue as many animals as
you can, keep your friends and family close, surround yourself with
people who can show they care about you, and screw the rest.*

*He finally came home around eleven fifteen in the morning and said,
"Do you want to do something, just the two of us?" (I thought yes,
more than anything, but I know what will happen, and it won't be
good.) I said, "I am going to the movies and lunch with our daughter.
If you want to go, you're welcome to." Shockingly he did. So it became
the four of us; my stepdaughter also came. After the movie we sat
down for lunch, and the girls were on their phones and no one had
said a word for like five minutes, so I finally said, "It is so sad that
our family is so disconnected no one is talking. We all talk when the
rest of the family is around."*

*After lunch I got in the car with my husband to go home, (the girls
drove separately) and he said, "You were so rude." He said, "You are
separating us." I said, "What are you talking about?" He said, "Your
comment about when the rest of the family is around, we all talk." I
said, "Yeah, when they are around, we all talk, but the four of us, we
don't." I told him he was a joke and took everything out of context and
twisted my words around. Even though I explained what I meant,
he just wanted to argue.*

*I got out of the car, walked to the nearest store, and called for
another ride home. Since my daughter had to work she said to call
my stepdaughter she was heading home. A big part of me believes he
didn't want to be with us in the first place, so he created this problem
that didn't exist so he could go drink and use me as the excuse to do
so. That was such crap. Try and be part of our family, you selfish*

jerk. I seriously need a miracle. My guardian angel, something, please help us.

June 30, 2012

I decided to try to take a lighthearted approach with my husband. Last night I kept it basic, no serious talk, and it went good, no tension, no arguing. Well, that was a nice break. Maybe this way somehow we can work on making some progress. I guess I really do grab onto any little thread of hope—is that bad? I don't know, but it is what I do.

I got up this morning, and he said to me, "So, you still feel the need to go through my wallet." I said, "No, I don't." He said, "Well, it isn't how I left it." I said, "Well, maybe it got bumped or the cat knocked it over, but I didn't touch it because I know if you're going to hide something, it isn't going to be easy for me to find in your wallet, so there's no need to look and put myself through that." But the fact that he feels he needs to set me up when I am not the liar is messed up; grow up! I did wake up in a good mood; thanks again for ruining that for me.

I went to go pick up my cat from the vet's office; she is being treated for kidney disease. Some jerk plowed right into the back of my truck, pushing me into the other lane, and then this idiot just backs up and takes off. Awesome hit and run.

What the hell else can I be put through here? I do good things, I rescue animals, I help people when they need it, I have a big kind heart, I go above and beyond. What the hell did I do to deserve to be this unlucky?

July 1, 2012

He did his usual not-come-home-till-the-early-morning hours, slept on the couch, and then told me I need to be nice to him. Oh yeah,

you bet, I will get right on that because you have been so good to me.
This is what I know to be true: he doesn't take care of me. He stays
out all night like he is a college kid, comes home, and tells me I need
to be nice to him. I got to thinking to myself … why is it when he
stops drinking, nothing changes, and nothing gets better?

I always said to him that it is because his behaviors are the same, just
without the alcohol, and that didn't make sense. I mean, it did to
me, but I couldn't really explain it. Then he would say, "Well, then, it
doesn't matter if I drink or not." So I went on the Internet and looked
up the characteristics of an alcoholic who has stopped drinking.
Such a person is called a *dry drunk*, which makes sense. People will
occasionally stop drinking but not deal with all of the "*ism,*" meaning
when they don't take care of their emotional house and only stop the
drinking, they're only dealing with one aspect of the disease. That is
why even sober, he seems the same. Hence, alcoholism.
I stumbled into this site about alcoholics, and it talks about selfishness
and alcoholism going hand in hand. Unfortunately, I know the
selfishness from him all too well. Basically every word I read I have
said to him, but he says I am just mean, when really it is just truthful;
that is what he doesn't want to hear, he wants to hear it is okay to
be a drunk. Maybe that is why he gets really pissed at me. Does he
know somewhere deep down that what I say is really the truth? Does
he in fact really hear me at times and know in his heart that he is
doing all these terrible things, but he doesn't want to even conceive
these things as reality so he can stay in denial and continue to blame
me? Is that his free pass to drink without accountability? I wonder.

July 1, 2012 (continued)

I went out into the living room. I asked him when the last time he
had a drink was. He wouldn't answer. I said, "Why are you ignoring

me?" He said, "I am just a liar. Everything out of my mouth is a lie." (Here we go with the manipulation again.) I said, "I just want you to tell me the truth about going to meetings and not lie about it." He got up, put on his shoes, and said, "Fuck you. I am not saying a word to you," and left.

Left and abandoned once again; this is a great life. How many times can he call me nasty names or tell me "fuck you" before he realizes that it is hurtful and very unhealthy? I just wanted to share this info with him. I thought maybe it would mean something, but I was wrong. I just need to let him go live his life without me so he can drink and do whatever he pleases. I am tired of being hurt and ripped apart every day by him. He can say any words he wants to me. His actions show every intention, and there isn't one good one. I say time and time again that I need to let go and this should be it, but I can't seem to let go or walk away. I don't like to feel hurt and what he does is not okay, but gosh damn it, he is my husband, he is my heart. I can't leave; there has to be a better way. I have to stay strong for us.

July 14, 2012

Last night I sat down with my husband to talk, no tone, no arguing, just simple talk. I said, "What are your intentions with our marriage?" He kept saying, "I don't know." The phone kept ringing, and I said, "Don't answer it; a bill is late." So he started questioning whose bill it was—that's all he cared about—and I told him one of his. He immediately got pissed and said, "Why?" I said, "You told me to do what I wanted about bankruptcy. I told you I stopped paying the bills, and then ten days later, you say you won't agree to do bankruptcy, so I had to catch up on the bills that were already late. Several of mine have been late."

Then he said to me, "You want to know what my intentions are. They are to have my paycheck rerouted into my bank account and pay my bills." I said, "What about the ones that are in my name?" He said, "Go get another job and pay your own." I said, "They aren't just mine; they are ours, just in my name." He said, "I don't understand." I said, "Are you frigging serious? Every time I tried to talk to you about bills, you didn't want to be bothered so I didn't tell you." Then he got even meaner. He said, and I quote, "I think you have a parasite in your brain from all the cat litter you have cleaned up; you have that toxic disease because you're fucked up." Wow, yes, he is that awful of a person. Those words came out of his mouth because he is an alcoholic. My best friend feels that he is manipulative and dangerous at this point, and she worries about me.

I mean, what man just stops paying his wife's bills and tells her she is a fu**ed-up parasite? I am just amazed at the coldness. He said he is a self-made loner, who has nobody close in his life. What the hell does that mean, a self-made loner? And he does have someone close in his life—me, his wife. I am sorry, but who is messed up? He treats me like shit on the bottom of his shoe; he said he has provided a roof over my head for the past twelve years. Wrong, I have worked my butt off just like you, so no, you alone did not provide for me; we did that together. Here is the other thing: he simply doesn't comprehend he has drank and gambled away thousands and thousands of dollars over the years, so no matter how much money you make, when you piss away a lot of it, you don't make shit. For whatever reason, he seems to feel that the more money you make the better you are, but he couldn't be further from the truth on that concept.

I told him I would rather be alone than to be with a man who makes me feel like this isn't my home and I owe him. I don't owe my husband for anything. What man thinks that way? It is so wrong. I have worked all these years too. I have done so much here, and this is the gratitude I get. How do you belittle your wife like that and feel good about yourself? He just did me a favor. He can take his money, shove it up his ass, and go fu** himself. It isn't right to say things

*like that. At least I don't feel good about it, but at times he makes
me crazy and my mouth just goes off, but I do apologize when I am
wrong. I do know how to take accountability and responsibility for
my wrongdoings or mistakes and try to make them right. I don't like
acting like that. I just come down to his level, and it gets nowhere
except for hurt feelings. Yeah, I am that pissed off at the moment.
This morning I heard him and our daughter talking, and she said,
"You should be home more. You're always gone." He said, "What does
it matter?" She said, "You're a dad. You should be here. Every time I
come home, you're gone." Again he said, "What does it matter?" She
said, "You're like fifty years old. You should be home with your family
instead of always running around drinking and stuff. She said I am
young and should be acting like you do, not you. Fix your relationship
with Mom." He said to her, "You need to back off of me." I jumped
in because he was getting angry. I said, "No, she doesn't. She has her
own feelings, and you have yours." She then said to him, "Instead of
always being gone, just don't come back."
Then I noticed a while later, he took off his wedding ring. I said,
"How convenient for you to go out without your ring on, so you can
act like you're a single man. That is cruel and unforgiving." So I
decided, you know what? If he wants to play the I-make-more-money-
than-you-and-I-am-going-to-pay-just-my-bills game, then screw it,
let him. So I got all his bills together, put them on his desk, and left a
note that said, "Here are your bills. Pay them yourself." At this point I
don't care what happens with mine. I won't pay them, and then I can
file bankruptcy. What he doesn't seem to realize is we are married and
any debt incurred while we are married is joint, so he is just screwing
himself too? He doesn't think before he opens his mouth.
I can't believe he took his ring off. It just shows me how he has no
respect for me or the sanctity of our marriage. There was no reason
to take it off and go out; now ask me again why it is I have a serious
problem with trusting him. He has no loyalty to me, so he doesn't*

deserve to wear the ring I gave him. The way he has been dragging our daughter into our arguments and the mean things he has been saying to her, he has become this smug, controlling, self-absorbed, childish, egotistical, alcoholic asshole. I believe the only reason he is still here is the house is in his name; otherwise he would have left a long time ago. He has no loyalty to our family. It is all about money, material things, and alcohol for him. He doesn't care about people, only possessions. At least this is how I feel. All I can say is what a serious life lesson for me to learn.

My daughter was put into this situation by me. She had no choice, and I carry guilt for that. I have always done everything in my power that I felt was best for her, and the one man I thought would be a good role model and father to her has turned out to be the opposite. She deserved so much more from him. He adopted her; she is his daughter too. He was supposed to provide love, support, encouragement, and protection; instead, he hurt us all. We are all damaged emotionally, but I feel our daughter had it worse than the other kids did because she lived here 24/7 for thirteen years. Now he is so lost inside of the bottle, he doesn't have time to see anyone else, and he certainly isn't going to stop and take accountability for any of the emotional damage he has caused all of the kids all these years. Have I destroyed my daughter's future by holding on and staying and believing that my husband, her father, could be so much more? Or maybe it will turn out where I taught her the biggest life lesson of all: to not give up and find hope and believe. Will her future hold the same type of fate? It is true what they say about wanting better for your kids than what you had.

I remember one time when the girls were about ten years old; he called me drunk, saying he was hiding in the alley behind this bar because he took someone's puppy. He said the puppy wasn't being properly taken care of; they were feeding it beer from the bar and canned cat food, and the puppy had diarrhea and appeared sick. So although I told him what he did was so wrong, I am also a huge animal advocate, so the girls and I drove down and met him in the alley. He gave them the puppy and said he was going back to the bar; he was going to tell them that someone jumped him in the alley and stole the puppy from him. He had asked if he could take the puppy out to go potty and then proceeded to call me. I told him to just get on his bike (pedal bike) and leave because when he went back in without this puppy, he was going to have a big problem. He said they would believe his story of being jumped.

The girls were in the backseat hiding this puppy when I drove around to the front of the bar. I saw my husband standing outside, and he was circled by about twenty people. My adrenaline kicked in. I thought they were going to beat the shit out of him, and with that many people, he could be severely injured, so I drove my truck up onto the sidewalk, jumped out of my truck, and started screaming at these people, telling them to step away from my husband. I was trying to protect him. He told me he was fine and I could go; he would meet me around the corner. I stood there glaring at every one of them, making sure they knew I was not afraid; I was standing my ground. So I left, and about five minutes later, he called and told me to meet him so he could put the bike in the truck and we could go home.

Once my adrenaline calmed down, I thought, *what the hell was I thinking?* There were like twenty or so drunk people outside this bar, and I am talking big guys, and here I am, this short five-foot-four-inch woman trying to take everyone on, and my girls were in the backseat with a stolen puppy. Even in the foolish situations he gets into, I am there trying to get him out of them. My husband said they told him that his wife was crazy, but at the same time, they all said that they wouldn't want to mess with me, trying to jump in and protect him by taking on a whole bar of people. Hands down, it was probably one of the dumbest things I have ever done without thinking, but it just goes to show you when someone you care about is in trouble, or seemed to be in trouble in this case, your adrenaline kicks into high gear and you just react. It's just another example of a really bad situation that his drinking put us in, and this time our girls were also involved. What if something had happened to them or me? He never stopped to think about that, and what's worse is I got sucked in and forgot to think of the girls' and my safety as well for a moment. What if when I did that, these guys grabbed both him and me and beat the shit out of us in front of our girls, and then found them with this puppy? We got lucky it turned out the way it did. This time.

Chapter 13

July 16, 2012

An unexpected turn of events has happened here. My husband came home Sunday night after we had talked about splitting up. I guess it hit both of us in an emotional way. After all, we have been together for over twelve years, so to think this was it, this is over, was very sad for us. He put in for his vacation time so he could find a place to live and have time to move his stuff out. We had a deep emotional talk. He hugged me so tight, which he hadn't done in a long time, and said he was so sorry for hurting me and that he had been so stubborn about not leaving because he didn't want to go or give up our marriage. He didn't want to leave me. He didn't want to live life without me. I needed to hear that!

It feels like he has been hurting just as much as I have, and he is tired of running; it isn't getting him anywhere. For the first time in years, he seems to be sincere. It feels real this time, like this could turn around and we can start over, maybe? So he started sleeping back in our bed instead of the couch. We have cuddled a little bit, which is huge for us. We are going to give it a shot and see if we can save our marriage.

July 19, 2012

My husband told me that my stepdaughter is getting married this weekend; however, I am not invited to go. Not invited to go? I can't imagine a more selfish, hurtful action from someone I had a part in raising. My husband said he is conflicted because he doesn't want to go without me and he also doesn't want to miss seeing his daughter get married. He said he talked to his daughter and told her it was mean and wrong to not have her stepparents there. I find her to be very selfish, plain and simple!

I am the one who took care of her here when she was sick, made her meals, did her laundry, took her shopping, helped her read better, pushed her in school, watched her schoolwork, tucked her in, put together every birthday party, shopped for every holiday, took her places, and so on ... the list goes on, but in the end, I meant nothing. For me being a stepparent was really difficult and at times agonizing, to try and be the best stepmom I could to kids who were told that they could hate me and didn't have to listen to me by their mother, according to what they told me she would say.

I just don't know what is going to happen with us. I want to love him and be with him if things can be different, but I need to be his first choice, not his last or a convenience. I need him to stand by my side. I am his wife. For now I am just trying to keep myself a little emotionally protected, but if you're going to try, you have to go all in. I ate dinner alone. He hasn't spent any time with me, but he keeps coming in and asking if I am okay (like three times now)because of what his daughter did; he gave me a hug and then went out to play his drums. I needed more from him; don't just check on me, sit with me. I can tell he is distraught about this whole situation, and I am so disappointed in her for putting him in that position. I mean, how selfish of her. I would never do that to him. I would never ask him to miss that as much as I want him to stand by me and stop letting the kids have this kind of control. I wouldn't feel right. If he did it on his own, it would be his choice. That would be the only way. Otherwise, as in years gone by, I just deal with being made to feel insignificant by kids I took care of and loved. I seem to mean absolutely nothing to them, and that hurts very much. Being a stepparent is not an easy deal. You come into a situation where children are already there and no one said you have to love them, but you end up taking care of them and loving them, but usually you go unappreciated and somehow always made out to be a bad guy, it's very sad. I think only other stepparents can completely understand how this really feels when you're trying to do your best only to be disregarded all too often!

July 22, 2012

I know it has only been a week since we started trying, but I am sad and disappointed that he isn't trying harder or showing really much difference, except there is less tension. We aren't arguing; that is really nice. I guess that is something—small steps, right? Things won't magically change overnight; I have to have patience.
All weekend so far he has spent maybe an hour with me total—that's it. He has either been busy going out with his brother, spending the day at his daughter's wedding, or trying out for a new band. I guess I just thought, when you're trying to rekindle and save your marriage, you work hard at it, and at least put the effort in. You actually have to spend time together, and really, shouldn't we be a priority?
I guess the emotional realization that happened for him last week has quickly faded.

July 28, 2012

We went to an amusement park with our daughter and her best friend. We had a nice day; it was fun. It was for my husband's work; they do it every year for employee appreciation day. They mostly went on the high-adrenaline rides and I watched, which was totally fine. We saw animals and went on a water ride; it was a good day. We got to laugh, hold hands, and spend time together; it was nice. Today we were so close and in love. We were smiling at each other and so happy. What a great feeling for us to have.

July 30, 2012

Yesterday he went to a motorcycle race with his brother and he told me he would be home between five o'clock and six o'clock. I had a bad feeling about it, but I let it go. So he called around six o'clock and asked if he should bring something home for dinner. I said I wasn't sure yet I wasn't very hungry at that time. He said he would call back; he was setting up a Facebook page for his brother. I knew in my heart it was just an excuse to stay and drink. He has been doing so good the past two weeks not drinking like he promised. Please, just don't drink; don't mess this up for us.

Then he called back around eight thirty and said he needed to get something to eat because he had been drinking. I hung up the phone. I was so disappointed in him, my heart just broke. Then around midnight, there was another drunken phone call to tell me he wasn't home yet, he was still out. No shit, that is obvious because you're not here. Anyway, I hung up again. When he called back, I told him I didn't want to talk to him. He said it wasn't fair that I was mad at him. No, let me tell you what isn't fair: you broke another promise. We are supposed to be working hard at repairing our marriage that you say you don't want to lose, and you're out getting drunk again— that isn't fair. Only two weeks, and it starts again. He is so far into this disease it is going to kill him. We are going to lose everything, including our family.

He walked in the door about three fifteen this morning. He was gone for over seventeen hours; that is pure selfishness. I got up this morning and got ready for the day. He got up shortly after me. I said, "We need to talk." He said, "Oh no." I said, "It has only been two weeks. I told you that this behavior wasn't going to be okay with me and

*that you needed to work on changing some of your behaviors." He
said that I just need to be okay with him being who he is, and if he
wants to go out and drink, I need to just deal with it and let him do
what he wants.*

*I am very upset, and he doesn't seem to care. Matter of fact, it's like
he played a big mind game with me, saying this isn't a big deal. Even
though I kept saying, "You really hurt me by doing this," he kept
saying, "No, I didn't," so now he is dismissing how I feel as well. Will
I ever be important to him? Will I ever matter? I was so hopeful of
turning things around for us. I missed him so much, and being close
to him for those two weeks was the best feeling. I had hoped we could
find our way back in love. He left, and then came back around noon
and said, "Are you done being mad at me?" I didn't say a word, so he
worked on his computer for about three hours, and then left again.
Hello, old behavior; you didn't go very far, did you? He isn't capable of
change as long as he continues drinking, and even if he didn't drink,
I don't know if he would be any different. I don't even know who he
is anymore, and neither does he. I am sure he will be out late again. I
can't take this anymore. It just isn't fair to me. I am not giving my all
to him just so he can take it and give nothing in return but heartache.
I am beyond devastated and heartbroken. Over twelve years together,
I let myself get caught up in what could be, instead of what really is. I
need to be more honest with myself and stop believing in the fairy-tale
bullshit that I have in my head.*

I love with all my heart, I give with my whole soul, and I go above
and beyond for family and friends. I will help those in need, I am
an animal savior, but mostly I am just a woman who wants to be
loved, adored, cherished, appreciated, protected, complimented,
spoiled, accepted, and understood. I think I can go out there and
make a difference and save people with my love and kindness and
show them the way, but really, who the hell am I? I am just one

woman going after my own happily ever after with the man I love. There is nothing wrong with that, nothing at all.

How many of you out there have had these thoughts? If only I am more patient and understanding toward him or her, he or she will be different. If only I didn't make him so angry, he wouldn't have done this, that, and the other thing, so it must be my fault. How many excuses can we make for them and ourselves? How many lies do we not only tell for them, but how many lies do we tell ourselves? There has to be a better way; there has to.

August 11, 2012

Let's play catch-up on what's been happening here. So after he came home a few days ago at three o'clock in the morning, we had a bad few days. He finally said to me, "Can we just start over? I promise you I will control my drinking." You already guessed what happened. I fell for it again. What is this, the millionth time? I just hang onto that hope like there is no tomorrow, praying that each and every time will be different than the last because surely one of these times, he will follow through, right? We had plans for the past week before he drank again to go see our daughter's boyfriend play (he is in a band). At the last minute he said he was going to watch another band play. It is always about him, zero regard for anyone else, so selfish. I said, "We had these plans for the past week. I was looking forward to us going together." He said, "I would rather see these other guys play." Our daughter wanted us to be there, but none of that mattered; he just left. Around eleven thirty he texted me that he needed a ride home; because he was drunk. I said, "You need to take a cab."

He didn't walk in the door till five thirty in the morning. Fuck this! He has ruined everything for us. I was so upset about his behavior two weeks ago, and then he does it again—no concern for me at all. He makes promises he has no intention of keeping; it isn't right to do

*that to someone. He breaks my heart over and over again. When will
I learn? I have to be done with the games, done with the bullshit. I
throw my hands up! I have to be stronger than this. Why can't I be
stronger? Why do I keep allowing myself to go through this? Because
I love him so deeply I don't want to give up on him.*

*I said, "You told me you would control your drinking, and then you
come in at five thirty in the morning." He said, "You should have come
to pick me up." Ahhhh, there it is once again, the blame. And the vicious
cycle goes round and round. He takes no accountability, and it is* my
*fault he drank because I didn't go pick him up. After all, he can't be
responsible for his own drunken ass and take a damn cab home.*

August 14, 2012

*Last night my husband said to me a few times that I need to go find
another man. I said, "Are you serious? How can you say that to me
and feel good about yourself? All I asked of you was to not spend the
night out and come home at a decent time." He said, "My wife is such
a bitch. Why would I?" He said that to me because I said, "You're the
type of man that makes a woman want to go toward another man."
That wasn't nice of me to say; I realize that it was hurtful. He just
continues to blame me for everything and say things to me like I need
to pull love out of him and pull him closer. I don't know what he is
taking, but if I pull him close right now, I might punch him in the
damn nose for being such a selfish man.*

August 15, 2012

*Oh today was such a fun day (I say sarcastically). After I got up this
morning, I went onto my Facebook page, and my husband had sent
me a message because he can't talk to me. Anyway, his message to me
read like this: "I see you didn't waste any time Mr. Fucking, believe*

*it's true." I had no idea what he was even talking about until I read comments under my post. All this is because I posted a picture with a quote that was called "**Get Off the Scale**." It read like this:*

> *You are beautiful. Your beauty, just like the capacity of your life, happiness, and success, is immeasurable. Day after day, countless people across the globe get on the scale in search of validation of beauty and social acceptance.*
>
> *GET OFF THE SCALE!*
>
> *I have yet to see a scale that can tell you how enchanting your eyes are. I have yet to see a scale that can show you how wonderful your hair looks when the sun shines its glorious rays upon it. I have yet to see a scale that can thank you for your compassion, sense of humor, and contagious smile.*
>
> *GET OFF THE SCALE ... because I have yet to see one that can admire you for your perseverance when challenged in life. It's true; the scale can only give you a numerical reflection of your relationship with gravity; it cannot measure beauty, talent, purpose, life force, possibility, strength, or love. Don't give the scale more power than it has earned. Take note of the number, then get off the scale and live your life.*
>
> *YOU ARE BEAUTIFUL!*

So let's be honest: how many people out there have used the scale to validate themselves? How many of us have looked at it and beat ourselves up for being too fat or too skinny? The numbers we see set the mood from that moment on, and it is usually in a negative way. So I commented above it and said, "I love it. This is awesome. I wish I could believe it about myself," and a male Facebook friend commented and said I should believe it. Just being nice; nothing more than those simple words. So because of that, I am accused of cheating. Wow, that is unbelievable to me. Because someone simply said I should believe it, I have such a terrible self-image of myself, so suddenly I am a cheater. My husband missed the point of me feeling really bad *about the way I look, obviously. It isn't like my husband says or does a damn thing to make me, his wife, feel beautiful, special, and appreciated. I said, "You know what? At least other people recognize when I am feeling bad about myself and take the time to say something nice to me, even if it is just to make me feel better; it is more than my own husband notices or says." I am so hurt by this. How can he really think I would cheat? I am the only one who has been committed to our relationship. I have morals and values that I wouldn't sacrifice to go sleep with someone else. I am married, period; my husband is my heart. Being with someone else is of no interest to me. I have been devoted and dedicated to him and us since day one. I am* not *that kind of woman. I left to do my housecleaning this morning. When I came home I took a shower. He came in and was all pissed off because in his mind, I went and screwed someone and came home to "wash off." What a total jerk! Is this man serious right now? Our daughter lives here; this is* our *home! That is just disgusting. Never in my life have I been unfaithful. I will not be treated like a whore! If anyone has shady behavior, it would be him, and maybe that is it. Maybe he is lashing out at me because he is guilty of being unfaithful to me. I mean, look at all the lies, betrayals, bad behaviors he has been doing lately. I know that he knows I would* never *do anything like that. This is just his messed-up manipulation mind games he is playing on me again.*

August 16, 2012

He came home last night around eleven o'clock. He came in the room, took his pillow, and went to sleep in the other room. He said something to me under his breath before he left the room about going out and making things "even" with me, so I said, "Did you go out and cheat to make it even like you think? Is that what you're saying to me?" He was mumbling and walking away. I was pissed. I couldn't stop my mouth, and at that point my daughter walked in. She just went in the bathroom to get ready for bed, and I was standing there taking his emotional beat down yet again and trying to convince him that I wasn't unfaithful.

I am the one who was standing there devastated that he could even consider me of all people to be unfaithful. I sat and cried and begged *him to believe me that even in our worst moments, I have never done anything that he is accusing me of and I never would. He said I am a stark-raving bitch, how I came home and showered, and then the Facebook post and my comment to him about how he pushes women away. He kept saying I have a big mouth and I don't know when to shut the fuck up, so we went back and forth.*

Then he got up to turn the cooler on in the hallway, and our daughter was standing there. He said to her, "I'm sorry." She said, "You're a jerk. I'm done with you." He said, "Fine. Pack your shit and move out. This is my house! *" He walked away and shut the spare bedroom door. She was so pissed off she walked up to the door and banged on it really hard. I haven't seen her that angry ever.*

I asked her what happened. Why did she freak out? She said because she felt like he was treating me like a piece of crap and she didn't appreciate it. I was up most of the night; I couldn't sleep. I surrender. I can't take this emotional beating anymore, and the way he talked to our daughter is sickening. He treats us both like shit. He has made it perfectly clear that even though we have lived here for over twelve years, this is his house! *I have news for him: this is also* my home. *It is* ours, *so I don't know what more to say.*

Ever feel like you're stuck in a rut, and no matter what you do, you feel like you have no place to go and you have no idea what you're going to do? That's how I feel. I am confused and so lost, I just don't know what to do. I know realistically I should leave, but I can't leave my animals that I take care of. They depend on me every single day, and I just want our marriage to be happy. I don't want to leave our home. I think I need to continue my therapy and work on growing stronger emotionally and not make any hasty decisions out of anger, frustration, and hopelessness. I don't know why, but I'm not ready to give up; maybe I should be, but I'm not ready to do that yet. I have my moments, but in the end, I love my husband very much.

I know people are probably asking why? What do you love? But it isn't about what I love exactly; it is how I feel, how I love. He is my husband, and I get to see the amazing man inside sometimes, and that keeps me believing.

I have to believe that somehow he will find his way and be that man I have always known him to be and good or bad, I love all of him. I know he doesn't mean to be this bad, this dysfunctional, this out of control; he is so consumed in his alcoholism he can't see the reality of any situation. He needs serious help. At this moment I have no answers, but I am growing each day and even on my weakest days I still get a little stronger. Even when I don't feel it, I know I am learning from this, and one day I will be able to understand—if nothing else, just for myself. I know there is a place for my heart, and until I find that place, I am never giving up. I can't.

Chapter 14

August 21, 2012

So the other night, my husband went out to watch his brother's friends play in their band. First he invited me to go with him, but then he started to say things to make me feel like he didn't want me to go, so I ended up not going. I could tell he didn't want me there. I knew he wanted to drink and he didn't want to hear me complain about it. We were doing okay, though. He told me he wouldn't drink very much and he would be home at a decent time. All I could do was to have faith in him.

Well, that was short-lived; he called me at 11:30 p.m., slurring his words so badly I could hardly understand him. I asked him to please come home, and he kept giving me excuses and the runaround. Then I asked him where he was so I could just come and pick him up. He said he didn't know, and he hung up on me; he wouldn't answer the phone even though I kept calling him back. My daughter and I were watching TV.

After several drunken phone calls, I found out which bar he was at, so we went to pick him up. He was stumbling out the door slurring his words and falling down on the street; he stank like smoke and booze. I was trying to help him, but he was falling into the walls and then on the ground. I recorded this drunken episode, hoping I could show him at a time when he was sober and maybe he could see what he looks like, how he acts, and maybe, just maybe, then he would have an aha moment and want to change things if he could see how out of control his drinking has really become. What he really looks like and how he acts once he has been drinking.

He finally passed out on the bedroom floor. I put a blanket on him and left him there to sleep; I finally got to bed around three o'clock in the morning.

August 22, 2012

I got up around eight thirty to find that my husband had crawled into bed at some point. The floor where he passed out was soaked. I thought he had spilled his water. Then I went into the bathroom to find that it wasn't water because the stench of his urine-soaked clothes on top of the laundry basket made me gag. Completely saturated, are you kidding me right now? Is this really happening? It has gotten to the point where he has no control over his bodily functions? Christ, someone help him.

So before the smell got any worse, I got cleaning towels and a soapy bucket, and I was on my hands and knees scrubbing the carpet to get the urine out, hopefully before it soaked into the padding. He woke up because I was scrubbing so hard. He was like "sorry." Not "let me do that" or "you shouldn't have to do that" and take over for me. Not this guy! He does nothing; he just sat there and watched me.

This is just disgusting; it is really sad. I mean, how did it get to this point? How can my husband not see how sick he really is? How is it that he feels like he is so self-entitled that this behavior is okay? I feel like someone threw me to the ground, kicked me, spit on me, punched me in the stomach, slapped me in the face, wiped their feet all over me, and then threw me out like yesterday's trash—that is what his actions make me feel like. I feel completely worthless right now. I am not quite sure what hitting bottom looks like for him, but I would have to say this seems like a pretty good place. When you urinate all over yourself and leave it for your wife to clean, how do you deny at that point that you have a serious drinking problem?

August 26, 2012

Just as I expected, he didn't come home again last night. I worry about him so much. It causes such anxiety and stress for me to the point where I feel sick.

Right now it is about seven thirty. I guess he thinks he is punishing me, but really he is punishing himself. I am trying not to allow it to upset me physically, but who am I kidding? This hurts! This is so hard for me because I want to help make it better, fix it somehow, but I just can't keep burying my head in the sand. This is serious: he is going to die from drinking. Truth is he has pretty much single-handedly destroyed our marriage, our home. I know he is a man that lies to his wife and does things even when they hurt others. This is the sixth binge he has gone on this month alone that I know about. Imagine what I don't know!

I told him last weekend that it's his life and his choices. I no longer am concerned if he drinks every day; it is his decision. I have to start finding a way to help him in a healthy way without enabling him, to help him see the destruction before I have to plan his funeral because he has killed himself with alcohol. He has become not only selfish but also very self-destructive. It's very sad really, because I am willing to try hard, put my all into saving our marriage, to have something better than we ever had; however, he is clearly more consumed with himself. I feel emotionally shut down toward him, and I refuse to do any more than what I have already been trying.

His drinking is completely out of control. He is spiraling down very fast, and he doesn't care who he takes with him. He has a false sense of reality through the eyes of an alcoholic who can do no wrong.

August 31, 2012

What a seriously messed-up night. My husband and I were going to pick up my dad to go to the rib cook-off, and something came up about money, I'm not sure what. My husband said to me, "Why don't you transfer some of your money to cover some bills?" I said, "Are you kidding me? I have used several thousand dollars of my money for bills already, and all you have done is taken your money and pissed it away on drinking, gambling, concerts, and so on. You play and I pay!" Then he had the audacity *to say to me, "You're just trying to get me to spend all of my money so I can't go out anymore and you will be in control again." I said, "Are you kidding me? I have never had control. I just asked you for $100 so I can go get a few things I need for the house. You piss thousands away on booze, and you throw a fit about $100?" I got so upset I started crying. I felt so hurt. He makes me feel like I owe him. I am his wife. Why should I owe him? I don't owe him for shit! Once dad got in the car we put on the pretend faces and stopped arguing. I just forgot about the money and didn't ask him for a cent; I didn't eat. I don't want anything from him. He drank the six or seven beers that he brought from the house and then bought a few more; we can't go anywhere without him consuming massive amounts of alcohol. We dropped dad off a few hours later.*

When we got home, he went outside and drank some more because he hadn't had quite enough yet. Obviously he was drunk, and he was in an argumentative mood.

Our daughter came home, and she made a joke about something he was eating and said not to eat them all; she didn't know he was in a crappy mood. He said something mean. I told her to just ignore him, he had been drinking. I could tell he was trying to start a fight, so I just let it go.

I went in and said good night to her, and as I was walking to our room, he yelled, "Good night, all you other fucking assholes in the house."

He started getting meaner and louder, and then he called me a fu**ing bitch. My daughter got mad that he was talking to me like that, so she jumped in. They started arguing, and then he started saying he was going to evict her and throw her out. He was saying she had better wise up because this was his house. What the hell makes him think he is superior to the rest of us? Why would you talk to your daughter that way, especially when you damn well know you started a fight because you're drunk again and she was only protecting her mother?

By this time, my daughter was totally pissed off, and justifiably so; he was drunk and mean. I told him she wasn't going anywhere that she was staying with me. He said, "You can go too." I said, "You'll be going before I ever do!" Then I couldn't believe he said this, but he said it very loud so she could hear him. He said, "You're just a bitch, and she is a bitch in training." Now as a mother, it took all I had not to punch him in his damn mouth, talking to our daughter like that! What the hell is wrong with him? Why has he become this way? Now you're verbally attacking our daughter—why? How do you talk to your wife like that, and how do you as a father say something so mean about your daughter, not only about her but about her mother? He has created such a distance between them. They used to be so close. It breaks my heart the damage he has done. What's worse is he can't even see it. She has grown up with an alcoholic father who has mostly been unemotionally available to her and now he is verbally abusing her, words can't express my heartache for our daughter.

She came out of the bathroom crying, saying, "You should be proud of me. I am in college trying to do something with my life. You'd think you would want to try and help your daughter out with college." He responded to her with another ignorant cruel response and said, "Stop begging for handouts. Pay for it yourself. You got a scholarship." She said, "Yeah, but I will still have like $36,000 worth of debt once I am finished." He said, "Good." She walked away and went to her room. At that moment my heart broke like it never has before, and I *prayed somehow someway the means I needed for my daughter and I to live on our own would fall into my lap because I didn't want to spend another second with this monster he has turned into. In that moment a rush of guilt came over me and I thought I didn't bring a father into her life that loves and protects her. I brought this man in who is unable to be a truly nurturing father to any of these children and I felt such shame because as the saying goes "any man can make a baby but it takes a real man to be a daddy" he certainly wasn't any kind of man I was proud of. To be so demeaning to our daughter who already had such a hard start in life with her bio dad you have to wonder what is wrong with him!*

He had the nerve to say to me, "She better wise up. She is not going to disrespect me like that. She is a spoiled brat. She has been given everything." Then he started trying to blame me, saying this was all my fault, that I drag her into our arguments. I said, "This was all you. You started this fight. Be proud the way you talk to your wife and daughter." Tonight he was very destructive with our daughter, very hurtful, and he doesn't even have the ability to get it. Why is this so damn difficult?

His oldest daughter moved out in one weekend because she failed her second year of college and he told her she was not allowed to go out of town because of her grades. She said she was nineteen and she would do whatever she wanted. He told her that was fine, and to pack her stuff and move out. Sure as hell she did just that! I don't want that for our daughter. I want her to move out when she is ready, not forced, not thrown out, not in a hateful way, just when it is time for her, but I don't think it will happen in a good way, not with him like this.

He doesn't make anyone feel welcome. He kept going on and going on. Then all those beers weren't enough; he went for a bottle of wine. At this point all I could hope for was that he would pass out soon so I didn't have to listen to his bullshit anymore! He said it was wrong of her to treat him like that. I said, "Yes it was; however she was defending me because you were attacking us. Also, you are her father. It is also wrong for you as an adult. You don't talk to your daughter like that, and you don't treat your wife like that." He doesn't get that she is modeling his behavior. He can't see that right now, but maybe one day that reality will set in.

September 2, 2012

So he has been gone for over two days without a word. I tossed and turned all weekend, and against my better judgment I caved in. I called him at 4:00 a.m. to make sure he was okay. I knew he was; I knew he was doing this purposefully. As soon as I heard his drunken voice, I got pissed at myself for calling. Normal healthy people don't live like this; they don't leave for days without any contact. He had an all-out verbal attack on our daughter and me and then he leaves for days, so destructive, so selfish, and so disheartening!

I just wish we could be adults and talk and do what is best in this situation at this moment, which is he moves out, even for just a few months, because right now there is too much pain. I am just afraid he is going to screw me over. Why won't he see how mean he has been? What does he care if I have nothing? He would take it all. I have no doubt about that. He is way too selfish right now to care about anything besides his next drink. There has to be a reason why he is still here besides just being selfish, doesn't there? He was deeply and madly in love with me at one point in time? Is that love buried deep down? Is that bond what's holding us together?

I thought if I loved him enough and showed him how much I cared that he would be better, that he wouldn't need to drink, I would be enough. Sadly it doesn't work that way with an alcoholic; until he is ready and him alone, there isn't a person who could change his mind. I feel emotionally exhausted, I feel broken, and I feel like I will never be enough for anyone. I am sad, overwhelmed, and scared.

I am praying for a higher power to wrap my daughter, me, and my husband safely in love and help us get through this very difficult time in our lives, watch over us.
I just pray he doesn't throw us out.

September 8, 2012

If I could say anything to my husband and he was capable of retaining information, this is what I would say … You are killing yourself. You have destroyed our family and yourself in the process. You have become very mean, selfish, and cold. You are volatile and emotionally abusive with our daughter and me. You have wasted thousands and thousands of dollars on drinking and gambling. I am not a convenience for you. I can't take the lying, the loneliness, the mind games, the emotional abusive behavior, the abandonment, and so on. You have all but destroyed our marriage. You are an alcoholic. Your drinking has taken control over your life. Stop blaming everyone else for the destruction you caused. Man up and get yourself into rehab before it is too late to save even yourself from this addiction.
It is really very sad, because I have always loved you deeply and stood by you. I would have helped you if you wanted to help yourself, but much like the destruction that an earthquake causes, some things you can't put back together. You need to rebuild, but even when given that opportunity, you didn't have what it takes.
Some things you have to call a total loss. Are we really a total loss after all these years? Is it time to say good-bye to all the passion and love we once shared? Our friendship, is it lost forever? Your empty apologies, the broken promises! The day will come soon enough when you will find yourself alone, but even then, I don't think it will matter what you lost because you will just medicate with alcohol. I am so disappointed and hurt by you. All I can do is pray for you and try to find forgiveness and hope that one day you reach for my hand and

make up for all the pain you have inflicted upon my heart and soul and the spirit and trust in our daughter that you have crushed.

From the end of 2011 through 2012 has been so difficult and heartbreaking. At times I didn't want to get out of bed; I just wanted to lie there all day. I had no energy or desire to do a darned thing. As the days and months go by, I see his binges are closer together, and the physical effects from his drinking are starting to appear. He is starting to cough and gag all the time, especially in the morning, and I can't help but feel like it is due to his drinking. Like maybe it is affecting his esophagus? His hands have become shaky, he has horrible sleep apnea as well; he doesn't take care of himself. His doctor earlier this year put him on antidepressants for depression (also hand in hand with alcoholism), and I asked him if he told his doctor how much he actually drank. He said no. I told him that I read that if you drink alcohol, the medication isn't going to work because of the way the alcohol counteracts the meds. Not that he would ever listen to me, but it is true. I asked my doctor about it; that is why I told him.

Honestly, growing up, I never thought my life would ever be anything like this. I never knew how hard it was going to be to have a good relationship that is healthy, to have honest good people in my life. There are a lot of people out there who pretend to be something they aren't, and it is very confusing because you grow to have feelings for someone so your judgment gets clouded. Isn't it true that you shouldn't give up when you love someone? How much is enough, though? This is why at times I feel as though I failed not only myself, but my daughter. Do you ever feel like you know what you need to do, what you should do, but something keeps you in a place where you know you shouldn't be and at times don't want to be, but you stay anyway? Maybe it is faith, hope, optimism, love—all the above? How many of you have had a similar feeling that your heart and mind conflict and you are more confused or overwhelmed than ever?

I tell myself, isn't that what marriage is about? Choosing to stand by someone else's side for the rest of their life because you love them? Then I think, if I am always sacrificing myself to be there for someone else, who can't be there for me, then who do I turn to? Where do I go? Where is my safe place? All my life growing up, I wished upon the stars that I just wanted to be happy. Into my adult years, I still look at those same stars and wish and pray for that same happiness.

Sometimes life seems so dark and hopeless, and in those moments it truly is, but we have all had times in our life where all hope seemed to be lost and we found it once again. We can all look back and say, "I remember this painful time. I never thought I would make it through," but look how happy you may be today all because you never gave up. Even if you are in a bad place right now at this very moment, there is always, always, strength in hope. Hold on and believe that just around the corner, your tomorrow will be better than today. You have to keep moving forward to achieve that goal!

Chapter 15

September 19, 2012

My dad called. He was emotional and said he needed to talk to me. He told me that the doctor told him that they think he has rectal cancer; he was so upset. My husband heard me talking to him; he asked if we should go over and check on my dad. I said, "Yes, that would probably be a good idea." We went over shortly after that, which is a good thing because we found him on the kitchen floor where he fell again. He has been falling a lot more the past year, and it is very concerning. We got him all set up. I went back the next day to clean for him. I phoned the head nurse, and she told me that he has a walnut-size tumor in his colon that needs to be removed, but first they need to know if it is cancer. The next day I went to see my mom. Just as I walked in the door, my dad called me because he fell on the floor again and needed help getting up. I went over to help him up, and one of his neighbors came in. She helped me get him back in his wheelchair.

I worry about my father because I think he should be living in an assisted living environment because of how often he falls, but he doesn't want to go. He also doesn't want to go to a nursing home; I don't blame him, but it creates more stress for me because when I call him and he doesn't answer his phone, I worry he has fallen again.

One day a few years ago, he called me at like three in the afternoon asking me what day and time it was. When I started asking him questions, he said he fell in his bedroom and hit his head; he didn't know how long he had been on the floor. I called for an ambulance and told him not to move. Well, he couldn't move. He can't walk without assistance, so he could only drag himself on the floor. I called my husband and asked him if he was closer to my dad's than I was because it would take me about ten minutes to get over there. When he arrived, the firemen and ambulance were there, but they couldn't get in because his door was locked and they couldn't reach the manager or the janitor, so my husband kicked the door down because he could hear my dad calling for help. Thank God for my husband being there for him. Turns out that his kidneys were starting to shut down. He went into renal failure, and the doctor at the hospital said he was knocked out on the floor for much longer than the twelve hours he told us he was. This is why I don't want him living alone, but he is stubborn. He stayed in the hospital for five days while they treated his kidneys aggressively with a fluid regimen. He was okay, which was good news—no permanent damage.

My husband is going to Texas for three days for training for his work, so I asked him what his plans were for the weekend since he will be gone for three days next week. He said, "I am going out riding tomorrow and Saturday." He just got home and he was only home for about ten minutes and left again. He is only thinking of himself again, no plans to, I don't know, spend time with your wife and work on our marriage. Maybe because we have been together for over twelve years, I just expect him to care more and just be different, or maybe he doesn't think he has to try anymore or put in that extra effort. That is where taking things for granted gets you into trouble. We should try to do things every day for the ones we love.

September 22, 2012

My husband and I were on our way out to dinner. I unintentionally started a problem between us. I had things on my mind, and I had to say them. I felt like he felt guilty and he was only going to dinner with me to make himself feel better. I stopped, pulled into the parking lot, looked at him with tears in my eyes, and said to him, "Look at me. This is pain, not happiness." He said, "Look in the mirror. You will see that you are the cause of your own pain." We just came home; I couldn't have dinner with him like that.

I started thinking about what he had said to me, and he is right in the sense that I am the cause of my pain because I choose to stay with him instead of leave. He is leaving early tomorrow morning for Texas, like 6:00 a.m., for a few days, so maybe some space will be good for us at this point. I know I am looking forward to a break. But of course it gave him the excuse to take off and drink. As soon as we got home, he left and went to the bar.

September 23, 2012

My heart was palpitating so much last night. I was so stressed out. I had so much anxiety. I finally had to take a Xanax just to relax so I could sleep a little.

He called me at 1:00 a.m. drunk, slurring his words and letting me know that he was at a bar with his sister. This seemed odd to me because I had just talked to her earlier in the week. I broke down about how bad his drinking had become and how concerned I was about his health. One minute she was worried about how much he was drinking, and the next she is at a bar taking shots with him? This just didn't sound right. I found that to be really weird because he said he was doing shots with her and her boyfriend, but she doesn't drink hard alcohol, so I have no idea what's happening at this point. Regardless, he is responsible for himself; it is no one else's responsibility. It's not up to his sister to control his drinking it is his. I think maybe he was just using her as a cover so if I knew he was with his sister, I wouldn't get as upset with him. That's typical of him to use others as a shield and not worry what relationships are harmed or who gets hurt in the process.

Anyway, he was like, "I can't drive home, so I was going to get someone to bring me home." I said, "Then why did you call me?" He said, "I don't know." He didn't get home until 4:00 a.m. so stinking-ass drunk, and yep, he found someone to drive him home—himself! Seriously, he is leaving for a training seminar in two hours for work, and this is how he wants to present himself? Hung over and reeking of booze? Why is it that this guy can drive drunk and never get caught? I just wish they would pull him over when he has been drinking so he can hit bottom, realize he has a serious drinking problem, and finally get help for himself.

I don't wish anything bad for him; just the opposite. I want him to get better and get help for his addiction and put our family back together. I mean, the kids are all grown now, but he could sure stand to work on our marriage and fix what has been broken with his wife, because it's going to be just the two of us so it would be nice if we could have a happy life together. You know, happy wife, happy life. If he doesn't want to try, then at the very least, he should be honest with me and let me go if he doesn't want to be here, which seems pretty clear to me at this point. I have waited to be happy with him for so long. I just wish I was worth as much to him as he has been to me all these years, but I don't have a shot in hell competing with the alcohol.

He ran out the door; didn't say bye to me or even let me know he was leaving. I just heard the door slam shut. How inconsiderate is that? What if something happened to him while he was gone? He was getting on a plane and didn't say good-bye. Has he ever thought about the fact that every day we have no guarantee and we should love and respect those that are closest to us and let them know how we feel? Really, though, my mind runs like a machine on overdrive. I just can't quiet my thoughts. It sucks. It is worse at night when I try to sleep.

October 6, 2012

Yesterday marked one week where my husband didn't drink at all. I was shocked, but he seemed to actually be trying. We didn't fight for a whole week; that was huge for us.

Then he went to band practice this morning. He left around nine thirty in the morning. We were not arguing; there were zero problems; things were good with us—they were really fantastic. I sent him a text that afternoon and asked him if he could bring me home a tea. He called me about six forty-five and said practice was just over; he was with the band and they were getting pizza. I immediately got a really bad feeling in the pit of my stomach. I said, "Why don't you just come home? We can watch a movie and spend time together." That was what we were planning on doing anyway. I knew the way he sounded that he was drinking again; he was an hour away from home. As the hours went by and he didn't come home, I knew he was bingeing again. I went to bed around ten o'clock watching TV. When I tried to sleep, I just tossed and turned. Even when things were good with us, he still drank, so there blows that excuse for him. I felt so sad, lonely, defeated, wondering why even when things were good between us he couldn't come home. Why was I not more important than the alcohol? Why wasn't he stronger than that? What was it going to take for him to see me? Would he ever really see me, love me, care about me? Would I ever matter to him the way I should?

I finally got up since I wasn't sleeping anyway. I thought maybe writing this journal entry would help me sleep. Now I'm going back to bed.

October 7, 2012

At 2:09 a.m. I got a phone call from an 800 number. I didn't answer it. I thought that was an odd time for a marketing call. There was a voice message, so I listened to it; it said something like depending on which facility, I would get a certain number of minutes. Suddenly my stomach started fluttering. At 2:13 a.m. the phone rang again— another odd number this time I answered. It was my husband, clearly slurring his words beyond drunk.

He said, "Hi, honey. I have been arrested for a DUI." I said, "Are you serious? Is this a joke?" He said, "It's not." Then he explained how he wasn't even driving; he had actually pulled off the side of the road to sleep it off because he was so drunk, and the police woke him up. Seriously, all the times he actually physically drove drunk, he never got pulled over, but the time he is sleeping it off on the side of the road, he gets busted. The one thing I worried about and prayed for finally happened: he was caught. Let's see if this changes anything. Will he see now that this is serious? Will he take the steps to get help for himself? I hope so. I love this man so much. He has lost himself. We have lost each other. We need a miracle; maybe this is it.

I talked to an officer and found out how much bail was and how much the impound fee was to get his car back. At 2:30 a.m., I was sitting at the table, alone, numb, and crying, wondering how things got so bad. I had slept for about an hour and a half; my eyes were burning from lack of sleep. I was beyond stressed trying to figure out how I was going to get all this bail money. What could I pawn or sell? This is ridiculous! I had just paid all the bills.... There was a little left in the bank; I took out what was left and collected all the change jars and turned those in for cash; I had to borrow the rest ... ugh ... not again. Here's another bad situation that his drinking has put us in. Why do I feel embarrassed? Why do I take the shame on? I am his wife, that is why and when he hurts, I hurt, and that is how it should be. I am so mad at him, I just want to shake him and say, "Now do you believe me? All those years I tried to tell you that you had a drinking problem. Now do you get it? Now do you believe me?"

My mom drove out with me because he was an hour away and I needed to pick up his car because he wasn't allowed to drive. Once I

*was finally able to get him, it was about 2:30 that afternoon. They
don't let them leave until they blow a certain number and they are
sober. My mom said she wanted to follow me for a while to make
sure I was going to be okay; she is so worried about me. I hate for my
parents to be so involved with this situation; it is so stressful.*

*We didn't get very far down the road before he had me pull over so
he could throw up. I was already so overwhelmed. I got out of the
car. I was pacing up and down on the side of the highway, tears in
my eyes, both pissed off and scared, taking deep breaths, feeling like
I was going to go into a full-blown panic attack, wondering what
was going to happen now—and meanwhile, he was puking all over
the place. I got back in the car and continued to drive home, first in
silence, and then we started to talk.*

*I said, "We weren't even arguing. We were getting along. Things were
good, and you still went out and got drunk. It still caused problems.
That is what I mean when I said you can't always use the excuse we
were fighting, because it hasn't always been that way. Even when
things have been great, you still drink."*

*He said he would sell the motorcycle, he was never going to drink
again, everything was going to change this time, how sorry he was
for putting me through this. He was so scared about losing his job. It
seemed to me that was what was most important, that he could lose
his job. Don't get me wrong. Of course it is important, and even more
so when he is the main financial provider in the house, but how about
the people that have been affected by all of this? I have no words at
this moment. I need to process some more; I am too numb right now.*

October 11, 2012

*My husband called his boss first thing Monday morning. He had to
tell him what happened. Thank goodness his boss has the attitude
like "things happen." The biggest concern, of course, is if he loses his*

driver's license, he will lose his job because his job is all about driving
a lot. His company has an FMLA, which stands for Family Medical
Leave Act, which means he can get the help he needs and still keep
his job. With that program they can also provide an attorney; you
take a loan from your 401-K and pay it back every paycheck. As long
as he goes into treatment and doesn't lose his license, he can keep his
job. They follow him for a year, and then it is as though it never
happened. I think most companies you would lose your job, so I am
grateful that there is some protection. I don't want to lose our home
and everything else. It wouldn't be fair to the rest of us since we didn't
make the decision to ruin our lives; he made that for us.
Tonight was his first day in the intensive outpatient program, which
is three hours a night four days a week for five weeks. He said when
he first got there, he didn't feel like he fit in, but as the night went on,
he was able to start relating to other people and the things they were
saying. He said there was a young woman who was upset and crying.
She was saying that she was an alcoholic but still does everything like
cooking, cleaning, raising the kids, shopping, working, paying the
bills, and so on. All she wants is for her husband to tell her he loves
her and acknowledge her. He said it reminded him of me because she
just wants the love of her husband, like I do.

October 18, 2012

I guess twice a month is family night with his group, so I went with
him tonight. I have to say, it is pretty emotional and tense listening
to all the different family members talk about how the addict in their
lives has affected them. I feel like it is really good for them to hear this,
and us as well. I am not sure at this point that I can put how I feel
into words; I am just trying to process all of this that has happened.
I feel as though the past twelve and a half years have just slammed
into our life in one fell swoop; it's like playing a movie in fast forward

from beginning to end, and all those feelings in all those years hit you at once. It is pretty damn overwhelming. It's like being on eggshells waiting to see if he loses his license, if he keeps his job, if he drinks again. It is a day-by-day process really, and I for one am terrified of how unsafe our environment is and has been for some time.

October 25, 2012

It has been a busy week. My father had surgery two days ago to remove a tumor; he is home now and doing well.

My husband started his third week in the treatment program. I ask him every night when he comes home how the meeting went and what he has learned. This is good for us because he comes in and sits with me and we talk, something we haven't been able to do in a long time. I am being supportive but still trying to take care of me. He has no idea what I am going through; the focus is still all on him.

He was pretty emotional tonight. He said he realized tonight that he treated our daughter different this whole time. He said, "You tried to talk to me about it many times and how hurt she was, but I always disregarded your feelings and her feelings—and I blamed you. I feel so bad for her because she had to give up her dog. I made the kids share everything. I never realized it was okay for them to have some of their own things. You always tried to tell me that, and I never wanted to listen to you." He said he has abandoned us all these years, and he hasn't been there for any of us! He said he had this false sense of self-entitlement and control because of his drinking.

I was in tears here, feeling such a sense of hope that he is starting to get it. He is able to feel some of the heartache he has caused, and I am proud of him, so very proud of my husband for being able to say out loud the things he has done wrong. This program is helping him to see without his drinking glasses on for the first time in his life. He is starting to see things more clearly, the way they really have been

instead of what he would tell himself they were like. I am sure he is
feeling so much shame, anger, guilt, sadness, and so much more. He
has missed life up until this point, and I am sure that must be a huge
shock to his system because he isn't used to hearing or seeing things the
way they really are. This is a great place to start over.

This has all been so overwhelming for me emotionally; it has
been really hard to deal with. I have been stressing about his
job and what will happen with that whole situation. I have been
sober and felt every single thing; I remember everything that has
happened all these years together, but he doesn't. He doesn't live
in the cruel words, the abandonment, the disrespect, the lies, the
betrayals, the feelings of worthlessness that he has created with
his actions. At times he has been so drunk or blacked out that he
doesn't remember things that he has said or done, but all these
years, day in and day out, I have lived every moment of it. I don't
know that he will ever get what that is all about and what it feels
like to be the person on the other end of what he has done. It is
easy to say, "I am sorry." It is much different to really be able to
listen and put yourself in someone else's shoes, to try and feel and
understand how they feel and what their perspective is without
letting your personal feelings interfere with that.

I thought it would be a good idea to interview other wives
of alcoholics and get different perspectives and emotions in
regard to the addiction and how it affects every person and
every relationship in a different way, but there are also a
lot of commonalities we can all relate to. It's like we all have
different stories, but we are all in the same damn boat. Like for
example, does it affect women in a different way than it does
men? This interview is with Wife #1, who has been together
with an alcoholic for eleven years, married eight of those years.

Question: *Was he drinking when you first met?*

Wife #1: Yes, he was, but I didn't realize it was a problem. I didn't know what an alcoholic was. We dated for three years before we moved in together. When we would have date nights or I would stay over, it was usually on a weekend, and we would have a bottle of wine with dinner. It was on the weekend that we drank and had fun. Once I moved in, I saw right away that the bottle of wine with dinner was every night. Suddenly it dawned on me that this was a problem for him. We were engaged to be married in three months, and I felt that things would change and his drinking wasn't as big a problem as I first thought it might be.

Question: *What is the worst memory you have with your husband?*

Wife #1: When I was twenty-nine, I was diagnosed with breast cancer. I was going to start an intense chemo treatment program in one week when a friend asked me if I wanted to help with drinks at a booth for an event here in town. I knew I wouldn't be doing much during my treatments, so I thought it would be fun. We made awesome tips and had fun. What I didn't know at the time was that my husband was drinking beer during this event; he would sneak down to the casinos, sit at a 21 table, and drink gin. When we were done around ten o'clock at night, we were going to have a free dinner for helping with the event. At this point my husband was so drunk he could hardly walk. We sat down, and he proceeded to order more alcohol with dinner. We were with about twenty people. When the drink came and he went to grab for it, I reached for it and moved it away from him, at which point he got up and become volatile, yelling at me, calling me nasty names, so my friend took him aside so he could calm down.

When we left, he was yelling at me in the car and continued to call me nasty names, so I jumped on the highway driving about ninety miles per hour. I was praying a cop would stop me for speeding so I could ask them to take him away for being so drunk—but no cops stopped me. The next day he was sorry for what he could remember, which wasn't much at all, but I should have left. I was just diagnosed with cancer, and all he could do was get drunk and be verbally abusive and not have any regard for how it affected me. In that moment I thought, what is wrong with him? *Instead of being there for me in what was a terrifying time in my life, he just wanted to keep drinking.*

Question: How has his drinking affected you emotionally, physically, and financially?

Wife #1: *Emotionally I am tired of always being sad. I want a happy life. I have so many feelings of uncertainty, resentment, anger, anxiety, and sadness. Financially, it hasn't had so much effect. He made great money when we got together, and now I make great money as well. We have family money and we used to travel to like Europe and have two big trips a year, but we stopped that a few years ago due to him losing his job going to work drunk so finances were an issue all caused by his alcoholism. Physically, it has aged me, and I have started to have heart palpitations from anxiety and the stress of it all.*
Possibly it even caused the breast cancer. Breast cancer doesn't run in my family and I was healthy before, so maybe the stress helped bring it on. He lost his job last year because he went to work drunk twice. The first time he was given a warning, and the second time, he was fired. I have been the sole financial provider ever since, which puts a lot of stress on me.

Question: What is your best memory with your husband?

Wife #1: *Traveling together. He used to plan everything from where and what we would do; we had a lot of fun together doing that.*

Question: If you knew then what you know now, would you change anything?

Wife #1: *If we weren't engaged, I would have left. I had a false sense that once married, he would get it under control. I know he is a good guy. When he isn't drinking, I catch moments of him, but then he relapses again and becomes mean when he drinks.*

Question: Has the intimacy in your marriage changed and in what ways?

Wife #1: *It's hard to be intimate with someone who has hurt you over and over again. At some point you just don't want the intimacy anymore. I shut down emotionally over a year ago. If it happens, he initiates it because I just don't want it. Even when it does happen, I am just not into it anymore.*

Question: How do you feel you have compromised or sacrificed yourself for him because of his addiction?

Wife #1: *I have sacrificed my heart and soul for him, as well as my health and social life. I never had heart palpitations until all this stress started with him, surrounding his drinking. I have sacrificed my right to have a glass of wine in my own house if I want to. The list goes on and on; it makes me angry to think about it!*

I was happy to meet someone who could understand how I felt, what I have gone through and continue to go through. Here we were, two strangers who had never met before, from different walks of life, and yet we have a strong common bond: our husbands are alcoholics, and so a friendship began. In the midst of trying to unravel the pain and devastation caused by this horrible disease, two women came together for the sake of their husbands and leaned on each other for support. Even in the worst of times, there is a lesson; something good is always found in the bad. You just have to be open enough to feel it and hear it.

I am grateful to have this woman in my life and call her a friend. She is a beautiful-spirited person and a great person to have a conversation with. I want to say thank you for taking the time to do an interview with me and for being so open about something that is so painful and personal and for being my friend. She feels if it will help benefit someone else by telling a piece of her story she was happy to do it.

Chapter 16

November 2, 2012

Last night was family night at his group. This time it was him, me, our daughter, my mother, and her husband. One thing that really bothers me is that he turns everything into a joke. Even when he needs to be serious, he just makes light of it—and it isn't funny. I realize this may be a defense mechanism, but it can be hurtful.

I had to protect the kids, protect our families, our life together. It was me doing the protecting, when it should have been him watching out for our family. I mean, the floodgates of emotions are open, and even though it is hitting me hard, I stop myself from feeling it to the full extent, but I need to so I can heal. The emotional and financial damage he has caused over the years have taken their toll. I am irritable and moody because I am processing all these years of emotions now. My therapist tells me that it is okay, it is normal to feel like that. I am proud of him for taking the steps he needs to so he can be sober, get his mind healthy, and understand things that he has never taken the time to understand. I want to be here for him through it all. Anytime he needs me, I'm here. I also need that from him. I am hopeful for our future but scared just the same because in the past, the other shoe has always dropped, and I have always been disappointed. Just when I started to believe and trust that things could be different, it goes back to the same way it always has been.

I am praying he never drinks again, but more importantly that his behaviors change. We have many years to work through, and that is obviously not going to be easy; it isn't happening overnight. Patience, lots of patience, with a whole lot of love, that's what is needed. He said he wants to know what life is like without alcohol, and that makes me so happy to hear.

I feel overwhelmed a lot of the time right now, and some days I can't control where and when I cry. I was in a drive-through the other day getting a milkshake with my daughter, and I started crying at the window, like uncontrollably sobbing. My daughter was like, "Mom, what is happening? What do I do?" I felt so dumb, but I seriously had no control. My emotions just pour out at times. I have to feel like it is healthy to get it out because keeping that in is toxic and bad for me, right?

November 4, 2012

Things have been going good. He has been sober almost a month now, and the tension in the house has turned into a calmer atmosphere. For so many years, we had fun, we were best friends, we were so in love—and we lost it. We allowed other things in life to get in the way of us. We promised nothing would break the bond we had and nothing would ever come between us, but alcoholism did. It has such a strong evil hold on people; they don't realize it until they can stand back after being sober and look at the destruction that they caused. Then it's like a bomb of emotions exploding. I truly have such empathy for these people like my husband because that must be a total trip. Ironically today is the anniversary date of when we got engaged back in "2001".

I have used the example to my husband that his drinking behaviors are much like the effects of a tornado; there is so much destruction they leave in their path, you have to start piece by piece to rebuild, and at that point you make it stronger so it withstands the next storm. See, storms will always come; it is how you prepare for them and deal with them when they happen that makes the outcome different the next time.

We went to a movie today that was about an alcoholic pilot that crashed an airplane. Almost everyone survived, but the guy could never admit he was an alcoholic or that he was drunk when he crashed the plane. When we left, we got in the car, and he was very upset. When I asked what was wrong, he said the movie made him very emotional because he is an alcoholic and it is very hard for him right now. This may sound kind of crazy, but to hear my husband say, "I am an alcoholic" makes me proud. I get choked up because it means that he finally sees that he does have a problem, and that is the key to the first step in changing and helping yourself: actually admitting that you have a problem.

In the past when I would say, "You are an alcoholic," or I would ask him if he thought he is an alcoholic, he would say no and get very defensive and angry with me. He would say he doesn't drink every day, or he would say, "Don't call me names." He would never admit it; it was always met with denial. I mean, that is definitely something. I wish he could stay in this IOP (intensive outpatient) group for a lot longer. He seems to be learning so much about alcoholism, and it seems to be more like intensive therapy. I just hope the changes stick and aren't short–lived, in-the-moment type moments that leave you hopeful, only to be let down. We really deserve to be happy together. We have a rare kind of love. This is a clean slate for us to be more than what we have ever been capable of being.

December 1, 2012

Today is my dearest friend's birthday. We have been friends for over thirty years. How awesome and rare is that these days?

My dad's seventy-second birthday was yesterday. We are going over to have lunch and cake with him today. He hasn't been feeling so good lately. He had a tumor removed about five weeks ago, and I think because of his MS, his recovery may be slower than normal.

Things at home are going okay. My husband is now doing two meetings on the weekends, one each day. He tells me that he doesn't have time to go during the week because of work, but when he was doing IOP, he was going four nights a week three hours per night. I think that is just an excuse and he is getting lazy about this, and that concerns me. I have been through a few six-month sobriety runs with him before, so until he has at least a year clean and sober, I don't think I will relax. I have to say, though, this is the first time I have really noticed a change. He is really working on this. I am so proud of my husband, so proud. He tells me, "I will never drink again" and "I have no desire to drink." I learned in IOP that those can be dangerous words and that people who get too cocky can end up relapsing. Don't get me wrong, he is working hard at it, but I just worry because of the stress or if we argue, how he will learn to deal with that in a healthy way instead of running out to drink.

Me, I have been emotional, moody, resentful, sad, and happy—it is going to be a process for me. I can't thank my friends and family enough for standing by me through all of this drama all these years, and they are still here with a listening ear and an open heart when I need them.

December 10, 2012

My husband and I went to the animal shelter today. They had a puppy that was so skinny. (You already know what's about to happen here.)...

They told us he was the runt; people have looked at him, but no one has wanted him. Once I held him and felt how skinny he was, he was shaking and looked so pathetic, my heart hurt for him. Since our daughter has wanted a dog of her own, we thought this would be perfect, so we got him for her.

I have been fostering a little tiny Chihuahua puppy for my neighbor, and my daughter had said she wanted him, but I felt he was way too small and not the right fit for her. Nonetheless, I put him in a Christmas box and said, "Here's your surprise. Open it." It was the foster puppy. She looked at me and said, "What is this? Are you serious? This is my surprise?" I said, "You said you wanted him, didn't you?" I love messing with her. I laughed and said, "Okay, here is your real surprise." I gave her another box. When she opened it, out popped this new puppy; she screamed she was so excited. My daughter is eighteen years old, but to see her face light up with joy still makes a mom's heart smile. Priceless!

My husband has been sober for sixty days now, which is fantastic, but he is getting a bit too blasé. What I mean is that he wants to go sit at a bar, listen to music, and watch a band play. These are the behaviors that I was hoping would dissipate and wouldn't happen anymore— no such luck. I don't think he will ever stay out of bars, sober or not. It makes me very sad. This is the problem with that situation: I don't feel he has enough control or sobriety under his belt to deal with being around the same situation he has been around all these years that has led to his alcoholism. To me, if you're serious about staying sober, you have to change things and make sacrifices that you may not want to make, but in the moment you have to do what's best given the fact you're trying to stay sober. It's probably not a good idea to go sit at a bar, which is where you used to always run in the past to drown out your problems. Even if he isn't drinking, he doesn't understand it is the same behavior as when he was drinking; the dynamic needs to change somehow in some way.

I told him that I can't make the decision for him to stay out of bars. I was just sharing my feelings and my concerns, but he doesn't want to hear those. He just wants to play the selfish card. It is all about him.

January 1, 2013

I am so happy that 2012 is over; it was one of the worst years of my life. I mean worst*! Every year I say that, don't I? How sad is that. Christmas was better than last year.*

There is a bit more tension right now with my husband. See, he doesn't understand why I can't forget about everything and just move forward. I asked him for time and patience because it is going to be another long journey together. I deserve that more than anybody. After all these years, I need some time now with what I am dealing with. It isn't fair sometimes the way he is one-sided. I have been here for him through every bad day, standing by him, helping him, sacrificing by putting myself aside. Sadly, he doesn't sacrifice for me. I don't think he will ever put himself aside for me, or anyone else for that matter. He is still very selfish, and it seems to be getting worse. I don't understand this. I hope the selfish part of this goes away. Shouldn't things be getting better? The holidays were better. It was nice to be with family. I was so happy my daughter was here this year to celebrate it with us. I was very sad that our Emmy dog wasn't with us this year. I can't believe it has been a year already. Time seems to go by so slow in the moment, and then a whole year is gone in the blink of an eye.

So, the first day of the New Year, and my husband went from telling me, "I am selling my motorcycle," to "don't worry; it won't affect our bank account in any way," to now he tells me he needs more money every month to pay for it. I am so tired of paying for his mistakes. He blew ten grand last year drinking. He lied to me getting that damn motorcycle, so at this point, I feel like he should step up and be a man. Sell it for now, and when we are in a better place financially, he can get one, but the way he did it was deceitful and it will never be okay with me.

My mom had a mild heart attack two weeks ago, just before Christmas. One of her arteries was 95 percent blocked, so they put one stent in.

She is doing well. She only had to spend one night in the hospital. So much life is happening all at once, I feel overwhelmed at times. I am so grateful she is okay. I don't know what I would do without my momma. She needed to take it easy during Christmas, so I was mothering her and hovering over her, making sure she didn't pick up anything too heavy. Five pounds was her max limit for two weeks, and my mother doesn't do well with restrictions and not being able to do what she wants to do. She is my mom, and although she tells me not to worry, I do. I can't help it; I just love her so much. I'd be lost if I didn't have her to turn to. I have my concerns, though, because mom is diabetic, and she is starting to have a few health issues pop up. From a woman who is never sick to some serious issues with her health, I can't help but worry.

On December 29, 2012, I lost one of my rescue cats that I have had for eight years. They think that a blood clot may have passed through her brain because there was something neurological going on that they couldn't pinpoint, but her body temperature was so low. We could hear her crying. She was clearly in pain and suffering, so we made the hard decision to let her go. I held her as she took her last breath. My husband and I carry so much emotion with our rescues; it breaks your heart. I want to save every one of them. I feel helpless at the end of a life; I want to do more for them. I tell you, animal rescuing is so rewarding, and yet so heartbreaking at times too. No one can ever accuse me of not having a big kind heart, and if they do, then they don't know me at all or what I go through. Through all these years, I have kept up my rescuing. Sometimes my husband has helped, and others he won't lift a finger, but I am hoping now that things will change and he will be more involved and present in our life together with everything.

I am seeing that being sober takes a lot of work, time, and patience, or I should say, the recovery part of it will be a lifestyle change.

For the rest of his life, he will have to work on it every day, and we have to work on us every day. Everything is still all about him, and that is hard to deal with for me. Is it so wrong to want some attention for me? Is it so wrong to want some gestures of love, understanding, compassion, and assurance from him? What I am trying to do is be supportive of him while trying to understand myself and all that has happened and what continues happening. At times he treats me exactly the way he used to when he was drinking—calling me names belittling me, or criticizing me for things that have no relevance here, like my animal rescuing. How can you be anything but proud of me for what I do with animals? My passion for animals is all from the heart. I would be very sad if I couldn't do what I do. This makes me happy. Even when I am overwhelmed with it, I am still happy saving animals. Especially given all the years of sadness, why wouldn't he want his wife to be happy? Why wouldn't he feel good knowing he helped put a smile on my face or that he helped to save a life? We have saved a lot of lives together; he needs to remember that.

I know this is going to take time for him to get to a point where he starts to really grasp what his actions have caused, but I am seeing the man he used to act like rear his ugly head, and I don't like it at all. This scares me. I have a funny feeling that it isn't going to get any better. If you're going to really try, then start by telling yourself this: "You have hurt your wife; you have caused deep emotional damage. When she is upset, take her hand and ask her to come sit by you. Just hold her. Let her fall apart. Comfort her. Let her know you are still her safe place, and you will do whatever is necessary for her to believe that again." All I want is to be in his arms. I have loved this man from the day our eyes first met. I have loved him through every good time and every bad time. I adore him because he is my heart, and I wouldn't want to be without him, not for one day. Even though at times I felt like

I didn't want to be around him, I would never want to live life without him. I believe we will somehow find the strength to get through this together.

In the meantime, give me a break for what I have endured all these years. Be kind to my heart; when you repair something, it takes time to make it right. Allow me to have my feelings and feel what I feel. Even when you don't agree, be supportive. Do the opposite of what you have always done. Instead of calling me names, hug me; instead of putting me down, tell me you understand; when you see me struggle with my emotions, say, "I am here to listen"—don't ignore me. All these years I have been a mom, dad, stepmom, teacher, chauffeur, cook, shopper, referee, babysitter, therapist, friend, accountant, housekeeper, maid, animal rescuer, nurse, and so on … so I deserve a break more than anyone, don't I? Not every moment of every day can be about him; it needs to also be about repairing some of the damage he has caused, and you can't do that by creating more damage.

The second wife I interviewed has been with her husband for twenty-five-plus years. He is an alcoholic as well as a physical abuser. This interview really touched me because of all the heartache and pain that has been caused by one person's addiction and how he is oblivious to the fact that he is accountable for hurting so many innocent lives of people who have loved him and want to be loved, but he can't seem to take the focus off of himself long enough to see the reality of his situation.

Question: Was he drinking when you first met?

Wife #2: *Yes, but we really just got to see each other on the weekends for the first few months because of work schedules. I didn't "foresee" a* *problem with it. Social drinking with friends seemed normal to me. I was nineteen, and he was twenty-three. Being sloppy at that age when you were drinking was what I was used to seeing. Six months into the relationship, he got into a few fights and had trouble with the law as a direct result from his drinking. I was by his side through it all. I became the person who would rescue him and make things better.*

Question: What is the worst memory you have with him?

Wife #2: It's painful and embarrassing to relive …
The summer of 1996 I was off from work for the summer, and he didn't have his license due to a DUI suspension. I drove him to work every morning at 6:00 a.m. One morning he thought that if he took my car, he could give me and our daughter a break, and we wouldn't have to get up to take him to work. The cops in our small town know his truck, so he thought he was being sneaky this way. I agreed if he went straight to work and came right home. I was pacing the floor when he was two hours late, watching out the window, waiting for the phone to ring.
Finally he pulled into the driveway and fell out of the car. My blood was boiling. I said, "What the hell is wrong with you? You swore you would come straight home. You could have killed someone." He said he had a long day and stopped to have a few beers. "You had more than a few beers, and I don't care how hard your day was!" I told him. With that he grabbed me by the throat, and immediately I had no air. I could feel his thumbs pushing my throat as I tried to grip his hand. I woke up on the floor with one leg bent under my body and a kitchen chair on top of me. He was yelling my name. When I looked up, I saw a blur of his figure. I got scared and jumped to a sitting position. Our two-and-a-half-year-old daughter was in the hallway crying, saying, "No boo-boo, Mommy, no boo-boo, Mommy." He went in the bathroom and started the shower, so I grabbed my daughter and

ran to the neighbor's house. I explained briefly what had happened and asked if they would watch my daughter until my mom could get there and to call the police.

As I was making my way back home, I noticed my ankle was swollen as big as a softball and the back of my head felt like mush. The pain was setting in. The police came, arrested him, and took me away by ambulance. I had a concussion, a slight fracture behind my ear, a fractured ankle, and the bruising to my neck was really bad. Victim advocates came in and talked to me, but I don't remember what they said; I just wanted to get my baby and go home.

I was in complete shock and so sad that he would hurt me like that, so sad.

After he had three months of anger management, AA, and counseling, I let him come back home. I believed he would never mistreat me again. I truly believed that he blacked out and didn't realize he was hurting me, his wife that he loves more than anything. He was sober only about a year after that.

This was a big blow to my family; they wanted me to get out right then. They told me once was too many times for something like this to happen. They were right, and so hurt when I stayed; they have lived with fear every day since. From then on, I have been too ashamed to go to them again.

Question: How has his drinking affected you emotionally, physically, and financially?

Wife #2: Emotionally it has made me a very nervous person. I rarely enjoy a glass of wine because I need to "mother" everyone else. With my husband, anger comes with drinking; he is an angry drunk. If I have "too" good a time, I am accused of being flirty, checking out other men, and so on. I barely talk to other men, and that includes my own family members.

I can't control my words or hurt feelings after an incident because there is no getting through to him when he is drinking, so I wait a few days to pass before I express my feelings. I cry uncontrollably when I let him know how his drinking has affected me and the girls. He shows no compassion when I get like that; he's almost heartless.

Physically it is exhausting. Years of getting him off the floor, cleaning up after him pissing the bed, vomiting, and so on. I have had fat lips, literally kicked out of bed at night, black eyes, broken ribs, things thrown at me, ice-cold water dumped on me while I slept, spit at, personal sentimental items broken. He has even urinated in my dresser drawers and on my pillows. There's been twenty-five years of this, not constant but in between these things, he would "fix" and keep me around. The last four years have been torment, meaning he pushes my buttons, so I detach from him enough so he can keep using me as an excuse to drink. This has caused me anxiety, heart palpitations, and depression—not wanting to face the day. I have sought help for myself. I am not medicated for my depression because I can mentally talk myself down from anxiety. I have too many responsibilities; I have to keep moving. I am the wife, husband, mother, father, cook, maid, taxi driver, bill payer, all the while running my own business; I have learned to live a very sick life.

Financially—ha-ha. We haven't been able to make ends meet for a good ten years. He is no longer working. He is disabled because he had a heart attack eight years ago. He made great money when he was working, but his behavior and bad attitude got him laid off more than once. He has been alcohol-free for a few months now, but he thinks it's okay to ignore the electric bill to buy a bag of weed and smoke all day long until it is gone. My business is suffering because of the lack of attention I can give to it because the safety of my kids and house come first. Years ago I could have supported myself, but now I am financially dependent on the pension and social security he gets. I wouldn't survive on my income right now.

Question: *What is your best memory with him?*

Wife #2: *The best memory is yet another sad story ... This is really blowing my mind, talking about all this with you.*

Six months before our wedding, my sister and I had gone shopping for wedding stuff. When we got home, we found him on the floor counting change. He was messed up, but not from alcohol; my guess was some type of prescription pills. I started dinner, and he came in and said he was going for a ride and would be right back. I flipped out but couldn't stop him. He came back an hour later, but in a condition I had never seen him in—grabbing for things that weren't there, like hallucinating. It was scary.

I woke up at 4:00 a.m. to a horrible sound. He was gasping for air, and his stomach was bloated. I realized he couldn't breathe. I called 911. They were there within minutes and ripped him out of bed onto the floor. "Overdose" and "trachea" were the only words I heard. Next thing I knew, at the hospital they were putting me in this room with a couch and a black phone. They told me, "Call his family ... it's bad." His family came in grilling me, "How could you let this happen to him?" "How could you let him take anything?" My brother searched his truck and found a pill on the floor; it was morphine. The doctor said to prepare for the worst; his organs were not functioning on their own, and he might not make it through the night.

He was in a coma for nineteen hours. He slowly started to make progress—but was he going to live? Suddenly he opened his eyes. Seeing the fear in them, in that moment I saw the guy I loved and was to marry in six months coming back; it was the best feeling ever. My immediate thoughts were he would never do another drug in his life. It took three months of physical therapy—he couldn't walk or feed himself—but he got full brain function back. I wanted to postpone the wedding, but he insisted we go forward with the plans. Our wedding day was the best day of my life. He was perfect, handsome, healthy, loving, and in that moment, while his family seemed to blame me, he was thanking me for saving his life because if I wasn't there, he would have died that day. It's a beautiful memory, and he was clean and sober for two and a half years after that.

Question: If you knew then what you know now, what would you change?

Wife #2: *Ha, ha, ha ... I wouldn't be here. I was young and naïve. I would have stuck with my friends and run (fast) in a different direction. I had no idea what addiction or mental illness was. I thought his controlling ways meant that he loved and cared for me. I thought taking care of him meant that I was needed and special for being able to "handle" it. At this point in life, I have given up. We live like roommates now. His sister was recently diagnosed with lung cancer, and she is very sick. That is when I woke up. She has a wonderful husband and two daughters that take care of her like you wouldn't believe, and it hit me like a ton of bricks—I don't have that with him. My kids and family would take care of me, but not him. I tried to discuss this with him, but he got angry, insisting he would "be there," but I know he could never do it. That's when I had to face the reality that I've never really felt loved by him. I feel that he loves having a wife who would live in silence, he loves being in control, he loves the fact that I am here to do and fix everything that I do, but if one day I couldn't continue with this life, he would move on. I don't know if he has ever really loved me back.*

Question: When if at any point did you realize you became an enabler and codependent?

Wife #2: *I first realized I was enabling him after his overdose, when he was in rehab. I had to be told by therapists and counselors, and*

I was fully accepting of it; they were right on the money seven years into it. Even after a few years of sobriety, I fell right back into that role—covering up, making excuses, even letting him drink a little at home so he wouldn't go out and get into trouble. In twenty-two years of marriage, he has never really had any responsibilities; it has always been less stressful and easier to do it myself. We all learned to live a sick and dysfunctional life.

Question: Has the intimacy changed in your relationship due to his alcoholism, and if so, in what ways?

Wife #2: *Intimacy is a complicated thing I have always been a very passionate person; he never really was. Before marriage, sex was frequent but unplanned, which made things more exciting. A year into marriage, we bought a house and became more creative and comfortable; it was great, very intimate. When he began drinking again, he would be passed out almost every night. When it did happen, I felt as if I was with a stranger a lot of the time. After the first baby, less and less. Once he started using prescription meds, I felt like he was just doing it for himself, not ever to please me. I really started trying to avoid it. The feeling of being with a stranger, being sad, lonely, angry, and tired—no big deal, I could live without it.*

Then he has a heart attack, takes meds for everything, and suddenly ten years later, he notices it isn't working right, so now he gets concerned, and the doctor gives him Viagra. For some guy reason, he thinks if his tool doesn't work, then I will leave. Over those ten years, he has been to two rehabs for alcohol and drugs and done four months of jail time for DUIs. He has become most abusive since his heart attack because of depression and has become paranoid. Over the past five years, I just stopped making any effort; I guess I gave up. He literally thinks a wife is supposed to make her husband happy—no joke, everything is my fault. He thinks I am always looking for a new man. I have

practically been forced to have sex or perform just to prove I am not
unfaithful or to not be tormented or verbally abused by him.
The hardest part, I guess, is that he is all I have known since I was
nineteen years old. Currently we are cohabitating, and it's an awful
situation. Neither of us has anywhere to go due to our financial
situation. He fights with me daily about sex, and I despise him.
He insists that I cause him to be different—no responsibility or
accountability. It is like going round and round in a circle over and
over again. Sex only happens out of fear that he will drink or have a
breakdown. I just give in to avoid a bad scene; intimacy has been gone
for many, many years between us. He accuses me of cheating when I
go to work or that I am really sneaking off to screw someone else. He
knows my morals and values.
He tells me he hates me and then wants to have sex. He thinks having
sex, being intimate, will make our relationship better. He doesn't hear
me when I try to talk about all the hurt and resentment I have bottled
up inside. He doesn't understand that sex is not love. All this time I
have fought for my family, only for him to fight his. I can't keep loving
someone who is so far gone; he isn't even my friend anymore. When
that is gone, what is there?

As you can see, this was a very emotional interview—very
powerful. I heard so many commonalities in what she said. The
blame from him and from his family that it must be her fault.
More than that is the abandonment, loneliness, anger, sadness,
anxiety, self-worthlessness, resentment, feeling defeated, and so
on that we all feel. Alcoholics have yet to take accountability or
responsibility without *blaming* their spouses or someone else.
One thing I find so admirable in everyone who stands by an
alcoholic—something that we don't see for ourselves—is that we
love the alcoholic, we want to help the alcoholic, we take care of
the alcoholic. Our hearts are in the right place even if we don't

realize in the moment that we have enabled and that isn't healthy. What I mean is we all feel as though we are weak, but we are in fact very strong for standing true to our love, for our loyalty to the one who is going through the addiction. That is something to hold our head up high for.

I have had friends say, "You are so strong. I couldn't have done what you have done," and I reply with, "I am not strong; I am weak." My friends say, "No, you are the strongest woman I know, and I am so proud and honored to be your friend." I thought my friends were saying that to make me feel good, but they were reduced to tears when they would say these things. It really came from their hearts. So to all of you who feel as though you are not strong, know that I believe you are some of the strongest people out there to love and stand by loyally to the person in your life who is an addict of some kind. Hold onto hope, for one day help will come, and you will be glad you stayed true to yourself and to the one you love. Know that if you choose to leave, that does not make you weak. There are different ways strength displays itself, but don't mistake silence for weakness or even walking away for weakness.

We all have different beliefs, and what works for one will not work for another. Find your own strength and follow your own path. You do learn how to live a sick, secluded, dysfunctional life, and it becomes all you know. We women want to be heard and understood, free to let our emotions out. Whether we are calm, yelling, or crying, we are all feeling the same things. What alcoholics seem to forget is the people that have been affected by their disease have lived and had to remember every painful agonizing moment, while they are medicating themselves and therefore they are oblivious to what they are really doing.

It is a sad, lonely world, and all we want is to feel loved and appreciated. When a child is hurt, your instinct is to run and take care of him or her, hold him or her and make it better. The same thing goes for a verbal wound. Hold the one you love. Let the one you love fall apart in your arms. Feel the depth of your loved one's pain, and no matter how much it tears you apart to realize the pain you caused another person, think of how much that person was torn apart inside by you. Think of what that pain has done to the person who loves you and realize that person needs this; that person needs you as much as you need him or her.

No one said healing would be easy; you have to do it together. Admitting one's mistakes is a powerful emotion to come to terms with. Emotional pain runs deep in the heart and deep in the mind. We are all individuals, and no one person is exactly like another. We all feel, heal, and think about things differently than the person next to us, but one thing is for sure: we are all human. We all have feelings and deserve compassion, understanding, and kindness.

Chapter 17

January 16, 2013

I am having a really hard time trusting him. We got into a disagreement about him keeping the motorcycle he should have never bought last year. His words are becoming cruel again, and I am not sure why. I mean, I know when people argue, they can say things that they wouldn't normally say to hurt someone, but it seems to be a constant with him. He made it very clear that his material things are the most important to him over everything else. It only took him a few seconds to elevate his temper, telling me to get over him lying, being deceitful, his drinking, everything that has happened. I am just supposed to wake up one day and say, "Okay, we're cool." I am no expert, but I don't feel like this is what recovery is supposed to look like.

He told me when I picked him up from jail that he would sell the motorcycle. I should have never believed he would do the right thing for us; he would never part with anything that he wants. He is famous for saying things in the moment, but his actions do not follow most of the time. He is just over ninety days sober, which is so fantastic, but I feel like all he is working on is just not drinking. I don't feel like he is really working on changing his behaviors and what his triggers are because he behaves exactly the same, just without the alcohol, and honestly he is becoming more verbally abusive. I do not like this one bit. I am tired of trying to talk to him about anything of importance to me. We don't work on the past hurts. He doesn't console me. It's just,

"Hey, let's just forget all I have done and move forward," and you know that would be great, but my mind and heart can't seem to do that, so instead of being patient and understanding, he becomes cruel. Shouldn't he be working on making amends anyway?

January 20, 2013

What I have noticed is that I have been involved with his outpatient program, going to family nights, same with his meetings, asking him what he learned, what he feels, and so on, but he doesn't stop and think how I might be handling all of this or how I am feeling. Not once has he asked. He has never said, "Please tell me what all this has done to you or how you are feeling/handling all of this. What can I do to help you?" He says that I am always angry, and I say, "Mostly I am deeply hurt. You never say, 'I see how hurt you are.'" He said, "Because I don't see the hurt." That is baffling to me.

How can you not see the hurt? What do my tears say to him? Are they not an indicator that there is pain? How as my husband is he so disconnected from me that he can't feel my pain? He said that all he has done the past three months is try with me, but that isn't truly the case. I know he believes that to be true, but it isn't. He has worked hard to go to meetings and stay sober, but if he doesn't know how to communicate with me, really hear me when I talk without judgment and defending himself, and to feel empathy for me, rather than attack me verbally, then the only thing that has changed is he is no longing pouring the alcohol down his throat!

He feels that every day he shows me he loves me, but the truth is he doesn't. I don't feel it, and when I try to talk to him about it, he gets mad at me. If he would soften his heart, he would feel more of what I feel, and I think things would be better for us. This is so hard emotionally. It is overwhelming. This seems to be even harder to deal with than when he was drinking, and that doesn't make sense at all.

I thought things would get better. They were going that way the first few months, so what happened?

January 21, 2013

Well, when you go looking for things you really don't want to know and you find them, don't be surprised. My instincts told me to check my husband's messages on his phone, so I did. See, he still doesn't tell me things, and I don't trust him because of all the betrayal and lies, so I took it upon myself to see if there is anything I "should" know. Regardless of whether it was right or wrong, I did it anyway, and this is what I found: a text message from a woman from his treatment program saying, "Thank you for being there for me," and then further down, she says, "Love ya." Ummmm, what was that? So a woman who you knew in a program for five weeks and you see rarely at an hour-long meeting is sending you "love ya" messages? I don't think so; this is wrong. It is like I see the attachment that some of these women form, and it is a vulnerable yet dangerous place. He can't just shrug everything off and say, "Oh, it is no big deal," just because it may not be to him. It may be to them; it sends a wrong message, and that opens up more problems for us, obviously. Look what is happening right now.

So I told him I looked at his messages. I made it very clear that not only is it hurtful that he is there for these people he hardly knows and he can't be here for me, his own wife, but I am not comfortable with these messages from another woman to my husband, period, and a stranger at that. It makes me feel insecure and sad. Then I said, "Wait a minute. Have you gone to this woman's house?" He hesitated, and I knew right then I was not going to like this answer. He said yes, yesterday he went to her house because she relapsed and needed help. So, let me get this straight: you went to this woman's house alone because you think you now have all the answers because you're sober for three months and you can "save" people who are having trouble staying sober? She is texting you, she is single, and your wife doesn't know about it because you haven't told her?

There you have it once again, keeping things from your spouse and putting yourself in a bad situation that you should have known better than to do anyway. What I do know is that the program has some guidelines for appropriate male/female contact and why they shouldn't sponsor one another, but he also doesn't know how to set boundaries with people because he thought this was okay to do without talking to me, his wife, or bringing me with him for the sake of this very reason. You do not go into a situation like that alone, and other men told him the same thing. The fact is that he should never have gone alone; that is something you just don't do. There is a reason to not put yourself in those situations with someone of the opposite sex. He has got to be open and tell me things and include me, or else these problems will keep coming up and this will not work.

He was supposed to go to court, but his hearing was postponed again until March. This is ridiculous. Let's just find out what is going to happen with this so we can move on from this part of our lives at least. He said he went to his therapist today, and he talked about issues that happen with us. She said he needs to give me a break because I have been going through this for twelve years and he has only been sober a few months. Which is what I have been saying to him: give me a break for what I have endured with all of this. It isn't just him that has been affected by all of this.

I understand for whatever reason he doesn't seem to hear me or feel that what I say has any justification or validity to it, but I can't always wait for someone else to repeat what I say and then have him hear it; it doesn't seem fair to me. As for me, I am not sure what is happening here in my life with him; I am just taking it one day at a time.

I am friends with one of the wives I interviewed, and her husband is still drinking and having a hard time getting it together. She said last weekend he fell down, broke his nose, had to get stitches, busted his face open pretty good. He was so drunk the night before, she had to drive around town searching for his car; he couldn't remember where he left it. Oh, and did I mention it was her birthday? My heart goes out to her because not only do I know how it feels to have birthdays ruined, but also the frustration surrounding the whole situation. They are really great people, our husbands entered the program at the same time, and I pray that he finds a way to live a truly sober life for both of them so they can begin to rebuild together.

A friend of mine said to me that my husband seems to be preying on my seemingly never-ending optimism. Interesting thought I guess it could be true.

January 27, 2013

I was sitting at the table last night having a bowl of soup; he was on the couch watching TV. I turned to him and said, "Have you told anyone about the DUI yet?" As far as I knew he had not told our family, so I asked. He responded with, "Why ask me questions?" I said, "Excuse me?" He said, "Why ask me a question? You know I can't lie." I said, "What I do know is you can *lie. Why won't you answer the question I asked you?" Finally I said, "Forget it. I am tired of your games and your jokes. You can't seem to tell me the truth about anything. I asked you a simple question." Then he asked why I always have to get mad. I don't always have to, but this was just dumb. It was unnecessary. The way he was behaving made me feel uncomfortable. I knew since I went into his phone the other day and it turned into him defending himself again, that he was going to change his passcode so I couldn't get in. Sure enough, yep, he did. So what does that say to me? It tells me that he isn't willing to be transparent or have open communication about everything so I can feel comfortable that he isn't hiding anything from me and anytime I want to look at something*

I am welcome to because there isn't anything to hide. I have nothing to hide. I would share everything with him anytime. Funny he can't do the same with me.

February 1, 2013

My mom went back to the hospital this morning for shortness of breath, which should not be happening with the stent they put in. I really worry about her heart. She had open-heart surgery about two days before my daughter was born. Within a two-month period, both my mother and my daughter had open-heart surgery. Talk about stress!

My father is still not doing well, and my marriage is just a huge mess. My mom said that she feels okay, a little off, but they are changing some of her medications to see if that will help. They said they saw something going on with her heart; they just don't know what it is. Well, that is concerning.

My brother is healing as well. He is in a lot of pain. He had surgery for a deviated septum. That sucks, and he lives far away from the rest of the family.

I think for now I just need to keep my conversations with my husband casual, nothing of importance, so that way I can maybe be less stressed. Oh, who am I kidding? There is no way around this kind of stress, and along with everything else, it makes it worse because I feel like I can't turn to him for physical comfort, to be held, so I turn to my friends and family, but that makes me feel so sad and very alone. Damn it, I am married. I want my husband to be there for me. I want to turn to my husband, but it seems I don't know how to anymore. I am having so much trouble moving past the hurt from the past twelve and a half years. I feel as though every time I reach out to try and help heal what hurts me, he just defends, blocks, rejects, and runs fast and far, instead of trying to just be there, to be the man I need. All I want is to be heard. I don't want him to apologize for what happened; I just want him to care, that's all, to love me and show me.

February 10, 2013

He said that his therapist suggested that he come back to work on some marriage counseling with me and my therapist. I told him I asked my therapist, and she said that he needed more time with his therapist to get his feet wet and work on his triggers and to not be so defensive, or it wouldn't be of any help to us because he still wouldn't be able to take in what I am sharing. He didn't like what my therapist said, so he started saying things like, "We are in a power struggle right now." He said I try to control him. I said, "I have never tried to control you." He said I am sick and twisted.

See, what is that all about? It wasn't necessary to say that to me. I told him that he needed to work on his emotional stuff and his triggers before we would be able to communicate in a healthy way. I said, "When you put locks on all your stuff and keep things hidden from me, it is deceitful, instead of gaining trust back by being an open book and proving yourself and allowing my insecurities and fears to diminish because I would know that at any time I could look through things or you would tell me up-front about things. Then I wouldn't feel so distrustful of you, and I wouldn't even feel a need to look at anything because the trust would be there." He said he makes decisions and doesn't tell me because of how I react. I said, "You are still being a dishonest person if you think it is okay to hide things from me because of what my reaction will be." He said it doesn't make him deceitful. I disagree!

Then he started again with, "this is my house." I said, "Seriously? You're going to be mean and try to go there again? This isn't your house; it is our house." He said, "It was mine when you moved in here." I said, "Okay, I have had enough. If you want to get mean and play dirty this will get ugly real fast" I walked away and went to our room.

The next morning after I tossed and turned most of the night, he came in to get dressed. I said to him in a very emotional way that I want him to stop calling me names and stop threatening me about the house. There is no reason for us to use names. Choking back my tears, I said, "Please, let's just be cordial. I can't do this anymore. It isn't okay; it is mean." He looked at me, and with a nasty look on his face and a nasty tone in his voice, he said, "Do you see how you're doing all of this? Do you see all this is your fault?" I said, "Stop. You don't get to blame me for your behavior; I just want the hurting to stop."

He may be sober, but he sure as hell isn't recovering very well. He is more arrogant and self-entitled than ever, feeling like he can act however he wants. This sucks. I thought sobriety was going to be awesome. I thought the DUI was a godsend, but not right now in this moment it sure isn't, because this sober man is worse than the drunk one.

February 12, 2013

Today is a very bad day. I told my husband I want a divorce. I just don't know how I can handle any more of this by myself.

He told me that he doesn't have to report back to me with everything he does because he isn't a child (in regard to keeping things from me). I said, "When you lied to me and hid another woman's phone number and played games about it, then here we are. You go to another woman's house behind my back without telling me, even if it was to try and help her because she is an addict. When you don't tell me and I have to find out all this stuff for myself, that makes you dishonest and deceitful." He said this was an unfortunate similar circumstance. Really? That's what I get? An unfortunate similarity— are you kidding me? He isn't supporting me through my process of healing the pain that I endured from his behaviors over the years. He continues to add more pain to it.

And now because he is sober four months, he is the almighty and he knows all and judges. His damn ego is bigger than he can handle. I would like to pull this pink cloud he is on right out from underneath him and hit him over the head with it. He is telling me that what I feel is wrong and what I say is wrong. I mean, after almost thirteen years together, nothing is ours; it is still his house. I am not a priority for him, so why fight for something that never seemed to matter to him anyway?

It isn't just for me; it is for him too. Maybe he would be happier starting over with someone who hasn't been affected by his addiction problem and who hasn't been a part of all of this. That doesn't make sense either. We have so much history and so much love. We are lost. We need the time to find each other again. We will find a way to reconnect. I have to keep faith that we will be okay. Going out and being with someone else won't change how we feel about each other, and it won't fix anything, I know we can make it. We just have to keep believing and find the strength to grow from this.

I complain and talk about my hurt; I am sure he must hurt too. I want him to be happy. It would be nice if he wanted me to be happy too. I wish for things to be different with us, but I feel as though they are getting worse, not better. How many more years can one person be this unhappy before something has to change? It is a sick unhealthy life, and I have learned to live with it, but I don't want that anymore. I want joy in my life; I want to laugh and play. I want to be me, the fun-loving passionate person I am, and I want that with my husband. It isn't me to not want to be affectionate, but I got to the point where I am so sad and feel so alone that I don't have that drive to make that effort anymore. I just push him away and isolate myself. I have been emotionally beaten up so much, it has hurt my heart and my spark as a woman. I feel defeated.

February 13, 2013

As usual, before I opened my mouth maybe I should have really thought about it before I said divorce, but maybe it would be better for us. I don't know what the answer is. Why do we keep hurting each other? I don't want a divorce I just want him to get it!

I believe in marriage and I believe in standing by the person you love in their time of need, but this just can't be all about him all the time. It doesn't work that way. He is so selfish. I truly don't want a divorce. I don't know why I think saying that will make him suddenly pop out of this selfishness he has and he will see everything clearly and profess his love for me. I am being ridiculous, and I should apologize for even saying that. I need to find a better way to get through to him. What I said was wrong. I don't want to lose my marriage or my husband. I love him so much. I just need more from him. I need something significant at this point.

I tried to have a nice calm adult conversation with him, but he was in some kind of raw mood today, where he had the audacity to tell me that I needed him to be sick with his addiction and that I didn't stay because I loved him but because I am codependent and need him to be that way. Belittling my love and turning it into some sick cruel thing. I am so offended. See, what he does is he hears little pieces in recovery or therapy, and he latches onto them and twists them into what he heard, rather than what was actually said, and then attacks me with it because, notice, I am still being blamed here and he has stopped drinking.

I was hoping for a kind loving man; instead, he just attacks me emotionally to cripple me, and he knows it. What thrill does he get out of treating me that way? He is a coward. I do not like the man I see before me. Dare I say he is worse than the drunken man I married? Seriously, though, this is so much worse. This I believe is what's called a "dry drunk," or being sober but not in recovery. These are all things

I have read when researching alcoholism and trying desperately to still find answers and comfort in someone else's words of wisdom.

That is what I have read and learned about a "dry drunk" or "dry drunken syndrome." This was in some psychology article. It said, "Clients come to me thrilled that their loved one has stopped drinking, only to report that the relationship is as fragile and inexplicably worse than before! Confusion arises when both have desired sobriety, and yet now that it is here, wonder why the relationship seems to be on rockier ground than when the alcoholic was drinking." This can be the world of the "dry drunk." The term "dry drunk" is believed to have originated from twelve-step recovery groups. The description seems to be universal: one that abstains from alcohol, but is still struggling with the emotional and psychological maladies that may have fueled his or her addiction to begin with, and continue to have a stranglehold on his or her psyche. The only change such people have made is to stop drinking, but in other respects, their life remains the same. Friends and family complain that the "dry drunk" is almost as hard to be around as when he or she was drinking. In AA the term describes a person who hasn't touched alcohol in years, but has not yet managed to get sober.

People who turn to alcohol or drugs for comfort will do so because they find life difficult to manage. This is because they have poor coping skills and feel unable to deal with life on life's terms. They are still struggling to deal with life using their old flawed coping strategies. If any of us were to stop doing something that we were used to doing for years, something that was part of our everyday existence, we would need help emotionally and psychologically to work through that absence. Alcohol might have been a total embodiment of their being. Alcoholics *need* and *should want* to be responsible for all aspects of their recovery. Without working on and realizing that the emotional and spiritual aspects need just as much work as the physical part of recovery, the alcoholic may become lazy, irritable, easily annoyed, or quick to anger and will defend and justify at the slightest questioning or provocation. (*Wow,* are they talking about my husband here? They surely must be.)

See, everything makes sense when you take the time to understand and really absorb the meaning of all you learn about alcoholism. An open mind and positive attitude is a good place for recovering alcoholics to start, and it is imperative for them to deal with the painful issues that may have brought them to their addiction in the first place. It is the only way for any real progress toward a clean and healthy lifestyle to take place. Just because someone shows certain symptoms doesn't necessarily mean he or she is stuck in recovery; everyone has bad days, but these are symptoms to show that they may be stuck.

Individuals who have a low tolerance for stress easily get upset if things are *not* going their way. The dry drunk continues to *engage* in unhealthy behaviors. *Denial* can be as big a problem for the "dry drunk" as it can be for an addict. The individual may refuse to see that his or her life in recovery needs to change. Due to this denial, alcoholics may continue to live a miserable life indefinitely. Such people are likely to suffer self-pity because recovery isn't as satisfying as they expected and they feel cheated. The "dry drunk" tends to be full of pride and feels overconfident about his or her abilities. They will not seek help from others because they believe they already have all the answers. Such individuals may continue to engage in unethical behaviors.

Chapter 18

February 27, 2013

It has come to my attention that he is doing something that we both agreed would be looked at as a betrayal in our marriage. He justifies himself because it is something he "wants"; therefore it is okay to break your belief or your word that you have with your spouse because you're entitled. This way of thinking is very destructive, very selfish. Trust, once broken, I know is never the same again, but that isn't to say if you work hard at proving yourself, don't lie, don't hide things or do things that you know are wrong to begin with, then you may have a good chance at gaining trust back—maybe never completely, but it's better than someone believing you're a liar.

Because I found out on my own and asked him about it and he told me the truth, he feels that is being open with me, but that couldn't be farther from the truth. Did he tell the truth when I asked? Yes, I suppose he did; however, that isn't being up-front and open with someone. It is waiting until they find things out, and then when they come and confront you, then you admit it. It is still keeping things from your significant other when you should disclose something you know is wrong. He will say things to me like, "I know the choices I make are wrong. I just don't know how to change it." Clearly, if you're aware your choices aren't right, why not take steps toward changing that behavior? If you continue to make bad choices and not put forth the effort to change, everything stays the same, alcohol or not.

See, what's happening is he is in recovery, but he isn't following what's suggested in the program or putting this knowledge or the effort to work in his everyday life. He is in these meetings, and he tells himself he is doing good by going to them; to him that's change because, after all, he has all the answers already. But he can feel it too. I know he is wondering why things still suck. He knows he hasn't put his whole heart into this program yet, and until he can admit that and put 100 percent effort in, things will stay exactly the way they have been, and even get worse. You can't give up just because something is challenging for you; that is just the way life is.

No one said it is always easy, but if you love someone and want them in your life and you want a better life for yourself, you go to great lengths to make amends and try to resolve and understand why things went wrong in the first place. You tell them things like where you are going, when you will be home; you put no passwords, no locks on phones or computers. At the very least, they should be able to have your passwords, so they feel more secure; it would prove you have nothing to hide. If something comes up with someone of the opposite sex that you know he or she would not be okay with, then be up-front about it. Don't wait until they find out and start questioning you about it. That makes you look guilty as hell, even if you're not. This is something I live by, and everybody should.

When you are all alone with no one around and no one would ever find out what you do, you still need to make the right choices as though your spouse is standing right beside you; that shows good values, morals, and characteristics as a human being. If you're only doing the right things when someone is around, you're missing the lesson. One day at a time, one issue at a time, but when you're cold and closed off and don't want to hear about the things that you have done that hurt someone else, maybe you should have thought twice or three times before doing it in the first place. However, you can't change the past that is true. You can't remove the pain that someone feels in the moment, that is true, but people do heal. You will never be able to make up for everything, but you can show them what you're made of now. You can show them how much you care. You can clean up the mess you made piece by piece, but you have to be willing to do so. When we run from our challenges in life that is how we kill the power in ourselves.

There was a quote in a book I once read that said something like, "We leave one mess and go create another, and God doesn't get angry. We are thrown a towel to clean up the milk we spilled, to tell the truth, not lie, make amends, and if we spill the milk over and over again, we will keep being thrown the same problem and the same towel to clean it up, because God knows when we get tired of making a mess, we will stop spilling the milk." The quote means, "Clean up your mess. You can't run from it, so stop." I wish my husband could hear that. You can show that you are making changes. You can be a selfless person if you want to be. You can take accountability and responsibility, not only for you being an alcoholic but for the pain that came with your actions. You can't live in denial. You have nothing to lose by trying a recovery program, except for maybe terrible hangovers, blackouts, or forgetting how you lost your money. To me losing those things is worth it when you can gain a whole new life that is healthy. You can always go back to drinking, but why not give sobriety a shot? You just might find that life without addiction really has so much more to offer, and you feel great and have an opportunity to do the right things and make good choices. There is no failing if you try.

Instead of it being all about what you want or need, think about how it affects the other person and everyone else. Think about how it would make you feel if you had to spend a day in their shoes dealing with yourself. Sometimes people go through really hard times. The answer isn't to just leave and go from person to person, because everyone has troubles, some more than others. There will always be issues in every relationship, but when you love someone, shouldn't it be that you stand by their side and you get through it together as a team? Everyone on their own time will know when they have had what is enough for them. Some may have left early on, others stayed longer, and some never leave at all. We all have our own limitations, and no one has the right to judge that.

March 10, 2013

My mom went to the hospital again for another angiogram. Since the stent they put in during December, she has still been short of breath at times, and she knew something wasn't right. They put another stent into another blocked artery they missed when they went in the first time (go figure). They had to piggyback the first stent with a second, so now she has three stents in her heart. This is crazy; my mom who is never sick.

The doctor that came up to talk to us told us that my mom has progressive coronary artery disease. Sorry, what was that? Heart disease? Progressive? Are you kidding me? Those are not reassuring words to hear. She has never had anyone tell her anything about this before. This was really scary to hear. My mom has diabetes, and from everything I have read, 65 percent of diabetics have heart disease, but we were all shocked, no one more than my mom. She said it was the first she had ever heard of it. The doctor said that if she can find a statin that she can tolerate, along with an over-the-counter medicine that would help the muscle aches, it could give her fifteen more years of quality of life. What he meant was that the statins are very beneficial for someone like my mother because she will inevitably end up with more heart problems as the years go by, according to this doctor.

Lately, between my mother and father and their health, they are stressing me out even more. I love my parents. I want them to be around for many, many more years. I don't know what I would do without them. Mom just needs to relax and gain her energy back, and every day she will get stronger than before. I have faith in that. My mother is a strong little cookie. She is most definitely a bit of a spitfire. Hmmmm, I wonder where I get my attitude from. I love my mom. She is an amazing woman. She has always done so much for me and my family. She has a beautiful spirit.

March 21, 2013

I don't even know where to begin at this point. Let's start with my daughter's bio dad. He found her; however, he gave up his parental rights when she was a young infant, only ten months old. I tried for years after that for him to be a dad to her, but it never happened. He couldn't stay off the drugs long enough to get his life together, so when she was five, I had to put a stop to his inconsistencies and move on with our lives. He was rarely around anyway, and he was never a "father" to her, so that was that. She hasn't seen him and she doesn't want anything to do with him, but one of his family members went to her work asking her questions, being pushy; I consider it harassing her. She called me crying from work; she was scared. I felt a terrible pit in the bottom of my stomach. She was so shaken up, they made her go home. It's bullshit. I won't stand for it; I will put a stop to this if it happens again. I won't stand by and allow anyone to bother my daughter. I don't care if she is nine, nineteen, or thirty-nine; I will always stand by her side in any situation.

Then my dad went to the hospital again. He is having big problems with his colon. They admitted him for the night. He has what appears to be a blockage. Seriously, could my poor father catch a small break here? I mean, he retired and became sick. He was never sick while he worked. He worked so hard all his life, has always done good for others, and this is what he gets. He deserves so much more. He is a great man.

I see how the MS has caused him great depression. I want to see him smile and hear him laugh. They have to do further testing to see if they need to do surgery, and if so, how they will go about taking care of this situation. He is no longer able to walk alone without assistance. He has no balance, and his right leg is a dead leg, which he drags when he does walk with his walker. It is so tough to watch your parents not only age, but age with health issues. I don't want them to ever feel any pain or be uncomfortable. I want them to be healthy and happy to enjoy their lives.

I would be lying if I didn't say I am feeling the stress from all these things that are happening in my life, and all at once. I know it could be much worse, but my mom got out of the hospital, and a week later my father went in. We joke around though and say he had to show my mom up because no one was paying attention to him. I know so many others have it so much worse, and even on my bad days I need to be grateful for all the blessings we do have. But it is tough sometimes to find the blessings in the bad, but you really have to; otherwise you miss the good. We are all one big family, including my friends. I am so grateful for the bunch of goofballs I get to call mine.

Finally, we went to court for my husband's DUI on the nineteenth of this month and here is what happened. The DA was presenting his case against my husband, questioning the officer who arrested him, and his attorney cross-examining, and so on. Then it was my husband's attorney's turn, and guess what? Surprise *he called me to the stand, not my husband like he told us before court. I was in* shock. *What, why me? I wasn't nervous; well, I was a little, but I was more surprised. I did not see that coming! I was sworn in, and my husband's attorney was asking me questions about where the ignition is in my husband's car because there was a question as to whether or not the officer could see the keys hanging in the ignition from the window and so on.*

Then the DA cross-examined me, and he was all set to go; you could tell. Right off the bat he said, "Does your husband have a drinking problem?" My response was, "Yes, he does." I have never seen someone that speechless in court; he had a deer-in-the-headlights look. He had no idea what to do with my honesty—priceless. *I think he was expecting me to say* no, *but* surprise, *I wasn't about to lie, and I told my husband that a long time ago. The DA asked if he had a drink since the incident. I replied, "No, he has been sober almost six months. He has been to an intensive outpatient program for five weeks, and he goes to AA meetings most every day of the week now!" I believe the DA was also surprised to hear that. He asked if I was "partial" to my husband, and I said, "If you're asking if I would lie for him, the answer is no, I would not, but of course I am partial. He is my husband. That was a dumb question." Then he said, "Has your husband driven drunk before?" I hesitated and looked at the judge, and then said, "Do I have to answer that question?" (Obviously you know what the answer was), but I was told I did not, something that had to do with the law. That wasn't what he was there for, so it had no relevance. I mean, I get what he was trying to do, but you can't hold him accountable for anything but what he was charged for.*

After all was said and done, the judge explained why he reached his decision, which is not guilty, charges dropped. *Holy shit, are you kidding me? Really? Charges dropped? I couldn't believe it, but to be honest, my heart sank a little because for a moment I thought,* oh God, if my husband feels any more entitled or his ego gets any bigger, he may feel he is untouchable and 'look, I can drink and *not* get a DUI.' *All I could do was pray the lesson was strong enough and scared him enough to this point to realize that he feels so much better sober, and maybe now life could start to get better for us. Maybe he would be grateful enough that he got this chance to make things right.*

I couldn't believe it he was so lucky; we were lucky that he didn't lose his job, health insurance, the house, and so on. It was scary; I am so glad that part is over. The judge said they worry about the people who drive and impede traffic, the person passed out hunched over his or her steering wheel in a parking lot with the engine running, people driving while drunk, and so on. My husband did the right thing, even though he was drunk. Thank goodness this part is behind us—no extra fines, no insurance increase, and no job loss.

March 26, 2013

Today I went to the specialist with my dad. They are going to do a surgical procedure tomorrow to see if they can figure out if they can take care of his problem without doing a big surgery. He is worried. I am worried. He has been through so much with his health, I just want it to be simple and easy for him so he can feel good and enjoy the rest of his life without pain, without limitations, to be happy and not be so sad!

The DUI is behind us so now the real test begins to see what happens: if he continues his sobriety and continues to grow and starts to make the right choices, or if he stays selfish and just stays away from the alcohol but changes nothing more than that. Only time will tell. To me, my husband still has many of the same characteristics and behaviors as when he drank. I know change doesn't happen overnight, but I suppose I was expecting a bit more than what I have seen thus far. You can remove the drink or the drug, but if you don't make any spiritual or emotional changes, then life as you knew it will not change. Substance or not, it appears the same, but when behaviors and old thinking start to change, boy, that is when you really start to feel different and see things from a whole new perspective.

Everyone is different. It may be quicker for others, but every day is a new day to wake up and make a choice to not drink for today. If a moment of clarity shines and I get a sneak peek of understanding from him, I become so hopeful and I feel this could be the beginning of a changed man. But then within a short time, that clarity is gone

*and it no longer shines; the darkness appears once again, and in front
of me is the man I have known all these years—no change!*

*Recently over the past week, I was having a feel-sorry-for-myself moment,
dumping lots of emotions onto a friend; afterward I felt so awful about
it. I apologized for spewing my emotional baggage everywhere, and he
said to me, "Let me be the judge of what I can handle. I'm here to carry
your weight when you can't. Remember that always." I needed to hear
that. It made me feel not so alone in the world knowing I have people
who care about me every day, knowing I have a friend or two.*

April 11, 2013

*He knows that I feel as though he may be being unfaithful to me, yet
all he can say to me is that I am crazy. I am not crazy. I am feeling
completely insecure, and I'm hurting; I am hurting deep down in my
soul. What's crazy is allowing your wife to continue thinking you're
unfaithful because you apparently think it is a big joke.*

*I know I have hounded him about it the past few months, so I am
sure he is sick of the accusations, but I just want to know without a
doubt that it isn't true. I used to feel so loved, so adored. I felt how in
love he was with me, and now I feel very heartbroken, almost like he
can't stand me, and it hurts more than I can express.*

*I feel like he is manipulating me and wanting me to feel as though he
is unfaithful, like some kind of control mind game; maybe he wants
me to leave him, and he thinks that if he hurts me enough, I will
go. I don't know what is happening at this point; I don't get it. He
is always out from morning till late night, doesn't show any interest
in me or us, and if he does it is short-lived; I feel as though he has
given up. He has always shown that no matter what, he is going to
do whatever he wants to do, and he doesn't care how much it may
hurt me. The only thing that he cares about is feeling like he has the
control to do what he pleases and when.*

April 12, 2013

This morning I was getting ready, and he came into the bathroom and said, "I know you're in pain and all, but ..." There is no but; I am in pain, period. He said it isn't fair that I peg him as guilty; I said, "That is what it looks like, and I want us to talk about it and work through it, to know that what I feel really isn't the case at all." (Even though he has told me a hundred times before that there has never and would never be anything with this woman, or anyone else for that matter.)

You know what, though? He is right. It isn't fair that because it looks one way to me, I assume he is doing things that he says he has never done. At this point I am so convinced that he is unfaithful; I need more than just his words of, "I am not doing anything." In the same breath he will say to me who he talks to is none of my business and hides phone messages, so you do the math on where the doubt stems from. His actions aren't right either, so I continue to feel very insecure and unsure of his loyalty; when he treats me like, "hey, things are none of your business" and doesn't seem to care if I hurt, then what other conclusion could I possibly come to?

If someone would have come to me and said, "Hey, things are going to get worse when he stops drinking," I would have said, "You are frigging crazy. They will be so much better." Well, I was wrong; they are far worse than I could have ever imagined. I don't understand. I am baffled. I didn't marry a cheater or a liar, but over the years his behaviors have become so destructive, he doesn't seem to care how it affects anyone, especially me, his wife.

And to make matters worse, he texted me last night at 10:00 p.m. after the dinner he went to, saying I could close the gate; he took a room at the hotel. I called him immediately after that message three times, and he wouldn't answer. Now, ask me again how I could possibly think you are unfaithful. It is actions like that that make

me feel like he is messing with my head; it is so wrong and mean.
When I got that message, I absolutely freaked out. I got sick to my
stomach. I started crying uncontrollably. I mean, I lost it. I thought,
there it is; that is the sign that he is being unfaithful *we live ten*
minutes away. There isn't a reason for him to stay at a hotel room.
Realistically, though, it is probably because he is tired of this crap that
we go through, so why come home? But in the same breath, why do
that to your wife when she has already gone through so much hurt
and continues feeling as though you have betrayed her? Why not ease
her mind and heart? Have empathy.
I called a friend of mine. I had a complete meltdown, and he said,
"If you want to know what's going on, go down there and find out
for yourself." I couldn't do it. I couldn't stop crying long enough to
gain my composure. I probably would have been arrested, looking
like a crazy woman running through a hotel, when really I am just
heartbroken and want to know my husband is honest and loves me.
If I could have pulled myself together long enough I would have gone
down there to his room and seen for myself if anything was going on.

April 27, 2013

The past week I have been called a bitch, told I am an idiot, flipped
off, told to fuck off, fuck you, and so on, all because if there is an
issue that comes up that he doesn't want to talk about or he doesn't
like what he hears, he gets defensive in an aggressive nasty way. He
has been exceptionally terrible to me the past few weeks. It has been
hurtful and exhausting. What the hell has happened to us, to the
passion and great love we once shared? It is definitely lost. I hope
we can find each other again and not give up. I mean, he is going
on almost seven months sobriety, and these are the same behaviors
as when he was drinking, only intensified. How can he not see that
or feel that? And how, I ask, can he be worse than when he was

drinking? It doesn't make sense to me. I completely understand from a realistic approach when it comes to being sober but no living a truly sober life, but what I am saying is "why is he worse"? Why hasn't this helped him in the ways I had hoped for? Is this the man he really is underneath it all, worse?

He came home from work today and said he is sorry he has been such an asshole to me this week; he said he knows he has blown up at me and he doesn't know why he is so angry. He said, "I know it may look like I have been unfaithful, but I haven't been. I do love you. I don't want to lose my marriage. There has never and would never be anyone else but you." That is a start of what I need to hear. Finally some validity to how I feel, and an apology is always nice to hear. It makes me feel like he is starting to understand when he does something that is hurtful and tries to make amends for it. I said, "Words are just words at this point without action to back it up and show that what you say you truly mean. You can't justify lying to me because I get upset. That is wrong. A lie is a lie no matter what the other person's reaction may be!" He said he doesn't want to be that man who lies to his wife; he said, "I am trying to change." I really believe he wants to change; I believe that with all my heart. I just wish I could see it.

Sadly those words sound so heartfelt, but they are just words. There have been so many broken promises. My gosh, that makes me so sad to hear myself say that. It shouldn't be that way. Make one promise to me and keep it. I need to know he can do that. I just want to jump in his arms, have him hold me and tell me everything will be okay. Why do I prevent myself from doing that? Because I am so scared, that's why. I miss him so much. I actually ache in my heart for my husband. Please, God, help me, help us. I want to believe him. Please, just show me this time you really mean what you say. That is all I need, all I need to know. Give me a reason to believe you again, please, just one reason.

May 10, 2013

The past week he has been a monster, being terribly verbally abusive to me. Why? What did I do now?

So tonight he comes home after his meeting. He said to me that the guys would tell him if he is being a jerk and call him on his actions, which I think is great, that he has people that will be honest with him on things he may not be able to see himself and he listens to them. He said the topic tonight was relationships, and one guy said to him that he is willing to hold out a hand to welcome in and support a newcomer, but he doesn't do the same for his own wife.

He said that he didn't realize that until one of the guys pointed it out to him. It really stopped him and made him think. He said he was so sorry for treating me that way. He seems to be trying harder at doing things a little different, like correct himself when he does something that isn't right. I know change is hard and it is all going to be one day at a time, but we have to move toward that change every day for it to happen.

He was on the phone with some woman, and I heard something that sounded odd to me, so I asked him about it. His response was, "Are you eavesdropping?" I said, "No, you were standing right next to me." See? That is what I mean. It isn't okay; it is disrespectful and hurtful. Later that night he said, "I shouldn't have said that to you. It wasn't right of me." At least he corrected himself, and he was aware that what he had done was wrong. You have to be careful though because when you blurt hurtful things out an apology is nice but it doesn't take away any damage that has already been inflicted from those words. I read a quote recently that said something like "ten seconds on the lips, ten years in the heart" true statement.

It seems to me that he is learning and growing, and I am so happy about that. I am proud of him, and I should tell him that more often.

June 4, 2013

I have been totally paranoid. It is making me crazy feeling as though he could be unfaithful, but yet not really knowing if he is or not. In my heart I don't want to believe he would ever do that to me, but things have been so bad and impossible lately, I have doubts and thoughts I don't really believe in; they just take over and play with my mind. I need to just trust him, don't I? So he thinks because things still aren't good between us that it couldn't possibly have been the alcohol, it couldn't have possibly been his drinking. What he doesn't seem to comprehend is it is the alcoholism and the behaviors that come along with it that have been the problem all along.

Here are my thoughts about that ... I mean, yes, that makes you an alcoholic and it causes your mind to react in certain ways that others don't, but the addiction part, the mental obsession part, is where it gets tricky. You have to work on your mind, get in touch with your emotions, work on your spirit, strengthen your heart, practice doing what's right from wrong, take accountability and responsibility for the destruction you have caused, and make amends. That doesn't make you a bad person; it makes you someone that is getting in touch with real life, not the false reality you have lived in for so long. Living in a bottle shelters you from seeing the way things have really been. When you make amends, it has to come from deep inside your heart, not because you read in a book that it is something you have to do, so you half-ass it to make yourself feel better, because realistically, you will feel much worse. It all has to be genuine for it to work in your life.

I see this in my husband. He is trying to fool himself and everybody else. He isn't being real; he isn't being honest. He is hurting more than ever. He is lost more than ever. He just wants to be accepted. He is still spiraling out of control, only this time it is without the alcohol, and I think that scares the shit out of him, but he doesn't want to say anything or ask for help because he feels like people will think he is weak or he will have to admit he was more powerless than he once believed himself to be. For him to let someone in enough to admit that he doesn't have it under control isn't going to happen until he completely surrenders, and he hasn't done that yet, even eight months into his sobriety. I wish he could hear me and realize I am here to help him, realize I love him more than anything and I want him to be healthy, but he doesn't want to hear he is still making bad choices because he feels he is entitled and knows all because he is now sober so he can't possibly be out of control.

Oh honey, we're going to lose it all. We already have. Please, please, don't let this happen. I believe he still thinks that it couldn't have possibly done as much damage to me as he has to himself. He has no clue what it's like to be me, to be on the other side of him. Otherwise, he would have empathy and compassion for what I have gone through and continue to go through as part of the collateral damage that comes from an addiction such as alcoholism. Last week he said to me that I am not a wife; I am just a codependent enabler. Seriously? After all these years I am just a codependent enabler? Really? What the hell is wrong with him? Ouch. That one really hurt. That will take time to heal from. After all I have done for our family, for him, for us, that's all he sees me as? Funny how you can love someone so much, and they walk around clueless as to how much their words or actions affect you. I know I did enable him, although I didn't know it at the time, but that doesn't take away from me being the wife I have been. It doesn't make me less than what I am.

He said to me that if we aren't "fixed" by the time he is sober for a year, then he will know it wasn't the alcohol. How can he be serious about that? He doesn't see his own reflection of how he himself hasn't changed behaviors or actions. Just because he has stopped drinking, he thinks he has made all these changes. And somehow he thinks everything will magically be okay in our life without much effort from him just because he has removed alcohol from his life. The truth is he really hasn't done a lot more than stop drinking and attend meetings; if you don't work the steps, if you don't change old destructive behaviors, there is going to be very little change. Truth is, he is just lying to himself and everyone else. I know him better than anyone, and nothing has changed. Well, I take that back. Something has changed. He is more self- absorbed, smug, arrogant, and selfish than I have ever seen, and it makes me sick.

Don't get me wrong, I am so proud of him for not drinking. I know it is a process, and a lifelong one at that, but at times he gets too self-righteous, thinking he has done all he can to change, when really he hasn't done much of the real hard work. I believe he will be successful. I know he can do it. I believe in him. I know what kind of man he is, even if he doesn't yet. He will get it, hopefully sooner than later, before more destruction is caused. I know it sounds like I contradict myself. I am just real about things. I hold onto hope to find my strength, but that doesn't mean I don't see the way he really is right now.

I will proudly take his hand, and side by side I will go through this journey with him because I believe, once we find us again, we will be nothing short of extraordinary.

At times he has clarity, which is wonderful, and I know those moments will eventually expand and become longer moments until it becomes the way he lives his life every day. He is learning every day, much like a child who never really knew how to be. He is learning how to live without his crutch, his safety net of addiction, and what is most comfortable to him is turning to old behaviors. New ones don't feel right, but the old way is destructive. As time goes on, I believe he will start to make healthier choices and learn how to deal with things in a more positive way. When he spends most of his time away from home and keeps running from everything and doesn't want to work on us, how the hell can you expect it to be anything different than what it has been? When old behaviors change, then everything else will start to change too.

He found out today that a guy he was trying to help (who actually asked him to be his sponsor but it was too soon for my husband) that he met at a meeting a few months back took his own life. He said that this man drove down the street and he put a gun to his head and pulled the trigger, alcoholism once again has taken another life, it is such a serious disease and can be deadly that's why I just want him to be healthy and change things. I don't want to lose my husband, the thought of that just makes me feel so sick to my stomach; it is very concerning to me.

My husband was very upset. I came home, hugged him, and listened. I was trying to be there for him. Things are very strained between us. I am doing the best I can.

My own feelings started becoming overwhelming, and things got tense. I started thinking that could have been my husband that lost his life. I got very emotional, hoping it would have a greater effect on my husband in a more personal way, looking at his own life and wife and the tragedy that is left behind when something like that happens to a family. My heart goes out to that man's family, to his poor wife, who now faces life alone, with so many questions unanswered and the heartache she must feel losing the man she loves to his addiction. I will be going with him to the service for support. We do find ways to still come together. It's just sad the way this whole thing has turned out. We have to find another way, a better way.

At this point I don't know if I should just throw my hands up. I try so hard to be understood by a man who seems to have no interest in understanding my feelings; it is just about him and what he needs and what I can do for him. I thought once he became sober, he would grow and be different, but he is worse towards me. It is like he can help every stranger with an addiction problem, but he won't hold his hand out to help his own wife. Another fellow alcoholic took his own life, how does that not affect him in a deeper way thinking about his own life?

July 27, 2013

Mom's in the hospital again for some internal bleeding. They have to scope her to find out what is going on. My husband and I are not doing well at all. Things are worse than ever, and five minutes after I walked in the door, something was happening with my father. My husband heard that something bad was happening with Dad, yet he just got in bed to take a nap instead of putting his feelings aside and coming with me to help.

Once I got home a few hours later, he was on the couch using the I-Pad, so I took a shower and watched a movie. All this time he is still on the I-Pad.

Hours later he left to go out, so I got the I-Pad to play my games. I hit the history bar—honestly by accident—and I saw photos of half-naked/naked women come up. I was so disgusted that at that point, when I needed him to be there for me for family, with Mom in the hospital and Dad having problems after his surgery, he is busy looking at things he shouldn't be looking at anyway.

He said that I need to worry about myself and not what he is doing because he is going to talk to whoever he wants, look at who he wants, do what he wants, oh, and he is changing all his passwords so I can't "spy" on him. Grow the hell up. If you had nothing to hide and you weren't doing anything wrong, then your passwords and being transparent wouldn't be an issue for you. This is why I have trust issues with this man; he can't be open and he hides things. I mean, he even went as far as blocking me on Facebook. Seriously, I had enough, so I took it one step further; I became just as childish, and I just deleted him off my Facebook so he wouldn't have to worry about anything I saw that he did. Shit, he even blocked our daughter. I mean really, at this point, what the hell are you doing? You are a fifty-year-old man that needs to change. Stop continuing to cause havoc to our family and our marriage. Isn't the destruction that has already been inflicted on our family by you enough? I'm sick and tired of all the secrets. He can do whatever he feels he needs to. I can't take it anymore. He can keep his secrets, lies, and betrayals if that is the life he chooses to live, but I can't do it.

A week later he came home from work and said, "I know you're in a lot of pain, and I have noticed you haven't talked to me for a week." He said he knew it was his fault, and he wanted me to know he was sorry for the way he was acting. I said, "What are you doing? You're giving your number out to all these women you don't know and you're looking at naked photos." He turned the blame onto me and then said, "I am not cheating right now." I said, "'Right now'? What the hell does that mean?" That didn't make me feel good in any way at all. He said he didn't mean it the way it came across. Choose your words carefully.

When he came home from work today, I could tell he was in a mood. Right away he jumped on our daughter, and she jumped back. Next thing you know, they started to argue. It is a bad situation, and as much as I do not want my daughter to move out, I feel the sooner she can be away from him, the better, because, let's face it, their relationship won't get any better as long as she is here in the middle of whatever this shitstorm that has been brewing is.

August 6, 2013

He moved a bed into his office. He has decided he needs space to figure out if he wants to be married anymore. This is what it has come to after all these years.

The past five days I have been freaking out, crying a lot. It is very painful. Then it hit me when I walked in the door from work at 2:00 a.m. to find that my husband did not come back to our room and hasn't asked for his ring back. He really means it. He doesn't know if he wants to be my husband anymore. Maybe he doesn't love me; maybe this is really it for us. After all these years, maybe there is nothing left for us. I don't want to believe that to be true. I thought after our heart-to-heart conversation, that it would have made a difference, but he didn't want to make the effort to try. I guess maybe he won't ever be capable of loving me the way I want to be loved, the way I deserve to be.

August 9, 2013

My husband told me this morning he didn't know if he wanted to be married anymore and he wants to separate. Separate? *Are you serious? What has happened to us? What happened to the man who loved me so much, was so grateful for my love, and adored me like no other? The only woman he has ever had eyes for or been in love with? How did my husband become this sober man that is more destructive than the drunken one? He has become so cold and shut off from life; he is in a very dark destructive place, and I am terrified of the outcome. Why has he given up after all these years together? I weathered through the worst of life's tribulations with him, so he just bails on me? What am I going to do without him in my life, the last man I thought I would ever be with, that I ever wanted to be with? I have been here through it all, and after less than a year of sobriety, he is just going to walk out on our marriage. This is tragic.*

Is there any hope left? Can a miracle come out of this wreckage? I can't believe this. I am devastated. My husband wants to be apart; he has given up on me. I feel like someone just punched me in my heart. Life as I know it has been shattered into a million pieces. Where do I go from here? I realize that the way I went about some things was wrong. I was trying to get him to notice me and love me, and instead, I just pushed him away. We both took what we had for granted. Shame on us.

August 10, 2013

We talked a little last night, and he still said he wants to separate. When I asked what that means, he said he is living on the other side of the house and needs space and time to decide if he is going to stay and if he wants to be married anymore. He said for all intents and purposes, we live together; we are married, but not husband and wife.

Oh no, this sounds like bullshit. That isn't right. We are husband and wife. I said, "It is not okay with me for you to be with any other woman, because I wouldn't do that. This is not what this will be about." I made it very clear this is not about being with anyone else, period. It sounded like an excuse for him to behave badly to me. I don't know what is going on, but I am sick to death over it. I have made mistakes, but given all he has done over the years, he has no right to treat me this way. I want to start over and start fresh, but he doesn't know if he does, so all I can do is wait and see what happens. I handled things wrong, though. I shouldn't have suppressed my love and stopped giving affection. I don't know what I was thinking (I wasn't thinking). That isn't a way to get love; it is how you push someone away. I didn't see what I was doing, though, until now. I really truly didn't. It wasn't intentional to hurt him. I was so lost and hurt myself with his addiction. We all became sick from it, but I don't think he gets that it has affected more than just him and how much it has in fact made me very sick as well and in what ways. I guess after all this time, all his bad behaviors year after year are acceptable, but my mishaps are not. Talk about one-sided, selfish, and hypocritical. He stopped making an effort, I stopped making an effort, and we stopped being close. I got tired of chasing after him. He just kept running and running, never looked back, and I suppose it wouldn't have mattered, but maybe if he looked back once in a while when he was running, he would have seen the destruction he left behind, the broken hearts, the broken family, the tears, the broken home trying to be kept together by me and me alone.

We have been together over thirteen years. In my eyes we are worth fighting for. I feel like he just wants to be alone to do whatever he wants; he doesn't want to be committed in a marriage, and that is a very painful thought to feel. If he wants to walk away, I will have no choice at that point than to let him go. I don't know if I can do that or how to let the man I love go. As much as it pains me to say it, all I can do at this point is pray for a miracle that somehow someway he finds the love we share in his heart again. His wedding ring is still off, and he stays out all the time. I am an emotional wreck. I can't handle what is happening, not right now. I can't do this.

I want to forgive one another for the mistakes we have made and move forward hand in hand, not to be separated though in the same house. It is so hard. This is ridiculous. Then again, at the same time, I don't want him to leave either, because I feel like if he does, he will never come home; he may never find his way back. I can't go through this every single day. It is too painful, almost torture, for me.

He runs around and does whatever he wants with new people he has met, and he seems to have no regard for how much I am hurting and seems to be having the time of his life. He will sit in the other room and text women all hours of the night. He goes to lunch or dinner with other women. I have seen these messages, and he uses pet names like "babe" or "baby." It makes me sick. It makes me feel like a worthless piece of crap that he can carry on that way in the same house with me, his wife, and our daughter. How can he hurt me so deeply and not see the pain? Someone told me they saw him out having dinner with another woman one night. Talk about feeling embarrassed, so ashamed, and so sick to my stomach. My insides were just churning. When I asked about it, he lied to my face and had the audacity to ask me if I was having him followed. That is what you're concerned about, not the fact that you are a married man carrying on this way. Talk about degrading to me.

He may be sober, but he sure doesn't seem to be getting healthy. He seems to have gotten so much worse. His ego and self-entitlement are through the roof, and he tramples all over me like I don't exist, like he is God and has all the answers. This is not a man who is working his program in any way, shape, or form. It is easy for my husband to put on a face for those who do not know him. He may have everyone else fooled, but not me, sweetheart. I know you inside and out and at times better than you know yourself, and you're self-destructing again and making bad choices. You act like you're happy, but you are miserable and scared. This will come to a terrible ending if you don't figure this shit out now and stop this behavior and the terrible actions I can only imagine you are doing behind my back.

Someone is always watching you, honey. Even if you think he isn't, your God is always there. If my husband doesn't utilize the tools that are sitting right in front of him to change his life, I fear he will one day drink again, and along with the other terrible choices, he will have lost everything, created even more pain, and he will ultimately kill himself this time. I hope God finds you first or you find God, and he guides you down a good path of morals, values, self-confidence, and a pride you can be proud of, for I want my husband to be happy more than anything, but he has to be healthy first. This isn't healthy. He has become a very cold man. Where has the love of my life gone? Can he be saved?

Chapter 19

August 31, 2013

I had a little emotional breakdown yesterday. It was hard on me and him too, I suppose. At this point, with the way he is behaving, I am not too concerned if it bothered him. I am the one who is clearly having a hard time just functioning in everyday life. How about some compassion for me? I can't help it. I want to save our marriage. I miss my husband. I miss the love and passion we once shared. I made a terrible mistake by pushing him away and asking him to leave because I thought he might be unfaithful. I hurt him deeply. I see that now, and I want to make up for that.

He has told me from day one that there is absolutely zero attraction to this other woman that I suspected things may have happened with. He said there has never been anything and there would never be anything ever *with her. I should have believed him. Funny thing is, I knew there was no way, but somewhere in my mind because we had been in such a bad place, there wasn't anything less it could have been. The fact that we don't talk and he is sharing our personal issues with someone else and confiding in her, that bothers me. I know I contradict myself a lot, but my mind doesn't always think clearly right now! He has always said I am the only woman for him, and I should have let that be enough. The way he loves me should have been enough. I just wanted to be shown more is all I was looking for. Everyone needs more sometimes, right? It wasn't enough, not because I am greedy, but*

the way he behaved and treated me wasn't right; moments of love are
great, but it needed to be more consistent, more genuine.

Over the past six months, I have seen some of the messages this woman
has sent my husband, and she is way *too attached to him; she is*
married herself, and that is totally not acceptable to me, period. He
told me he finally saw what I was talking about with her recently
and that he took care of it she started trying to fish around for my
husband to compliment her and he let her know things she was saying
to him were not appropriate and it made him feel uncomfortable. I
was happy that he came to me and told me because he wanted me to
know that he did take care of it. Can I trust him, though, that he is
being honest with me? Do I have a choice? Did he really talk to her,
or is he just saying that to me? So much doubt for good reason. She
needs to worry about her own damn husband and pay attention to
her own marriage and stop with the messages to my *husband and*
back the hell off before I end up saying something. Normally I would
have said something a long time ago, but it is a situation that I can't
really explain at this time.

Enough said about that, because I know now that it was my mind
playing tricks on me and that he will now distance himself from
situations and women like that because it causes problems. He thought
it was just simple conversation he was having, he said there is no
attraction to her at all she actually tends to annoy him as he said
but he now realizes that he shouldn't confide in other women with
our personal issues. If he wants to confide in any woman, it will be
me, his wife. I swear when you think someone is being a friend, they
just have bad intentions; clearly she does. At least he sees the error
in his ways, and that is a learning experience for him. I surrender,
I have to surrender, my husband really needs to surrender, and I
mean wholeheartedly because what he is doing now is just inflating
his ego and he is becoming more self-centered. If he doesn't completely
surrender, he will never recover from his alcoholism.

September 1, 2013

He called me when I got off work last night and asked if I wanted to go meet him and watch this free country concert that was playing. He actually wanted to spend time with me. I was honestly shocked but excited. Maybe we can reconcile, save our marriage, and rebuild. I wanted to feel him hold me; put his arm around me, something, anything. I put my hand on his back and rubbed for just a second, and it felt kind of awkward from him so I stopped.

I asked him this morning what he was feeling last night; he said, "distance between us." I said, "Did you want to hug me, kiss me, hold my hand?" He said yes. I asked why he didn't. He said he didn't know; he said he was watching other couples being close, and it made him feel sad that we weren't like that anymore. I said, "You realize that you're creating distance between us, don't you? Don't stop yourself if you want to reach for me. Allow the process to happen. Let it be okay. I miss you, honey." We sat together in bed. I laid my head on his chest. I just wanted to be close to him again. I never wanted to leave that moment. After a while he was leaving. I said, "Wait a minute." I put my hands on his face. I said, "It will be okay," and I kissed him.

I feel so terrified, but I am trying. I am fighting through my pain, but it is not easy when you feel so defeated. I feel like he wants to be near me, he wants to come back, but he is fighting himself, and I don't understand. I don't believe he wants to live without me or our marriage. I feel like he is punishing himself for something, feeling almost as if he doesn't deserve my love because of all he has put me through maybe; I don't know. There is something, though. I can feel it, and I wish he would talk to me and get it out there so we can have a chance to move past whatever this is.

September 2, 2013

My husband told me today that he was unfaithful, that he had sex with another woman. I knew there was something terribly wrong; I could feel it. When he first came home, I went to his office and asked him to kiss me. He said, "You may never want to kiss me again after I tell you what I did." I stood in the doorway of his office, crying so deeply it took my breath away. I dropped to my knees, holding my stomach, yelling, "No, no, no, tell me you didn't, you didn't do that to me. How could you do that to me? How could you touch someone else?" He seemed so cold when he told me; I felt so alone, so betrayed. I know I have had my suspicions for the better part of the year that he was being unfaithful, but at the same time, he kept saying he wasn't. He would say, "Maybe those suspicions are heightened because of our lack of closeness," so I took that into consideration. I never had any proof, so I thought maybe I was overreacting—you know my mind was playing tricks on me. I know after thinking all this time it was a possibility, hearing it really happened seems like I shouldn't be so shocked, but I never convinced myself completely or wanted to believe in my heart that he would ever do something like that to me. I didn't want to believe it could be true. It was never real until this one terrible moment.

This was not with the woman I had my suspicions about. This was someone in a meeting he hardly knew that in my opinion took advantage of our bad situation to benefit herself, which pisses me off. My husband has his own responsibility in this tragedy he took part in. My worst fear came true: he betrayed me in the most ultimate heartbreaking way a husband could ever betray his wife. Shit just got real. How could he touch someone else or let someone touch him? Oh my God, just the thought of it, I am going to be sick. I feel like I am going to throw up. The pain I feel is heart-wrenching. How was I not enough? I loved him through every terrible thing he ever did, and this is how he feels I deserve to be treated? Oh my God, these images are going to keep haunting my mind.

He said it was a mistake. He isn't planning on ever talking to her or seeing her again. He said he didn't plan it; it just happened. How does it "just happen"? There's that old excuse: it wasn't my fault, it just happened! My husband was unfaithful. Are you fucking kidding me? This is a whole new level of destruction. He said he told himself that it was okay because he took his wedding ring off and he asked for a separation, but I made it very clear that it wasn't okay with me. He said he stopped the "indiscretion" just minutes after it started because he couldn't go through with it; he said it didn't feel right that it wasn't me. He said he felt so much guilt he had to tell me about it. I feel like I am going to be sick again. Oh my God, breathe, just breathe.

Oh, and this happened two weeks ago, so for two weeks he has looked at me every single day coming to our home, knowing what he had done, and me, I am running around like an asshole trying to save our marriage, showing him that I love him, pleading for him to give us a second chance and not give up while he is out screwing someone else. Damn it, we just went and watched a concert the other night. Did he feel guilty? Was he ashamed and thought he should do something nice for me? He did it to make himself feel better, I think.

I feel so stupid for going to any lengths I had to so I could show my husband the love I have for him and how our life together is not worth giving up on. Seems he already gave up on us. That really meant something to me. I thought that he wanted to spend time with me, like maybe he was starting to feel like he didn't want to lose our marriage. I was clearly wrong about that. He has completely broken my heart, destroyed any trust I had for him. I could write for hours about this, and I still don't think there are enough words to express the pain I really feel inside. I can't believe this. I can't breathe. I can't feel anything. I feel like I am going to die in pain right here on the floor, curled up in a ball, all alone. He cheats and then tries to justify it because he took his ring off and we were separated. Bullshit! *I guess I wasn't hurting enough. He really had to kick me while I was down. I wasn't in enough pain. Is this what "I don't love you" feels like? I feel as though I was worth so little to him; our marriage, our family, our whole life seems to have meant* absolutely nothing! *I stood by him all the years he drank, only to have him do this to me when he becomes sober? How is that for irony? I don't know what has happened to him, what he has turned into, but this isn't the man I know and fell in love with. My husband loved me, adored me. I was my husband's angel, his soul mate, the moon and stars. My husband was an honest faithful man. I don't know this cold cheating selfish monster he has become. It's like he is a shell of the man he used to be.*

He came up behind me while I was on the floor, curled up crying. He was hugging me; I just sat there. I didn't want him touching me. Then he left to go to a meeting, and as he was leaving, he turned and said, "I am dead inside." I guess maybe he is when he tells me, his wife, he was with someone else and then leaves me on the floor crying while my world is crashing around me. I thought to myself, he is dead inside? What an excuse, but hey, thanks, I feel fucking fantastic and so alive right now. I know he has no feelings toward this person, none. It wasn't about feelings; it wasn't about feelings. I can understand it wasn't something he intended to do or planned, but that doesn't take away the pain I feel deep inside. That doesn't make it right. He said he felt like he was taken advantage of because he had expressed how our marriage is really bad, how he moved into the other room, he didn't feel wanted, and we were separated, so someone took the opportunity during a weak moment. My whole world, my whole life as I know it, shattered into a million pieces in an instant because no one stops to think about what the consequences will be for everyone involved, especially the innocent who had no choice. How can we survive this? How can I survive this? I better never ever see this woman, especially in this moment. I will not be able to control how I will react.

September 7, 2013

I saw my therapist yesterday. Thank goodness, because I don't know which way is up or down. My mind is just spinning on overdrive. I feel like a zombie walking through life right now, not knowing how to function or if I can. This is truly devastating. I mean, the most heart-wrenching betrayal I could feel from the man who promised to love me till death do we part.

My therapist explained to me that what my husband did was not an intentional indiscretion; he didn't think about how he could hurt me, it just happened. Huh? What was that? This is ridiculous. This goes against everything I believe in. How is this remotely possible? I said, "How can I even have a thought about staying with him after this? I feel like I am crazy like there is something wrong with me for even thinking that. How can I still love him? Shouldn't I hate him? What is wrong with me?" She said, "In the past six months you had thoughts that he was being unfaithful, and the difference is that that would have been an intentional affair that was planned. I believe him when he says it just happened, it wasn't planned, and that is why he stopped it just after it started; he didn't allow it to finish because somewhere in his mind, he knew enough to know that what he was doing was wrong and he stopped it. Although that sounds terrible, I know, and doesn't excuse his behavior, it shows that there is hope for him. You're still in his mind and in his heart enough to stop what he was doing, knowing he made a terrible, terrible mistake."

I felt like I was going to throw up again. As cliché as that sounded, I got what she was saying. So does that mean there is a way to survive this? Can we come out stronger and more in love? How is that even possible? This goes against everything I have always thought. When I left her office that day, I was numb, but in the same breath it was like the fog was lifted from my mind and I got it. My A-ha moment hit me, and it hit me hard.

She said to explain to him how I was completely unaware at what I was doing when I withheld love from him, to share all of my feelings about what I experienced through our destruction. I didn't do it knowing what was happening; I was oblivious to what my own actions were causing. I didn't see he was hurting, because I was hurting so much myself. I was responsible for causing heartache to my own husband inadvertently while trying to achieve the great love we both wanted to feel from one another—that is a powerful realization for one to have. I own that. I take accountability for it. I must have hurt him terribly, and I didn't get it until now. I only saw my own pain. I do have things that I am responsible for doing wrong through our relationship, and I suppose it was just easier to blame him because he was responsible for causing most of the destruction, but that doesn't mean I didn't play a part in it too.

That is where I have to be honest with myself. I have to make my own amends to my husband for the ways I hurt him too, because that is the right thing to do. I wasn't the only one who was hurting. So was my husband, and I suppose in some ways, I thought that he couldn't possibly be hurting because of the way he was always out and seemed so cold, when in reality he was hurting just as much as I was. He just didn't know how else to express it except to run from the pain. My actions are part of the reason why he shut down. I in no way take any blame for his indiscretion. That was all him. It wasn't my fault. Then why do I feel like I am somehow to blame? I will tell you why. Because I have been blamed for years that everything was my fault; that is why I question myself, even though I know better.

I was where he is now, not being unfaithful but in a very dark hopeless place. You feel like you just want to give up and run. You become numb to life. You have little to no hope of coming out of it and ever feeling different. You can't give up. As painful as it is, you have to fight. You have to hold onto hope wherever you can find it, and that gives you strength in ways you never thought were possible. I have always loved him. I never stopped, and I never intentionally tried to hurt him. It hurts me to think that I did hurt him and didn't even realize what I had done. I can't explain it, but once she explained it to me from a psychological perspective, I felt something change inside of me that has given me the hope to give true and complete forgiveness to my husband, to let go of the past hurts and resentments and really show my love for him again for the first time in years. Would I be able to do this?

I know it sounds crazy that something could happen like that, but it did, and in that moment I walked out of her office feeling relieved. I know I sound insane, but I actually had a clear mind about what had happened. She gave me the hope that couples can come out of infidelity sometimes stronger than ever, so if forgiveness and a new start for us is what it would take, then I was going to give it my all because I still love this man and I still believe in us and a second chance at an amazing life between us. I feel crazy, like what's wrong with me to feel this way, but she assures me it is normal. The pain is still with me. It is deep inside my heart and soul, and I honestly don't know if it will ever go away completely, but I had to allow the healing process to begin so it wouldn't take over my life. I don't know how to feel better, but I had to try.

How could I ever trust him again? I will always question where he is, his messages, phone calls, e-mails, but you know what? That is something he will have to deal with and be open about. After all, look at what his actions have caused in our life. He has been fighting a battle within himself trying to get over the sadness and pain he feels from what our life had become and what his life had become due to alcoholism; he has love inside. He still loves me, doesn't he? Or is he really dead inside? I am determined to not believe that. I will find his heart again. I will show my love and persistence and melt away what he thinks is dead and the coldness that has grown around his heart. My perseverance will pay off. We will finally have the life we had always tried to have together. Wow, I do sound crazy, I find out my husband is unfaithful, and I am thinking about how things can be better between us. I have a lot to heal from. These are things he should be doing for me, for us.

Today he said he was ready to talk divorce. Wait a minute, what? It is because of the guilt. Divorce is ugly and mean; it is not a fun place to be or go through. I for one don't want that if there is a possibility we don't have to. If he wants to leave, I have to let him. I can't fight anymore. If forgiving the ultimate betrayal and loving him isn't enough for him, then there is nothing left. I have to turn it over now to help us heal and connect again as husband and wife because I don't know how else to be. I am in so much pain.

I don't know what to do to make it right. People say talk to God, he will listen. So I am talking and praying, hoping for a sign. For the first time ever in my life, I sat on my bed and cried for hours and hours until I felt like I had been punched and kicked till there was nothing left inside me. I had never felt more alone in my life. I was so ashamed. I felt dirty. I didn't want to reach for anyone. I was so emotionally exhausted, feeling pain like I have never felt before, and I had a newborn go through open-heart surgery. I know heartache, but this was excruciating for me in ways I can't explain. I was wondering how this could have happened, why it happened, and what I could have done differently to have had a different outcome?

And just then, through puffy clouded eyes, I looked over and saw a pill bottle on my nightstand full of Xanax. I reached for it and poured all the pills out in my hand, wondering with warm tears streaming down my face, how many it would take to swallow before the pain would stop, before the tears would stop falling, before I wouldn't feel so worthless, so unloved, so unwanted, so empty, before my heart would stop beating. I sat there in a total state of shock contemplating for a moment what to do. I didn't want to die, did I? No, I just wanted the pain to go away.

I stared at the pills for a few minutes, not knowing what to do, if I should just swallow them all or not—and then I thought about my daughter. How could I do that to her? I couldn't leave her. I love her way too much, and I didn't really want to end my life, and I certainly couldn't let her come home and find her mom in bed after swallowing a bottle of pills, so I made a choice to put them all back except for what I knew would be a safe amount, instead of taking the chance that I may never wake up again because there would be no hope for resolution if I was dead.

I knew he would come home and maybe not even realize there was a problem, and there was not a chance in hell I could do that to my daughter. My daughter has given me the strength in my life to be the woman I have become, and I raised her to be just as strong. So I had to be strong for her and for myself. I had to be stronger than my darkest moments of weakness, and I found some shred of hope to hang onto, and that became my strength. I would never want to hurt myself, but in a moment of great sadness and darkness, I felt so much pain that I understood how people feel so lost, hurt, alone, and defeated that in their minds there simply isn't another way to make the pain they feel go away.

After I put the pill bottle down and before I passed out, I sat there. I looked up. I put my hands in the air, choking back my tears and heartache, and said, "God, I surrender. I need help. I can't do this on my own. Please help me. Please show me the way." I kept repeating, "Please help me," and then I prayed for my husband. I closed my eyes, and with all my heart, I said, "God, please help him find his way. Help his heart to soften. Help him find the right path. Help him to completely surrender so we can find our way back as husband and wife. Please wrap your love around him today. Keep him safe."

As I sat there staring out in front of me through clouded eyes, all of a sudden from head to toe, there was a warm flushing sensation that went through my entire body slowly, as if I was being hugged from the inside out. I have to be honest. I was totally freaked out and felt a sense of calmness at the same time. That's when I must have passed out from the emotional exhaustion. This was truly a higher power working through me. I just can't put into words how phenomenal it felt, because in that very moment, my whole life would change.

I know I sound crazy, but my dearest friend is very religious, so later I called her and told her that she wasn't going to believe what happened to me. She cried and said, "That was God letting you know you aren't alone." She was so excited. I suppose in that moment when I needed a sign, I was sent one in the form of eternal love from a power greater than myself. I pray that others can find a way to deal with the pain as I have, because ending a life that is so precious to those who love you truly is a tragedy. Always reach for help; there is no shame in asking. We are all a gift on this earth. We all have a purpose. Never lose sight of that. Even in your darkest moments, hold onto hope; never let that go.

Our daughter knew something terrible had happened (more than normal), so she confronted her dad that evening the same day that he told me about the infidelity. She insisted on him telling her what had happened because she had never seen her mom in such a bad way. He was honest and told her what he did, and at that moment, she told him to get out of her room, that she was so disgusted that he could do something so horrible to her mom; she wanted nothing to do with him. Their relationship had become very strained the last few years because of his drinking being out of control, his behavior toward her, and how badly he treated me, but this sent her over the top. She was as devastated as I was. I think she felt a lot of pain, and she was pissed. She stopped talking to him after that. It was as though he didn't exist to her anymore.

This all became so overwhelming for me because of my pain, her pain, his pain. I couldn't take it. I had no idea how to make our house a home again and our family a family, not a house full of people simply coexisting together, all the while trying to cope with what just happened and find a way to heal.

September 8, 2013

Here we are six days after I found out what he did. He sat in bed with me this morning for about an hour; he said he just wanted to sit with me. I feel like he wants to be close to me for some reason. I know it is possible that he really feels terribly guilty and awful for the pain he has caused me by his actions. I am terribly sad and feel defeated. I feel so betrayed by the one person I thought would always protect me. I feel a deep, deep sadness in my soul, like I just lost my best friend, and really, haven't I? With all that has happened I have not given up. I am just allowing myself time to feel very sad right now and for today not do anything but just be and work on healing. I am exhausted and overwhelmed with the events that have happened recently. I need to give myself some time to take it all in and accept it. I also need to remember to be forgiving to myself. Will I really ever be able to get over this betrayal? Will I ever be able to trust him again? That's all I have for today. I can't do anymore at this moment, and that is okay.

September 26, 2013

Our daughter moved out two weeks after she found out what he had done; she couldn't take being around him. I asked her if she could just be cordial with him, and she said she didn't want anything to do with him right now so she left. As much as it pained me to see her go, I knew it was for the best. She wanted to spread her wings, but this pushed her much quicker. She needed space from him if they would ever be able to heal their relationship.
In those few weeks after I learned about the indiscretion, my husband seemed to become a bit colder. When we would talk, he would say

things to me like, "What if I can't promise something like that won't happen again?" One time he even said, "Maybe I don't love you anymore," so I said to him that if he wants to be with other women and he truly doesn't love me, then he needs to make the choice to leave because that isn't fair to me and I certainly will not put up with that behavior.

Before our daughter moved out, he came to me and said that he couldn't take her silence anymore and one of them would have to move out. I told him that I would not be choosing between my daughter and my husband. If he wanted to leave, he could; he was the one who put himself in this situation with his infidelity, and he should deal with the consequences for his actions. I said, "Not only that, but how much do you think she is hurting? She is devastated by what you have done; we both are. You're supposed to protect her mom, not cause her harm." All he is thinking about right now is himself. This certainly is not a time to be selfish. It is a time to really work your program and be honest with yourself and the role you played and take accountability. You need to take and ask for forgiveness and begin to make amends for causing harm to your wife and daughter again. The day I felt a presence of warmth wrapped around me was the day I was given the ability to forgive my husband completely and wholeheartedly for all the pain he had caused our family, for all the lies, the betrayals, the abusive behaviors, for all of this, and so much more. It was as though a huge weight was lifted and gone. The moment I said, "I forgive you," and felt it completely for the first time was the strangest, most unexplainable thing I have ever experienced, but I am grateful that all those years of feeling resentment are gone. The anger is gone. I feel true utter forgiveness, and what an incredible feeling because I am no longer a prisoner to my pain. Don't get me wrong, I still feel pain and hurt, but I am feeling it and I am healing from it. I am not engrossed by it, and that makes a big difference. It allowed me to open my heart completely and feel love like I have never felt love before. This was truly an amazing gift from above. I am so blessed. I thought I would always be a prisoner to the pain and resentments I felt, but I was shown I don't have to be. Forgive and love with all your heart and keep hope alive, and that makes you stronger every day when you believe in something greater than yourself.

To jump forward a bit, we have talked a lot, and we even spent a little time out together at a park. As soon as we got there and started walking, we saw a severely injured seagull. We picked him up. My husband put him in a box, and we rushed him to the emergency vet. I think that was a sign for us of our togetherness; something is trying to show us the way. After all this time apart, we still find ways to come together.

He told me yesterday morning that his sponsor had him read these pages in the big book of AA because of what we were going through; he wanted me to read them to see what I thought. He said he read them several times before, but this time it had a different meaning to him, and it touched him in a different way. He said it makes him feel like he wants to try to move forward with me. I was taken back. I wasn't expecting to hear anything like that, but I have to say, I got a little flutter, feeling guarded but hopeful that he feels like he wants to start spending more time together and trying to move forward to save our marriage. This is fantastic!

Anyway, I went to work, and when I got home at ten o'clock that evening, I went to his office to say hello. The bed he was sleeping on was gone and set up in the other room, but he wasn't there and I didn't see him anywhere in the house. My heart sank. I thought maybe he left me while I was at work (that would be a shitty thing to do to someone, I thought). I got ready for bed and I still didn't see him, but he was in our bed, waiting for me to get home. I was so excited I couldn't believe it. I haven't given up hope this is a sign. It has to be. That was such a huge effort from him to put the bed away and move back into our room. I am still in shock, though, that he was there and he made the effort. Maybe I am jumping the gun, but he felt sincere, like he really wants to try.

September 29, 2013

We talked a little when he got home yesterday, and then he asked if I wanted to go downtown with him to watch a band tonight. He introduced me to some of the new people he knows. We even danced a little. It was really nice to have fun together.

I rode on the motorcycle again. This is only the second time since he got it that I have been on it, and he has had it for about one and a half years. I never wanted anything to do with it because of the way he got it. However, if things were going to be different, which I could feel in me they were, then I would be a part of all that he enjoys, because that is how it should be. And you know what? I enjoyed it and having fun together again, even if it was a bit awkward, but I think that is only because we haven't spent time together in a long time where we actually felt good feelings with the separation and everything else that has happened, but in time it won't feel that way.

To be able to change the whole dynamic of our relationship with forgiveness is pretty awesome, just incredible. We have been blessed with a second chance, the gift of our life together. Time will make it grow into an amazing journey of a rare beautiful passionate love, and I for one can't wait. I am guarded, but each day I will learn to trust more, to believe that he is honest with me. I have to believe that what he tells me will always be the truth. It isn't going to be easy. It is going to take a long time. It will be a process for me, and he has to be willing to work on it and be transparent for me so I can grow to trust him again.

October 5, 2013

He has been back in our room for a couple weeks now. Things are going good between us. I would have never thought this was possible after all we had been through. The intimacy is back. We are able to communicate better than we have in a long time. He sent me a message yesterday that said he is ready to be close and spend more time together. I have waited so long to hear something, anything like that from him. I am happy to hear his effort. Life is a journey, and it is one we do not have to take alone. Something makes me very sad, though. I say, "I love you," but he only says, "I love you too." He never says it to me first. I suppose I need to be patient, but sometimes I feel like with all I have gone through with him; I deserve to be showered with love and affection.

A few weeks ago, a wise woman gave my husband some very insightful advice. She said that he needs to be very aware of certain women in meetings and women in general; they can be like vultures preying on men when they have moments of weakness. Also he needs to pay attention to the women who are befriending him now because their intentions are not those of good intent. She said to him that there is not a woman who could compare to his wife's beauty inside and out and that the miracle he is looking for is at home; he will find that in me. She said he is very lucky to have me for his wife to stand by him all these years, and that if it takes him spending the rest of his life making amends to me, then she said, "Do it; it will be worth it. You will not find another woman who will love you the way your wife does." When he told me about this, I was so touched that a total stranger would look out for me and my husband. I thought how genuine some people really can be. And let's be honest, she is right about other women—look what happened.

My husband now shares things with me. He will tell me or show me if a message come's across from another woman that seems too personal or not appropriate or just in general. I have to believe he will always be totally honest with me; he won't hide things. I believe he will do what is right and not make poor choices anymore. He wants what is best for us, and he wants to do right by our marriage and me as his wife. That is an awesome feeling. I still can't believe that this is happening after everything we have been through. I am amazed that this is possible.

October 12, 2013

Last Sunday was his one-year sobriety birthday, and he didn't bring me with him like we planned because we had a little hiccup the night before, but he shouldn't have excluded me from that celebration. He still needs to work on his anger and how he gets defensive so quickly. He still has a strong self-entitlement issue he needs to work on.

After he left, I thought, you know what? This is an important day for him, but it is also just as important for me, and I deserve more than anyone else to be there, *so I drove down and showed up at his meeting. I am pretty sure by the look on his face he was shocked to see me walk through those doors, but I am so glad I did because I am so very proud of him going 365 days without a drop of alcohol and now he is truly working his recovery. It is a monumental day, and I wanted to be part of that, to share it with him because it is part of us. I wouldn't have missed it for the world, and if I didn't go, it would have been a big mistake, so I made the right choice by going and being there with him, showing my support.*

Today I went with him to his Saturday meeting, and he was picked to talk so he stood up and he talked about being sober for a year and how his wife showed up at his meeting last week to see him get his one-year coin. He said, "My wife is here with me today," and you could hear all these people saying awwww. They were touched that I was there. I found it to be sweet and supportive of us. What a great feeling to have! I like when he asks me to go to meetings with him because I feel like it helps to create a stronger bond between us. We sit and listen to others tell their stories of addiction because we can both relate to what they are saying. We look at one another without speaking a word, smile, and know we are so blessed to be where we are now with each other;

we understand where we were. I feel so welcomed and understood by complete strangers—what a great feeling!

For the first time in years, I feel hopeful about the direction we are going; it is different. We are able to really enjoy one another in an amazing way. It is a good foundation we have started to rebuild, and from here it can only get better and stronger every day.

As wonderful as it is to feel us loving one another and having fun and growing closer, I still have a strong fear that at the slightest disagreement, he will just up and leave. I don't feel much reassurance, not much security. To come from a place where every day I waited for him to say he was leaving and to now try and feel like that won't happen is hard. We both became so saddened and stressed with what our lives had become that we lost a considerable amount of weight, didn't eat much, and couldn't sleep. It was tough on our bodies and our minds.

October 24, 2013

I have been riding on the motorcycle with my husband, using his jacket and an old helmet that is way too big for me, so today he stopped and bought me a helmet that fits and a jacket of my own with armor. It is so nice to be thought about. He wants me to be safe. That's all I want—to feel protected by him. He wouldn't have bought me those things if he wasn't planning on staying with me; he really never wanted to leave either. He has always loved me. We are doing so well. I am so happy how we are progressing, and the time we are spending together is nice. I love it.

November 8, 2013

Dad has been in the hospital all week. He fell in his bathroom and was down on the floor for about four days, maybe five. His oxygen guy came and was knocking on the door. He heard my dad call for help, so he got the maintenance guy. When they went in, they found him wedged between the wall and the toilet. They called for an ambulance, and then I was called and told how they found him.

When my daughter and I got to the emergency room, he was so delusional his eyes were bugged out. He was shaking terribly, and the stories of what he believed to have happened were crazy. One story was he believed his entire apartment was wrapped in Christmas paper, like every wall, cabinet, the floor. He was so dehydrated his kidneys were shutting down. He was in renal failure, he had blood poisoning (sepsis of the blood), and a very large pressure sore that was severely infected just above his tailbone it was all black and smelled of infection. It was so sad.

When I walked in the emergency room and saw the condition he was in, I had to walk out for a minute and catch my breath. I started crying. I was scared for him. The doctor said a few more hours on the floor like that and he would have died. This oxygen delivery man saved my father's life; thank goodness for him. I could have been planning my father's funeral. I could have gone to check on him and found him dead on the floor; that would have been a horrible tragedy.

They had Dad in ICU for a few days because of the blood poisoning; they needed to get a handle on that. He was a very sick man. My husband has been really good at being at the hospital with me and going to visit Dad. He is becoming the man I always knew him to be. I am so proud of him. For the first time in a long time, I can say that my husband is here for me. He is really here for me, and I am so grateful for that. We are putting our family back together. We are putting us back together.

I still feel like I need more assurance. All this emotional stuff with my dad, I am sure, is causing my emotions to be more heightened, but my husband still isn't wearing his wedding ring. He says he may never wear a ring again, which makes me feel so very sad because it is important to me. As I sit here, I realize that my birthday is right around the corner again, and I have to say it makes me feel a bit anxious because the past few years have been just terrible for me with him not being present and being so wrapped up in what he wants to do he has just pushed me aside and I haven't felt like a priority. I mean, spending your birthday without your husband being with you is a very lonely feeling. Just once it would be so nice to have him do the unexpected, to surprise me, to do things he would never usually do to make me feel special.

This man has meant everything to me from day one and every day in between. I believed if I tried hard enough, believed long enough, and loved him deep enough that he would come back to us. At least I hoped and prayed for that, so I guess looking at it that way, we are each other's miracle. He is quicker to apologize now and point out what he sees that he knows he is doing wrong, and he makes it right and kisses me or says, "I love you," and we don't fight about it. Yes, he says, "I love you" first now and often. I love it. He still has work to do. At times his temper flares very strongly, and he goes right back to old behaviors like threats, running, and calling me names. That is what he needs to work on for himself to be better every day than the day before.

We are both growing together and handling things much differently than we used to. I am proud of us and all we are and have yet to become.

December 12, 2013

This year my birthday was different: my husband was here to spend it with me. My husband said I could open a present, so he gave me this little box and inside was a round black titanium ring that looked very large. I said, "Is this for my thumb, because it seems really big?" He laughed. He put out his finger and said, "Look, honey, I will show you," so I put it on him. I was still confused, not catching on here. He said, "Honey, it's my new wedding ring." I said, "Are you serious? You told me you would never wear one again." Tears in my eyes, I was so excited. I can't tell you how happy that made me. I jumped and hugged him so tight.

He said he decided a while ago he was going to get a new ring for our new beginning. He said, "You almost blew it for me a few times," because I kept getting upset when I would ask about him wearing his ring and he felt bad telling me no, so that was an awesome surprise. I was shocked. I had told him that all I wanted for my birthday was for him to put his wedding ring back on, so he did, but a new one for our new beginning and our new life together.

December 31, 2013

The last day of 2013, and let me tell you what happened on Christmas this year. This entry will not say "worst ever." It did not suck for the first time in years. It was amazingly wonderful.

Our daughter stayed the night Christmas Eve, which was so wonderful for us. Recently she shared this with me. She said, "When he first got sober, he acted like the world owed him something, and our fights got much worse. When I learned about the infidelity, I was infuriated. I wanted nothing to do with him. But then I saw how you forgave him, and I started to see him trying to be a better man, like the one you deserve, so as long as he continues to be the best man possible for you, I will continue to resolve my resentment toward him and start over with my dad. I am so proud of his sobriety." My daughter, I am so proud of her as well; she has grown so much. We opened presents in the morning with her, and then she went to her boyfriend's house with his family.

After she left, we opened our gifts to each other, and there was a little jewelry box he gave me to open. Inside there was a beautiful *twisted ring, white gold with black diamonds. He said, "I thought if you wanted to change it out sometimes with your wedding ring, you could." I said, "Thank you; it's beautiful." He said, "What's wrong?" I said, "My wedding ring was given to me years ago with 'I do.' This ring doesn't have that same meaning. I don't want to change it out." He said, "I'm sorry. I didn't mean to upset you." I said, "It's okay; you didn't. I will wear it on a different finger. Thank you for the ring. I am going to get ready now." We had a lot of family to see that day. I was getting ready in the bathroom, and I heard a knock on the door. He said, "Why is the door locked?" I said, "It isn't locked." When I opened it, he was down on his knee with the ring, and our little dog was next to him. He said, "We want to know if you will marry us again." I was so excited. I said, "Are you serious? Why didn't you ask me when you gave me the ring?" He said, "I needed to be reminded of what is important." I jumped in his lap. We were hugging and kissing. We could feel ourselves falling deeper in love at that very moment because we knew that what we shared is truly a gift. You see, we lost the very best part of ourselves—each other—and to get that back is phenomenal. The fact that we get another chance to love one another and save our marriage is a true blessing that we are so grateful for. The Christmas card he gave me this year brought me to tears. I was so touched because he taped his very first one-year sobriety coin that he received inside. One thing he said was he not only maintains his sobriety for himself, but for us and to be the man that I deserve.*

This is the story of our life together and how alcoholism affected us. I am not here to judge anybody else's life or their addictions because we are all different. My hope is that in some way we have helped touch others in need. This is not the end of our story; it is just the beginning of a whole new chapter for us.

There's one other thing I want to share (with my husband's blessing, of course). It is a post my husband put on the Internet for all our family and friends to see. Because he had created such an upsetting environment, he said he thought what he wrote would help make things better, so January 1, 2014, his post reads like this:

> *I will not forget the past, nor will I shut the door on it. I can now say I have truly learned from it.* Happy New Year *to my lovely wife … may we grow closer, love deeper, be happy in the good times, and the hard times too.*
>
> *For those of you that don't know, I have asked my best friend to marry me all over again because I love her with all of my heart. On June 22, 2014, we will renew our vows and our life together, which was all but lost for so long. My alcoholism almost destroyed eleven years of marriage and fourteen years of being together with a woman that would never leave my side. Why she stood by me I will never know, but for this I will be eternally grateful.*
>
> *Today I am 452 days clean and sober. I have not been sober for this long since I was fourteen years old. 2013 was my first sober year. Today I can be present for my life and the lives of those who know and love me. This is my choice alone. Even my friends and family who drink stand by me and respect my decision to be sober. I will never judge or ask anyone to do what I do. I will always show respect to those that make their own choices and do whatever makes them happy.*
>
> *To all my friends and family, thank you for your love and support. Today is the first day of 2014 and the second new year in a row I woke up without a*

*hangover (wow, what a trip) … and to my wife, I
truly love you with all my heart.
Life is good today.
Be happy. Be yourself. Love who you are … because
I sure do.
Happy 2014.*

Chapter 20

Interview with My Husband

Question: How did your drinking start?

Husband: I had my first drink at thirteen. A friend's brother was having a kegger, and my friend said, "Let's try the beer." I said, "No, we better not." But we ended up filling up two cups of beer anyway. I spit it out; it was terrible. My friend said, "Let's hold our breath and drink it as fast as we can so we don't taste it," so we did. I threw it all up, and then about fifteen minutes later, I started feeling good, so we had another. And from then it was on. I drank whenever I could, and I have been drinking ever since.

Question: What was it about getting a DUI that was your wake-up call?

Husband: I knew I wanted to do something about my drinking, and this seemed to be the straw that broke the camel's back. Sitting in the jail cell, feeling so sick. I poisoned myself again from the amount of alcohol I consumed the night before. I said to myself, "This is it. I can never do this again," knowing I was facing the possibility of losing my job. I have never not worked in my life since I was a very young kid. I knew I had pretty much lost my family and shut them out to the point where I couldn't be there for them even before this day. So something had to change.

Question: How would you describe yourself when you were drinking?

Husband: For the most part, I was a binge drinker. I would maintenance drink during the week. I would describe myself as having no control whatsoever, and I would consume as much as I could without any regard to the consequences of how it would affect me physically or emotionally or those around me. But at the same time, I always thought I was in control of my drinking.

Question: How was the beginning of your recovery different from now?

Husband: At the beginning, I just wanted a quick fix, and I wanted to go back to drinking occasionally and not overdoing it. I started with IOP (intensive outpatient treatment) to try and find a way to do that. I learned so much about myself in this program about what the alcohol was doing to me physically and how destructive it was to everyone around me, especially my family and the ones that were closest to me.

Then someone asked me to go to a meeting so I did, and that's where I caught the disease of alcoholism. Once I realized I was infected with it, I was able to surrender at about the third month, or in my mind, I thought I was surrendering. I asked someone to be my sponsor, and I realized after a couple weeks, I wasn't ready for a sponsor because I hadn't truly surrendered yet.

The problem I had with my sponsor is he wanted me to call him every day, so every night at 7:00 p.m., I would look at my clock and think, oh crap, I have to call him again. This sucks! I thought to myself, why can't I do it my way? Why the fuck do I need a sponsor? But I kept going to meetings and I started hearing something different. I began to see people who were actually working the steps and how it was having an impact on their lives. They were happier and somehow stronger. They were comforting to talk to, so I decided to give it another try. I started to go to more meetings. I decided since I could drink every day, I could go to a meeting every day. Twice a week I went to men-only meetings, which I found to be the most supportive when it came to my recovery because men who were like me seemed to have a better understanding of what I was going through and I didn't have the distraction of female interaction. On Fridays I started doing service for a halfway house.

Then I decided it was time to find another sponsor. As luck would have it, I found one that didn't own a cell phone, so I wouldn't be burdened with calling him every single day. He asked me to meet him twice a week and call twice a week on days I wasn't meeting with him, so I did. At our first meeting, he asked me first and foremost if I was willing to go to any lengths to stay clean and sober. I said yes. He said, "On to the next question. Are you ready to take the first step?" I said yes. He said, "Wait a minute. I want you to think about this. Take a few minutes and really think about your life." Then I said, "I have come to believe that I am powerless over alcohol, and my life has become unmanageable." Then I moved on with the following eleven steps as suggested to me. After completing those steps, I felt better and confident that I was able to stay sober. Along the way I completely lost the obsession to drink and began to live what I thought was a sober life in recovery. Little did I know you can live clean and sober without alcohol and yet not be living a sober life. For me, some of my old alcoholic behaviors began to creep back in. I started to go back to the bars to watch musical events and stay out late, with the reasoning that I wasn't having alcohol so it was okay for me to be there. I was so high on what is called the pink cloud: because I was going to meetings every day, I felt I had the right to go wherever I wanted and do whatever I wanted because I wasn't using alcohol. In the beginning, my wife thought my recovery was going good and we did have good communication with each other, but as I started to relive old alcoholic behaviors, I started to pull away from the relationship because I felt entitled because I had stopped drinking. The more the arguments would come, the more I would run. I started to isolate and do whatever I could to stay away. We were both unhappy.

As I was heading into my tenth month of sobriety, I asked my wife for a separation and moved into my office. Then I did the worst thing possible: I took the thirteenth step, which is recognized as having an intimate affair with a newcomer in the program. All this time my wife was trying feverishly to restore our marriage, leaving notes every day telling me how much she loved me, throwing herself at me intimately. I didn't know what to do. I was in a tailspin, spiraling down again, so I reached out to my sponsor and other men in the program and they helped guide me through it. I came home that night, and my wife said that she wanted me to kiss her. I said, "You may never want to kiss me again." I told her what had happened, and I watched her heart break to pieces right in front of me. It was the most painful thing I have ever experienced in my life, and I wouldn't wish it on my worst enemy. In the days following, our daughter that was still at home questioned me as to what I had done that made her mom so upset. Because I felt I needed to be completely honest with everything in my life, I told her what had happened. This was just as devastating as when I told my wife. At this point I was sure there was no hope to reconcile our relationship or save what I had destroyed once more by not living a sober life.

This is where I had my second moment of clarity. Where my first was lying in a jail cell stinking drunk, this time I was lying in a bed in my office all alone, thinking of how I destroyed my family once again with my alcoholic behaviors without the alcohol. Once again after being humbled by the effects of my disease, I began to reach out to other alcoholics in the program. They offered suggestions on what I needed to do, what they would do, and how hard it must be for my family to understand. They all had the same solution: to pray for an answer and keep coming back. God started to do for me what I couldn't do for myself, and for some reason, my wife wasn't ready to let me go. She kept leaving me notes daily telling me how much she loved me and wanted us back, but I was refusing because I had betrayed her and hurt her so deeply. I felt in my mind I didn't deserve her. By the grace of God, she stood by me, not letting me go for a second, and helped us find our way back to each other's arms. Since all this has happened, I feel like she has forgiven me completely. Even though thoughts and feelings of pain creep up for her, we work through it. Our daughter moved out, and over a period of time with her not speaking to me, we have slowly started to rebuild our relationship. My wife and I have become closer than we had ever been in our lives. We go everywhere together now. She rides on the back of my motorcycle, something she vowed she would never do in her life. She goes to meetings with me, she helps me set up my drums when I have a show, she is a part of everything I do now, something that never happened before, or if it did, I was too drunk to be present or appreciate when it was happening. Life is good today. I am sober, and I am starting over every day. I get to renew my vows with my best friend and truly the only person I ever wanted to be with for the rest of my life.

Question: What regrets if any do you have?

Husband: I have a tremendous amount of regret, mostly from the damage I caused those around me and the people I hurt. I feel if I would have sought help sooner, I might not have those regrets today.

Question: What message would you like to get out there to others who still suffer from alcoholism?

Husband: Today is the day you don't have to drink or drug, no matter what. You can live your life and be present for those you care about and those that care about you. My sponsor told me they have a saying in the military called "get with the program." At 515 days of sobriety, the best advice I could give anyone would be to do just that: get with the program, reach out to other alcoholics in the program, get a big book, go to meetings, get a sponsor, and get into service. If you're lucky enough to still have a family, involve them in your sober life and be present for them. It's the best gift you could ever give yourself and your family. Always reach for help before you reach for the bottle. Pick up the ten-thousand-pound phone and leave the twelve-ounce bottle in the trash.

The past is an important part of recovery because the reality is I am an alcoholic, and I never want to forget where I was and the man I never want to be again. I am always an arm's length away from devastation if I pick up that first drink. I know now that is something I never have to do if I work the program the way it is intended and not the way I feel it should work.

Question: What would you like our family, friends, and strangers to know about me as your wife?

Husband: I support my wife 100 percent in writing this book, and as embarrassing and heartbreaking as the things I have done are, they are all true. I have to be honest about my behaviors as an alcoholic if I want to continue my sobriety.

My wife is the bravest person I know. She did a beautiful job in writing this book. She is one in a million to be able to stand by me for so many years when I couldn't be there for her; she is truly amazing. I think to myself, why would somebody do that? All the years of emotional abuse from myself, my family, and my children assuming she was the cause of all my problems, yet the whole time it was my disease that was causing the destruction. All the while my wife struggled to get me help and help me show my family what is right. There were years of marriage counselors and children psychologists trying to help her stepchildren and do what was right. Even while my family turned their back on her thinking she was keeping me from my children and them, it was my disease. I was consumed with working as hard as I could. I had to be the best at everything, but there was one thing I was never good enough or strong enough to do, and that was to put down the bottle. That was my escape, my excuse to let my family assume that she was the cause of why I was distant from them. In other words, I would go out and get drunk and blame my wife for my drinking. I would blame my wife for why my kids were messed up, and the whole time she was doing the best she could to keep our family together, always supporting our family, trying to point my children in the right direction and get them help when they needed it.

Now looking at my wife through sober eyes, I am able to look back over the years and see all the damage I caused her. Not only was I isolated from my disease, but I caused her so much emotional damage, she started to isolate even from me; she isolated herself. I made so many broken promises of "this is the last time; I will never drink again." I saw in her face every time she believed in me that I would turn this around and how much disappointment she had when I would drink again, and she started to withdraw from me.

But she is still here with me today. She tells me how proud she is of me, how much she loves me. She still writes me love notes, and today I get to be present and truly love for the first time without alcohol in my body clouding my judgment. I am truly grateful and blessed to have her in my life. I don't know what I would be without her.

Chapter 21

A Love Letter to My Husband

I would like to take a moment to thank my husband for all of his support and his blessing for me to write this book in its entirety, to be so open to give the world a look into our most personal detailed daily life living with alcoholism. Thank you for your touching interview.

On that note, I would like to say that I am so very proud of my husband for all he has accomplished. He is growing every day, wanting to be a better man and husband than he was the day before. He still has some old behaviors to overcome, but we work through them together. He is no longer running and leaving the house or abandoning me to hide. He has the ability now to recognize rather quickly when he has done something that isn't right, and he will come to me and we talk about it and he apologizes. The wrongdoings now are not in the form of betrayal, lies, or broken promises; they are issues that are part of everyday life. Sometimes when the past rears its ugly head, we work through it. That isn't always an easy conversation to have, but you learn how to navigate through the storm and ride it out together.

My husband, you are the absolute love of my life. I couldn't imagine being without you for one day. Although there has been so much heartache and destruction, we have somehow managed and been blessed to find our way through the wreckage of it all and save each other. There was a time for years it seemed I would go to bed alone, missing you, because you were always running; now we get to go to bed together every night, knowing we will never be apart again and that we never want to be. I am most grateful to have the ability to completely forgive you and feel all the resentments and anger fade away so I can love you wholeheartedly and unconditionally. You are my very best friend, the closest person in my life, and soon we get to say "I do" all over again. I don't know if anyone can imagine how very precious that day is for us. It's even more powerful than our wedding day.

Every day I fall deeper in love with you. I have respect for you. I admire you. I appreciate that you work so hard to take care of us. I adore you exceedingly. My husband, you are my heart, you are my everything, for when I honor all that you are, I feel full and complete with love for you. I know there was a time we never thought there was a possibility for us to rebuild anything, but we have witnessed a miracle in our own lives. We have truly been awakened to the deep abiding love we have always shared for one another and our life of togetherness. This may sound completely insane; however, through all the pain, anger, disappointment, tears, happiness, love, and hopelessness, I wouldn't change a thing (as much as I would like to forget certain instances and would rather they hadn't happened). Without them all, I wouldn't have learned all the lessons I did about myself, life, forgiveness, and loving unconditionally.

For many years I was truly suffering, in so much pain the resentment was killing me, eating away at my soul, and at times I felt like I wanted to die. I couldn't find a way out. I almost gave up completely until it had consumed every part of my heart and mind, where surrendering was the only way I found myself feeling alive and free again from the emotions caused by your alcoholism that I allowed to take me prisoner. Instead of looking at you with disgust and feeling resentment, I now look at you, my husband, even on our worst days, with great pride and great adoration. How is that possible? I had to surrender my pain and ask for guidance on how to find myself again. When I did, it was a day I will never forget, because I got my life back. My heart was whole again, full of forgiveness and so much love. I wanted to love life and live again, be happy with my husband, and I wasn't going to stop until that happened. By the grace of a higher power and my husband working his recovery program the way it is suggested to be worked, we now have an amazing life, full of more love than we could have ever hoped to have with one another.

My husband will always be an alcoholic, and I know that every day there is a chance he could relapse and take that fatal fall with alcohol. Even if there were a relapse, I would love him just the same and be here with him every step of the way because he now has the ability to get right back into line with the program that saved his life. I choose to have hope and believe that my husband is a great man. He has great strength, and every day he wakes up and chooses to not have a drink, to go to a meeting. Every day when he says, "I love you" and chooses to be with me instead of in a bar drinking, it is a great day. Every day that I wake up and open my eyes, it is an amazing day because I get one more day to spend with the love of my life. I get to fall asleep in his arms every night and wake up every morning the same way. I know he will never leave me alone again because my husband is choosing to be the best part of himself that he can be. Today he is the husband that makes me proud. Every day he makes the choice to live a true sober life, and when he goes to sleep at night, he can say he hasn't hurt anyone today, he didn't have a drink today, he loves his wife, he helped where he could, and tomorrow he will wake up and do it all over again.

Those that don't know my husband very well or at all, I want you to know this: he is an amazing man, the best I have ever known, one who has overcome a great deal of adversities in his own life and fights a battle every day with alcoholism, because it is a disabling disease. I have asked before that you not be hasty in judging my husband or myself for past behaviors, but instead take something that you have read and allow it to benefit in your own life. Understand that this has been our path and our path alone, and as the saying goes, "Unless you walk a day in someone else's shoes, don't judge their lives. Take a look at your own," for we all have a story to tell, and this is just part of ours.

My husband wakes up every day and has the ability now to know right from wrong and make a better choice, to not hurt me ever again, to not abandon me when things get tough, to be honest and tell the truth, to be a kind loving man, to be gentle with my heart and help me heal, to be present and supportive, to communicate with me about real-life issues, to have fun without drinking. For all these things and so much more, we wouldn't have been able to have a life this full and complete if there was not a recovery program in place to help guide people through it step by step to live a life completely free, without alcohol or drugs.

I share in my husband's sobriety by being supportive. I go to a few AA meetings with him every weekend, which has been a blessing for us because there are so many stories that we can both relate to. One woman would say to me every time she saw me, "I am so happy when he brings you with him." These people are happy to welcome me and get to know me as well. The way AA is designed as a program is just remarkable, as is how it changes so many lives. People who never thought life would be fun without alcohol are having more fun living without it. It has saved and helped transform so many lives. I have seen firsthand in my husband, when you follow the program, what miracles it can work in your own life if you just do the work.

Honey, I love you. I am so proud of you. Thank you for taking this journey with me through life. I can't wait to see what the next fifty years has ahead for us as we take every day one day at a time, but I know no matter what, we will face it all together side by side. My husband, you are a survivor. You have strength and determination like those of a great warrior. There is a great quote from Tao Te Ching: "He who knows others is wise. He who knows himself is enlightened." You are the breath I take, you are the beat of my heart, you are the light in my soul; with you I am everything. Thank you for your encouragement and the love you give me every day, for now I know what being loved unconditionally feels like.

I have learned to never judge a book by its cover. Take the time to open it and read it first before you decide you don't like it, because it may be the best damn thing you have ever read. Much the same is true for people: don't judge what you don't know. I wish you all a safe journey on your path to recovery and healing. Hold on to hope, don't lose your strength, and never forget there is a power stronger and greater than any of us. I pray that this book has brought hope to those that feel hopeless, guidance for those that feel lost, peace to those that still suffer, and a belief that even at their worst, things can and will always get better. You just have to take that first step. I hope the words on these pages have touched you or someone you know in ways you never thought anyone would understand.

If you have been unsure whether you had an addiction problem but can relate to some of the people in this book who have shared their stories and you now realize you need help, congratulations. Know we are all proud of you, and most importantly, be proud of yourself for taking that first step. Never give up, and always find hope to hold onto. Forgive yourself, believe in yourself, and remember, tomorrow always starts with a blank page, and you decide how it will begin. Be safe in your journeys.

Wishing you Serenity,
Harmony Rose.....

Printed in the United States
By Bookmasters